GLOBAL
ECONOMY:
POST-CRISIS TO
SUSTAINABLE
DEVELOPMENT

GLOBAL ECONOMY:
POST-CRISIS TO SUSTAINABLE DEVELOPMENT

IRAKLI KOVZANADZE

GLOBAL ECONOMY: POST-CRISIS TO SUSTAINABLE DEVELOPMENT

iUniverse books may be ordered through booksellers or by contacting:

iUniverse
1663 Liberty Drive
Bloomington, IN 47403
www.iuniverse.com
1-800-Authors (1-800-288-4677)

ISBN: 978-1-5320-4703-9 (sc)
ISBN: 978-1-5320-4704-6 (hc)
ISBN: 978-1-5320-4702-2 (e)

Library of Congress Control Number: 2018901945

Print information available on the last page.

iUniverse rev. date: 05/22/2018

Contents

From the author

The consequences of the devastating global crisis of 2008-2009, which affected not only the economic but also the social and political development, have not yet been overcome. In a number of countries, including Greece for example, we see a dramatic deterioration in the situation. However, in recent years, there has been certain economic stabilization observed. Growth rate of the world economy in 2015 and 2016 were 3.4% and 3.1% respectively. According to the IMF forecast for 2017 it will reach 3.5%. The GDP of developed countries in 2015 increased by 2.2%, while in 2016 - by 1.7%. The growth in 2017 is expected at the level of 2%. Economic growth in developing countries in 2015 was 4.3%, in 2016 - 4.2%, and in 2017 it is projected at 4.5%[1]. In the next review of the World Economic Outlook in April 2017, the IMF noted positive developments such as a cyclical recovery in manufacturing and trade, although it pointed at short-term problems adversely affecting growth in the medium term: low growth in labor productivity, high income inequality, strengthened requirements in developed countries for a transition to policy measures aimed at the domestic economy[2]. The book examines the causes of the crisis, including a dangerous triad of deregulation, financial innovation and the speculative nature of doing business. Because of the uniqueness of the crisis scale, its origin, development and transition to the stage of the global pandemic were investigated in a systematic manner.

The economies both of developed and developing countries could not reach sustainable development for a long time. The situation was significantly

---

[1]   IMF. World Economic Outlook databases, April 2017, www.imf.org.

[2]   IMF. World Economic Outlook, April 2017: Gaining Momentum?

complicated by excessive debt in many countries where economic growth was hampered by deflation or low rise in prices. Of course, considerable efforts are being made to change the situation. The basis for certain optimism was the latest measures of monetary authorities, for example, the creation of the European Fund for Strategic Investments in the amount of EUR 315 billion (in 2015-2016 this fund began implementation of investment projects worth EUR 138 billion[3]),as well as the steps taken in many countries to develop specialized investment institutions.

At the same time, the scale of the problems requires more decisive and comprehensive steps in the economy and social sphere, in the area of public finances. In order to realize such measures, serious theoretical studies are needed to research the nature of the economic crises and ways for its resolution. This study continues a series of monographs on this topic. I hope that the work offered to readers will contribute to the search for solutions to current socio-economic problems at national, regional and international levels.

---

[3] The Investment Plan for Europe, www.europa.eu

Introduction

Almost 10 years have passed since the onset of the global economic crisis, but so far, scientists, businessmen, bankers, and politicians continue to argue about its causes, feasibility of its prevention, efficiency and consequences of anti-crisis measures, as well as about the possible recurrences of crisis phenomena. There is no complete agreement among theorists and practitioners as to whether this destructive crisis has been completely overcome and which direction the global economy is heading to.

The book *"Global economy: Post-crisis to sustainable development"*, offered to readers, is a continuation of the author's research on the nature of economic and banking crises. The aim of the monograph was to study the entire range of opinions on the global economic crisis of 2007-2009 and the possible ways of forming a new, more stable and dynamically developing economy. At the same time, one cannot but agree with the majority of respected experts and politicians, that the way to a new economic model lies through profound and consistent reforms in the economic and social areas.

Unfortunately, geopolitical risks have significantly increased in recent years which seriously impeded the emerging positive trends in the economy. The explosive nature of growing terrorist threats around the world, including the emergence of the terrorist state "Islamic State of Iraq and the Levant" (ISIL), endangers the economic and social stability of many states, primarily the Middle East. Another negative factor was the crisis in Ukraine and subsequent economic sanctions, which had a negative impact primarily on the socio-economic development of post-Soviet countries. At the same time, terrorist threats, political tension in the post-Soviet space, and the threat of their proliferation negatively affect the entire global economy.

Any complex socio-economic phenomenon requires systematic analysis, including the study of historical experience. This approach is also valid in studying the nature of economic crises that are integral companions of human history, especially since the rapid development of market relations around the 17th-18th centuries. As Professor N. Roubini, a well-known researcher of economic crises, rightly points out, "... irrational euphoria, pyramids based on credit levers, financial innovations, speculative bubbles, panic, depositors' raids on banks and other financial institutions ... are typical for many other cases of financial catastrophes"[4]. That is why the proposed book begins with an analysis of the history of economic crises, their genesis, how they arose, developed and were overcome.

The analysis of historical experience, conducted by us in the first chapter, convincingly shows that crises are a common phenomenon of the world economy. At the same time, the global crisis of 2007-2009 became not just another link in the chain of recurring phenomena, but its destructive scales have a certain similarity with the Great Depression. It's hard not to agree with Professor N. Roubini who said: "The fact that the recent crisis has so many frightening similarities with the events that unfolded decades ago is not a coincidence: the same forces that initiated the Great Depression for several years created the basis for the emergence of a catastrophe in modern history - our own Great Recession»[5].

However, historical experience gives us examples not only of destructive economic crises, but also of effective anti-crisis policy, for example, the new course chosen by F.D. Roosevelt, which allowed the United States as well as the global economy to emerge from the Great Depression. Experience of a fairly long and dynamic economic development after the Second World War (approximately until the 1970s) was very valuable from a theoretical and practical point of view. In addition to the historical aspect, the first chapter of the monograph is devoted to the study of various theories of the origin of the crisis, starting with the views of the founder of the crisis theory of K. Juglar, and ending with the studies of modern economists such as J. Stiglitz, N. Roubini, P. Krugman, R. Rajan, F. Jordan, J. Akerlof, K. Azaridis, L. Kaas

---

[4]   Roubini N., "Crisis Economics: A Crash Course in the Future of Finance", M., EKSMO, 2011 (in Russian language);, pp., 20-21.

[5]   Ibid, p., 20

and others. Along with medium-term cycles and long-term economic cycles, whose founder was the outstanding economist N. Kondratieff, we focused our attention to so-called "Juglar cycles". The theory of long economic waves, developed by N. Kondratieff, found its further development in the works of many modern crises researchers (E. Mandel, D. Dixon, J. Goldstein, F. Jordan and others). Considerations of the scientists of this direction that the last crisis is at the junction of the ascending and descending waves of the fifth extended economic cycle deserve attention and explain its destructiveness and protracted nature, as well as make it possible to forecast the forthcoming major changes in the economy and the social sphere.

In our study, the whole palette of opinions on the causes of the crisis is presented, including the theoretical views of Keynesians, monetarists, institutionalists, neoclassicists, Marxists, representatives of the Austrian economic school, since there is a rational grain in each theory. The recipes of various economists can be taken into account in practical terms when carrying out anti-crisis policies and building a new model of sustainable economic development.

The first chapter of the book addresses in detail the last crisis of 2007-2009, including its causes, a dangerous triad of deregulation, financial innovations and the speculative nature of doing business. Because of the uniqueness of the crisis scale, its origin, development and transition to the stage of the global pandemic were investigated in a systemic manner.

The second chapter of the monograph is devoted to anti-crisis measures at the national, regional and international levels. To overcome the crisis, many different instruments were used, including maintaining liquidity in the economy and the financial sector, restructuring credit and financial institutions, structural and institutional reforms. From the point of view of preventing and overcoming the consequences of crises in the future, it is very important to understand how the applied and applied anti-crisis measures are effective and sufficient. The acute phase of the crisis has been overcome, but overall, economic growth is still unsustainable and in a number of countries the recession is still going on so it is necessary to rethink critically the experience of applying anti-crisis measures. Moreover, it is still difficult to fully evaluate the consequences of the use of a number of instruments, in particular, large-scale quantitative easing.

The second chapter offers measures for reforming rating agencies that occupy an exceptionally important place in the modern global economy. The global crisis has convincingly shown that their activities, in particular, the procedures and methods for assigning ratings and the ratings themselves needed more transparency and effective regulation.

The third chapter of the book is devoted to one of the most important directions of building a more stable economic model - reforming the regulatory and supervisory system. We studied steps taken at the international level, in particular, through the Financial Stability Board and the Basel Committee on Banking Supervision, and at the regional and national levels. It seems that the further development of the Basel Accords, the special order of regulation and supervision of systemically important financial institutions, the improvement of the European stabilization mechanism can play a significant role in the transition to sustainable and dynamic economic development.

The fourth chapter of the book addresses the analysis of trends and the forecast of the development of the post-crisis global economy. To understand the possible ways of reforming the global economy, it is very important to identify both its disproportions and "weaknesses", as well as positive phenomena. The macroeconomic situation as a whole was analyzed, including the growth rates of GDP, the level of investment and savings, inflation processes, the dynamics of the money supply, the state of public finances, trade and balance of payments. The situation in the banking sector was studied separately.

The monograph examines the trends and prospects for the development of various groups of developed countries and developing ones (including their differentiation by region), with the transition economy. A separate section of the book is devoted to the analysis of economic and banking development trends in Georgia.

The fifth chapter of the monograph reviews the possible ways of reforming the global economy. Now most scientists, businessmen, bankers and politicians are in favor of profound and systemic reforms, although they have differences in the tactics. We have tried to bring a wide range of opinions on these reforms.

It is quite obvious that sustainable development is impossible without deep structural reforms, without modernization and giving an innovative character to the development of industry and agriculture. There is a need for changes in monetary policy, designed to make it an instrument for supporting deep structural reforms. Tax and budget policy should play a more active role in ensuring economic growth. At the same time, in order to maintain the stability of public finances, it is very important to reform taxes and optimize expenditures. For sustainable and long-term development, it is also important to preserve the social orientation of the economy.

According to most experts, a new quality of economic growth is impossible without a resolute fight against the problem of moral abuses in business, in particular, with the practice of super bonuses without linking them to the long-term performance of companies.

A crucial part of building a new model of economic development is the consistent reform of the regulatory and supervisory system, including such issues as the transition to countercyclical regulation, preventive control of systemic risks, further development of the Basel Accords, increased transparency and efficiency in the regulation of financial markets, financial instruments and structured products and increasing competition in the financial sector. It is necessary to improve the quality of regulators themselves, which requires constant attention to such issues as their independence, professionalism, transparency of activities.

A serious problem threatening the development of the global economy is the imbalance of trade and balance of payments in a number of countries. The solution to this problem lies in the plane of action both at the national and international levels. In the international sphere, a higher degree of coordination of the economic policies of countries, including monetary, taxation, regulation and supervision, is also needed.

In conclusion, I would like to note that the book is devoted to a wide range of problems related to overcoming the global crisis and building a more sustainable economic development model, as "under the old model, the financial sector took on outsized risk in pursuit of outsized rewards, causing outsized ruin—and precipitating the crisis we have been experiencing for the last five years. Since then, the international community has been struggling to build something better. This is not easy. It means throwing away old blueprints and designing new ones. It means dealing with the perverse incentives of financial firms and the inability or unwillingness of authorities to act."[6].

---

[6] Lagarde C. "Managing the New Transitions in the Global Economy", an Address at George Washington University, Washington DC, October 3, 2013., www.imf.org

CHAPTER 1
The 2007-2009 global crisis: development factors and socio-economic consequences

1.1. World economic crises: the historical aspect

Economic crisis as a manifestation of the accumulated imbalances in production, exchange and consumption is the constant companion of human civilization. The emergence and development of such crises are associated, as a rule, with a whole complex of interrelated factors, both economic and socio-political, with those economic factors linked to the spheres of finance, credit, and currency relations.

Before the formation of market type economies and banking systems, individual countries or even regions have also experienced economic crises, usually associated with the disorders in public finances and monetary circulation. So the problems with the public finances of Spain and the refusal of the Spanish King Philip II to pay his debts provoked the first exchange crisis in Antwerp. Economic crises before the industrial revolution did not have a cyclical nature, they arose mainly in the sphere of circulation or public finances. At the same time, prototypes of present crises appeared in that period.

The first well-known crisis in the history, which arose from a "bubble in the asset market" was the so-called "tulip" crisis in the Netherlands in the 1630's, when as a result of speculation and even the conclusion of futures contracts, the price of rare tulip bulbs was artificially raised at an exponential rate. Trading futures contracts has acquired a massive audience, it involves representatives of all social groups. Like any other, the "tulip bubble" in 1637 quickly burst, enriching a few and leading to losses for the main group of players. As a result, by the decision of the judiciary, contract holders could expect to receive only 5% of their nominal value.

With the emergence of commercial and issuing banks and development of the securities market, economic crises became sufficiently acute and large-scale. At that time, one could observe bubbles in the stock market and the desire of the state to solve its financial and economic problems, both through the growth of the state debt and active issuing activity. A vivid example of such a bubble was the Mississippi Company and the first issuing bank in France, founded in 1716-1717 under the initiative of the financier and economist J. Law, who was in favor of the theory that "the use of credit increases money supply in one year more than the most flourishing trade is able to reach in a decade. With money, additional manpower is bought, which creates more products in the country, multiplying national wealth. You can increase the same amount of money... by issuing credit money. " As a result, over five years of the bank's existence, paper money was issued for three billion livres and the money supply increased 20-fold. At the same time, speculative operations with shares of the Mississippi Company increased their price by 40 times. The next financial bubble ended with massive losses for depositors and the collapse of the bank as well as the company. A similar story occurred at the same time with the stock company of the South Seas in England.

Economic crises, with a clearly expressed cyclical development, in which successive phases of revival, recovery, boom, recession and depression change each other, appear in the period of the Industrial Revolution. They are first observed in the most developed capitalist countries (Great Britain, USA) and later extend to regions and the world as a whole. Such features of modern crises as overproduction, bubbles in the credit and stock markets and the exit from crisis through technical innovations are clearly traced in the crises of the initial stage of the industrial revolution (the end of the 18th and the beginning of the 19th century). The first crises of 1788, 1793, 1797, 1810, 1815-1816 and 1819 were observed in the UK and covered a rapidly developing cotton industry. At the same time, the cyclical development of crises was closely related to the state debt and the country's trade balance. The reduction of public debt negatively affected commercial banks, which traditionally held state securities in the portfolio. This in turn was reflected in the real sector of the economy. The trade balance was adversely affected by the continental blockade and trade wars. As a result, sharp expansion and contraction of cotton production and fluctuations in prices for manufactured products were observed.

The crisis of 1825-1826 was the first cyclical crisis that affected virtually all sectors of the economy, including the financial and banking industries. It spread from Great Britain to the USA, Latin America, France, Germany and the other countries involved in world trade (crises often occurring in one state, quickly spread to many other countries). It is interesting that economic thought did not yet know about the cyclical nature of crises, and a special parliamentary commission was setup to determine the reasons for such an all-encompassing recession. The factor of world trade played a major role in the emergence of the first world crisis. The countries of Latin America, which became independent, were regarded by English business as an endless market for the textile industry. At the same time, many stock companies were created to invest in emerging Latin American markets, whose activities were often limited to speculations with their own shares in the stock market. Banks were willingly lending to companies with rapidly growing market values, as they could rely on high returns from such loans. Such a rapid increase in production volumes increased raw material prices, but the factor of limited demand for finished products was not taken into account, which led to overstocking, a sharp decline in product prices, non-repayment of loans and bankruptcies in the industrial, commercial and financial sectors of the economy. Thus the crisis of 1825-1826 became a good illustration of the assessment of the world crises given by the well-known Russian Economist M.I.Tugan-Baranovsky: "Along with the individual characteristics of crises, strikes their extraordinary similarity in all significant features. The state of the commodity market that immediately precedes the crisis, changes in the circulation of money accompanying its development, the subsequent fluctuations of credits – are the features that make the crises similar... This determines a great monotony of crises history, but at the same time this monotony serves as the best proof of legality of the investigated phenomenon "[7].

The next cyclical crisis was observed in 1836-1837, the epicenter of which was again the United Kingdom. The rapid growth of depository banks in England, the fascination of British financial institutions by lending to speculative operations on the US land market, and the significant orientation of the English export of goods and capital to the American market were the factors contributing to the crisis development. The volume of operations on the American land market in 1834-1836 grew more than three times. At the same time, most of the operations were speculative. The trigger mechanism for the development of the crisis was the decision of the US President E. Jackson in 1836 on the sale of land exclusively for gold. As a result, American banks and speculators attempted to obtain a gold loan on the British market by placing a large amount of securities. However, there was no demand for such securities. The problems of American partners affected the British banks, including very large ones, which also began to go bankrupt. For example, one of the largest banks in England - the North and the central bank in Manchester, having 38 branches and playing a very important role in lending to the British industry, went bankrupt. Simultaneously with the problems in the financial sector, due to a sharp drop in exports to the US market, the crisis affected British industry.

The United Kingdom and the United States became the epicenter of the 1847-1848 crisis. The crisis affected almost all capitalist countries. The most important factors in the development of the crisis were a sharp and significant increase in the prices of agricultural raw materials and foodstuffs as a result of lean years in Europe and the United States. The rise in food prices had a significant impact on the decline in demand for manufactured goods. As a result, both in the real and financial sectors of the economy there was an unprecedented demand for loans, but the refusal of the Bank of England to carry out a massive refinancing significantly aggravated the situation. The crisis of 1847-1848, according to historians and economists, was extremely destructive and provoked the revolutionary movement in 1848-1849.

---

[7]   Tugan-Baranovsky M., Periodic Industrial Crises, M., 2008, Directimedia Publishing(in Russian language)p., 217.

The crisis of 1857 occurred against the backdrop of the world trade heyday and was caused by the abolition or reduction of customs duties in most countries (with the exception of the United States), the rapid construction of railways (from 1847 to 1857, the network of railways grew more than 3-fold), development of mining and metallurgical industries, large-scale growth in the volume of issued shares and bills, including banking ones. The economic crisis was preceded by a crisis in the financial sector, where massive bankruptcies of companies and banks keen on speculative operations with securities and commodity assets took place. At the same time, free world trade contributed to lower prices for raw materials and manufactured goods, which negatively affected the financial condition of American, and after some time English, companies. Although the crisis of 1857 was quite severe, it did not last long.

The crisis of 1866-1867 to a large extent was associated with a sharp increase in the volume of speculative transactions in the financial sector. The growth of high-risk and speculative operations was facilitated by changes in the institutional environment of doing business, in particular, by adoption of the acts of 1856-1862 in Great Britain on stock companies and providing for the creation of limited liability companies. This legal form of the company envisaged the liability of owners only in the number of funds contributed to the authorized capital. If prior to adoption of these laws companies could not engage in financial operations before the final formation of capital and start of real business, now companies could issue bonds and other kinds of liabilities even before the start of operations, which stimulated speculative operations. A good illustration of the negative effect that adoption of new legislation had on stock companies was the bankruptcy of the largest British financial company *Overend, Gurney & Co*. Having a 60-year history and reputation as a respectable creditor and investor (inferior only to the Bank of England, according to the famous English Historian L. Levy), after the transition to a legal form with limited liability in 1865, the company began to pursue an excessively risky policy, accepting promissory notes and other obligations, which were mostly not reliable. As a result, the company went bankrupt, and after it many financial companies and banks also collapsed. The fall in the stock prices was followed by the high demand for loans and cash. The financial crisis spread to the industry, where prices fell by 20-40%.

The cyclical crisis of 1873 was notable for the fact that its epicenter was not England, but the countries of Central Europe (Austro-Hungarian and

German empire), where liberal legislation was adopted in previous years on establishing stock companies. Respectively, from 1870 to 1873, more joint stock companies were created in these countries than in the previous 70 years. In the stock market, a significant speculative bubble was formed as a result of speculation with municipal securities, shares of railway and telegraph companies and land lots. So the number of land plots representing the objects of speculation on the Vienna Stock Exchange was so high that it would take decades to use them realistically. In May 1873 the Vienna Stock Exchange crashed, causing more than 300 companies to go bankrupt and share prices fell 2 times. The share price of German companies fell by 46%. The US exchange collapsed in September, where during the period of 1876-1878, around 10 thousand companies were going bankrupt each year. The stock market crisis triggered the general economic downturn all over the world, especially in Great Britain. Since the crisis of 1873, there has been a decrease in the duration of economic cycles from 10-11 years to 7-10 years.

Following the crisis of 1873, major changes took place in the world trade: there was a turn from free trade to customs wars, a universal gold standard was introduced in accordance with the decisions of the Paris monetary conference, the export of capital sharply increased from Great Britain (in 1881, 700 million pounds sterling were invested only in foreign securities), France and Germany to the developing markets, which constrained economic growth in the exporting countries. Simultaneously, a long period of the agrarian crisis (1875-1895) started as reflected in the long-term decline in prices for grain and the other agricultural goods. Serious innovations occurred in the financial market: speculative transactions with shares and commodity futures significantly increased and the role of stock exchanges and investment banks expanded. In such circumstances, the crisis of 1882 broke out, starting with the bankruptcy of the largest French bank *L'Union Generale*, which although having a very modest capital, was keen on founding activities, creation of various enterprises and banks and participation in foreign concessions and loans. The bankruptcy of *L'Union Generale* provoked the collapse of the stock market in France and a number of the other countries. In the US, signs of the stock market crisis were observed as early as in 1881, but then came a short-term speculative boom that ended in a major crisis in 1884.

The crisis of 1890-1893 occurred against the backdrop of the strengthening of monopoly positions, large-scale technical and technological innovations, continued massive export of capital from Europe (primarily from Great Britain) to the emerging markets of Latin America and Asia, the sharp rise in joint-stock companies, stock market growth and development of banking systems, cashless payments and short-term lending. The movement of capital was extremely speculative, which was particularly evident in Latin American countries, where the symbiosis of greed for capital and irresponsibility and corruption of the authorities was noticed. A precursor of the crisis was a loud scandal in 1889 with the bankruptcy of the Company in France planning to build the Panama Canal, when the merger of speculative capital and the government got disclosed. In 1890, in the United Kingdom, credit institutions and enterprises actively investing in Argentine securities (after a sharp drop in rates and private shares, and government bonds) began to go bankrupt. The outflow of capital from the markets of the United States and Latin America triggered a financial and industrial crisis in these countries. Thus, this crisis clearly demonstrated the destructive power of the chaotic movement of speculative capital for both developed and developing countries.

Economic cycles and crises of the 20th century had remarkable features due to influence of the two world wars, revolutions in many countries, loss of close economic ties between the territory of the former Russian Empire and China for a long time and the failure of the gold standard system.

The crisis of 1900-1903, the first one in the 20th century, was preceded by a significant overheating of the economy: the existing production capacities could not cope with ever increasing volumes of orders, electricity generation increased in the 90s of 19th century four times and previously peripheral countries got more actively involved in world production and trade. The situation was intensified by the Anglo-Boer War (1899-1902), which required even greater production of coal, metal, etc. As a result, commodity prices, primarily for metals and coal, began to rise sharply. The severe winter of 1899-1900 and difficulties with the export of coal from England further exacerbated the situation. The first signs of a crisis were manifested in Russia, where large firms *Mamontov* and *von Derviz* became bankrupt and a financial panic arose. The bubble in the market of metals that broke in 1900 led to a 30% reduction in prices in the US ferrous metallurgy. In May 1900, the American stock exchange crashed.

The sharp monopolization of markets, revolutionary changes in technology, a new surge in railway construction (in the period from 1900 to 1907, 72 thousand km of railroads were built in the world) and large unsecured issues of shares of monopolies (for example, the entire issue of shares by the *Morgan Steel Trust* for 508 million dollars had no security) preceded the crisis of 1907, which erupted in the United States. The New York Stock Exchange failure in March 1907, when the shares of railway companies fell by 20% in just one day, became the trigger mechanism for the crisis. Following the stock market crisis, a recession began in industry. In October of 1907, panic of depositors and a monetary market crisis began (the loan interest in the US rose to 125%). Although the crisis of 1907 seized the entire world economy, it was most acutely manifested in the United States, where the drop in production was the most significant compared to all previous crises. The severity of the crisis forced the US authorities to take systematic measures particularly in the banking and financial spheres, and therefore the Federal Reserve System was established.

According to a number of economists, another economic crisis began to form in 1913-1914, but the natural course of events was interrupted by the First World War, during which a number of world economic ties broke off, the world monetary system built on the gold standard got rejected and prices for many types of products and raw materials dramatically increased. In the warring countries during the war years, the economy largely acquired a mobilization character and the role of state regulation significantly increased. By the end of the war, the German, Austro-Hungarian, Russian and Ottoman empires disintegrated, and many new independent states appeared. All these changes had a generally negative impact on the economies of the belligerent countries, however, the economic situation of a number of countries (Canada, Japan, and especially the United States), on the contrary, had improved.

The transition from war to peace also had a strong impact on the economy. The economies of the United States and other belligerent countries saw a decline in production from the end of 1918 until mid-1919, associated with the cessation of military production. In the US, the decline was 17%, while in Germany, due to the transport, fuel, raw materials and food crisis, the economy was close to collapse. However, since mid-1919, consumer demand in many countries, both postponed during the war, and due to stimulation by the governments, has increased noticeably. And to a large extent, the growth of consumer demand in European countries was secured by loans from the US and an increase in the budget deficit of European countries. However, the increase in demand in 1919 was extremely short-lived. Due to the measures taken by the monetary authorities of a number of countries to tighten fiscal and monetary policy, primarily in the United States, consumer demand began to contract rapidly and its fall in the United States in 1920 was assessed at 25% of GDP. In addition, the economic situation in the world was exacerbated by US protectionist measures and the transition from inflation to deflation. Thus, in 1920, a new cyclical crisis occurred, accompanied by a significant decline in the share price (in the US, shares of half of the companies' fell 2 times or more), sharp drop in world trade (exports and imports fell by half) and an unprecedentedly high level of unemployment (in the UK, it reached 20% among members of trade unions). The crisis of 1920-1921 was quite deep, albeit short-lived. Already in the spring of 1921 a new economic upswing was noted, which was of a rather stormy character and lasted until the Great Depression of 1929-1933.

The crisis of 1929-1933 because of its destructiveness and duration, is still an object of close study by economists, since it most clearly manifested systemic problems of the economic order.

The crisis was preceded by a rather energetic rise in the American economy (Roaring Twenties). In the United States the automotive, machine-building, chemical, electrical and aviation industries were flourishing. The American miracle of the 1920s was visibly embodied in intensive housing construction, for which $30 billion was spent. The real estate market, especially for new homes was growing very quickly. Simultaneously with the housing market, the long-term consumer goods market was developing rapidly. American capital was penetrating quite actively into developed and developing economies. On the eve of the crisis, US investments in Europe reached $5 billion, Canada - $4.5 billion and in Latin America - $ 6billion. The United States was producing 44% of world industrial output (excluding the USSR).

However, in the most countries no noticeable economic recovery was observed. For example, in England, the total physical volume of industrial production could not exceed the pre-war level. Germany experienced periods of hyperinflation and was burdened with a huge indemnity.

Significant changes in the 20's took place in the international monetary system, where instead of the gold-coin standard that collapsed during the war, a gold standard was introduced. The role of the dollar as a world reserve currency has significantly strengthened, which was caused both by economic reasons (huge debt of the European countries against the USA, strengthening of American production and exports) and growing political role of the USA. During this period, various international political and financial institutions were also established, from the *League of Nations* to the *Bank for International Settlements*.

At the same time, due to the pressure of the trade unions, regulation in the field of labor relations and wages was tightened, which made the labor market less flexible, and according to a number of economists, contributed to unprecedented high unemployment rate during the Great Depression.

Economic recovery of the 20's also was not accompanied by a rise in the level of prices for commodities and raw materials (characteristic for this phase of the economic cycle), which could be attributed both to an excessive rise in prices during the war, and, for example, to the dumping of prices for bread and other raw materials by the USSR. At the same time, prices for financial and monetary assets increased significantly.

In addition, during this period, the share of financial services in the produced GDP has appreciably increased. If earlier the most significant industry in GDP formation was heavy industry, then in the 20's in the economies of the USA, Britain and France, the financial sector began to dominate. As a result of large-scaled issue of shares, an increase in participants on the stock exchange (at least 1 million players in the US alone) and expansion of services offered by financial, trust and leasing companies were noticed. In the United States, holding companies became more and more important in the economy, while minority shareholders increasingly withdrew from business management.

In the spring, the Federal Reserve System began to worry about excessive lending activity in the banking sector and large-scale speculation in the stock market. Indeed, from 1922 to 1929 the Dow Jones index rose from 103 to 381 points and the interest rate on short-term on-call loans reached 15-20%. In these circumstances, in order to prevent overheating of the economy, the Fed raised the discount rate, which did not prevent the crisis (and according to some economists, even contributed to it). However, some economists, for example, the distinguished Austrian scientist Ludvig von Mises warned about the stock market crash several years before.

In October 1929, massive collapse occurred on the American stock exchanges, which spasmodically lasted for several years, reaching the bottom in 1932 at 40 points (thus became an absolute historical record). Despite the statements and the measures taken by the administration of President Hoover (meetings with big business, the adoption of the housing construction program, etc.) another collapse took place on the stock exchange in May 1930, which was exacerbated by the crisis in agriculture due to a crop failure and at the same time a fall in product prices.

The measures taken in the United States in 1930 to protect the domestic market from imports through the introduction of protective duties caused retaliatory steps in other countries, which not only reduced US exports, but also destructively affected all world trade.

The situation was simply catastrophic in the US industry. In 1932, the index of industrial production was only 54% of the pre-crisis level (only 14-15% in the automotive and steel industries). According to Huerta de Soto, the famous Spanish economist and researcher of the crises in the United States, about 110,000 companies, 5,000 banks and 900,000 farms went bankrupt and the unemployment rate approached 25%[8].

The American crisis quickly "infected" the other countries. In the summer of 1931, the largest financial and banking crisis began in Germany and as a result of the panic of depositors, banking "holidays" were introduced. The collapse on the stock exchange led to its closure by the end of April 1932. Germany declared a default on reparation debts in 1931, which led to a chain of sovereign defaults in a number of countries and a deterioration of the financial situation in England and rejection by the country of the gold standard. Following the England, the US and other countries also declined the gold standard.

---

[8]   Soto de U., "Money, bank credit and economic cycles", Chelyabinsk, 2008, Publishing House., «Socium»(in Russian language).

In general, as a result of the crisis of 1929-1933, the world trade declined threefold, US industrial production fell to the level of 1905, in Germany to the level of 1896 and in England to the level of 1897. The economic crisis led to an aggravation of the socio-political situation in virtually all countries, many states established authoritarian or dictatorial regimes and prerequisites for the Second World War were created. At the same time, a new economic model of development with a strong regulatory role of the state began to form in developed countries.

Thus, in the US, Roosevelt's "new course" included rehabilitation of the banking sector, creation of a deposit insurance system, performance of public works for the needy, public investment, insurance by the Federal Housing Administration of mortgage loans, regulation of prices and production volumes, and compensation to agricultural producers. At the same time, it was possible to preserve democratic institutions and the rule of law.

In a number of countries in the 1920-40's (Nazi Germany, Fascist Italy) an economic model was used, based on subordination of business to the state and syndication of industry and trade unions. At the same time, democratic institutions were eliminated.

Economic growth in the mid-30's was unstable, restrained by the collapse of world economic relations and the decline or even lack of export of capital. A new crisis emerged in 1937 due to the unresolved disparities in the economy. In 1938, production decline in the United States was 30%, while in France it dropped 12%. The way out of the crisis was already associated mainly with the growth of orders of the military industry, which led to economic growth and a reduction in the unemployment level. So in the USA in 1940 the number of unemployed was 8 million people, and in 1944 (against the background of huge military orders) - only 700 thousand.

The Second World War significantly changed the world political and economic configuration, strengthening the United States as the world center. At the same time, restoration of Western European countries and Japan was carried out with active American participation, in particular, in accordance with the Marshall Plan. Post-war recovery, as well as the economic development of Western countries in the 50's - 60's was characterized by a smoothing of fluctuations in the economic cycle, a small depth and duration of the recession. So, the recession during the crisis of 1948-1949 was 1.7%, in 1953-1954 - 1.6%, in 1957-1958 - 3.4%, in 1960-1961 - 1.4% and in 1969-1970 - 0.8%. At the same time, during the periods between crises, there was a very impressive growth noticed: in 1949-1953, it amounted to a total of 28%, in 1954-1957 - 11.8%, in 1958-1960 - 11.4%, in 1961-1969 years - 47.8% and in 1970-1973 - 15.2%[9]. Many scientists, for example, the famous Belgian Economist G. van der Wee noted the uniqueness of the economic development of western countries during the 25 post-war years[10]. Among the factors that determined such a long period of economic prosperity for developed countries, one can note model of state regulation effective for that time, deep socio-economic reforms, integration processes at the regional and international levels, the scientific and technological revolution.

The crisis of 1973-1975 became the first post-war crisis, strength and duration of which greatly exceeded those of the 1940-1960 crises. The crisis was preceded by the actual collapse of the Bretton Woods currency system that was based on the dollar convertible into gold. The economic decline in 1973-1975 was combined with galloping inflation ("stagflation"), which was not typical for previous crises. Among the factors of the crisis development, the economists noted the monetary crisis, as well as the rise in prices for fuel and raw materials (in 1971-1974 - by 159%[11]). The crisis began to develop in the fall of 1973 in the United States, Great Britain, the Federal Republic of Germany, and soon spread to the other countries. As a result, industrial production in developed countries fell by 11-13%, unemployment in the US rose to 8.5 million, retail and wholesale prices increased by 16-21% and share prices fell by 43.4%.

The crisis of 1979-1982 developed against the background of an excess of capital (primarily due to capital flows from oil-producing countries), continued growth in oil prices and galloping inflation. During this period, due to taking power in many countries by neoconservatives the ideology of economic policy changed. It was followed by transition to deregulation and reduction of the government's role in the economy and the social sphere. In addition, the

---

[9]   Business Conditions Digest, 1975, April, p., 111.

[10]   VeeV., "History of world economy" 1945-1990, M., 1994, Publishing House., «Nauka»(in Russian language).

[11]   VeeV., "History of world economy" 1945-1990, M., 1994, Publishing House., «Nauka»(in Russian language), p., 174.

emphasis was made on monetary methods of regulation. In order to combat inflation in accordance with the views of monetarists, the discount rate of central banks was actively being used. So in the US the discount rate in 1980 rose to 13% while in the UK - to 17%, which according to many economists (e.g. P. Samuelson) aggravated the recession. At the same time, according to A. Greenspan, former US Federal Reserve Chairman, this measure was justified, and the crisis began earlier[12]. The crisis of 1979-1982 was not acute by nature, but was protracted and with a high level of unemployment.

Since the 80's of 20th century financial revolution had started, manifested in the continuous financial innovations, the emergence of new products, tools and technologies. Deregulation in the financial and banking sector was combined with the erosion of the borders between banking, financial and investment operations, and the growth of speculative operations. At the same time, globalization of the world economy, the elimination of borders for the flow of capital, goods and labor and emergence of new economic centers took place. Against this background, crises of the next years were occurring.

The crisis of 1990-1992 was caused by the rapid growth of the external debt of developing countries (in 1986 it reached $1 trillion), engagement of banks in risky and speculative operations, adverse foreign policy influences (for example, investors' expectations of rising oil prices due to Iraq's invasion in Kuwait). The complexity of the situation is indicated by the fact that the Fed, from July 1989 to July 1992, reduced the discount rate 23 times to stimulate business activity. In 1991, decline in industrial production in Japan began, which then developed into a prolonged recession. In Spain, the recession lasted five years, while in France unemployment reached 10-12%. The economic recession was supplemented by monetary crises in Great Britain, Italy, Sweden, Norway and Finland. Scandinavian countries also faced systemic banking crises, overcoming which significantly increased their public debt (in Sweden, for example, to 73% of GDP).

Between 1994 and 2002 it was possible to observe a whole series of national and regional economic crises: the crisis in Mexico and Argentina in 1994-1995, the Asian crisis in 1997-1998, then the crisis in Russia in 1998-1999

---

[12]   Greenspan A., "The Age of Turbulence: Adventures in a New World", M., 2009, Publishing House., «Alpina Business Books» (in Russian language), p., 92

and new crisis in Argentina in 2001- 2002. When reviewing the nature of these crises, it is to be noted that in general (except Asian countries) they were not classical cyclical crises but were caused by an external factor (tides and outflows of speculative capital) against the background of structural weaknesses and imbalances (high public debt and state budget deficit, an overvalued dollar against the national currency, socio-political problems). In case of South Korea, Hong Kong and Singapore, we can talk about the cyclical nature of crises, but the factor of the "hot" capital movement played a significant role.

The crisis in these countries usually was starting with a powerful pressure of speculative capital on national currencies. Their monetary authorities were delaying the smooth devaluation of the national currency, but the destructive pressure of running capital eventually led to the collapse of the currency, bankruptcies in the financial and banking sector and later in other sectors of the economy), hyperinflation, panic among investors and often to sovereign and private defaults.

In developed countries, in particular in the US, one could observe the cyclical crisis of 2001-2002, which occurred after a very long period of economic recovery (120 months according to US economists). During this period, a massive inflow of foreign capital into the American economy was observed (75% of foreign investment in the US economy for the period from 1951 to 2001 were made in the last 6 years before the crisis). At the same time, foreign capital largely attracted the growing stock market, primarily new companies associated with internet technologies (dotcom bubble). The emerging bubble is well characterized by the fact that 10 companies of a "new" economy accounted for almost 25% of the total capitalization of the US stock market. In addition, the share of the financial services sector in the American economy has steadily increased, reaching 32% in 2003. The first collapse in the US stock market occurred in the spring of 2000, followed by a period of short growth, to which the well-known American financier, G. Soros, gave a very figurative description: "The music has stopped, but people are still dancing." The total capitalization of the largest Internet companies fell by more than USD 1.2 trillion by December. In March-April 2001 there was another collapse of quotations. The situation on the stock market worsened after the September 11, 2001 terrorist attack. In October 2002, compared to the pre-crisis level, the Dow Jones Industrial index fell by 37.5%, the S&P 500 by

50%, NASDAQ Composite - by 78%[13]. In 2001, there was a general economic decline. In order to overcome crisis, the Fed 12 times lowered the discount rate in 2001-2002, which in October 2002 reached 1.25%. The cheapened credit resources stimulated a boom in financing the housing market, which created the prerequisites for a new destructive crisis in 2007-2008.

Thus, having reviewed economic crises in the historical aspect, we see better that "the crisis depends not only on random causes peculiar to a certain historical moment, but on the constantly acting common causes inherent in the modern cultural and economic system"[14]. Despite all the variety of crises, there are many common points that allow the researcher not only to establish the causes of the problem, but also to try to offer their vision of overcoming them.

1.2. Views of representatives of different directions of economic thought on the nature of crises

In economics, there is a fairly wide range of views on the nature of the socio-economic crisis, including such aspects as factors of its development, the possibilities and ways of its prevention, tools to overcome the crisis, the measures to minimize its consequences and so on. At present, with all the diversity of economists' views, the concept of inevitability and the cyclical nature of the economic crisis is dominant, which so aptly was formulated in the 19th century by C. Juglar, the famous French theorist of crises: "It seems that crises like diseases represent one of the conditions for existence of a society dominated by trade and industry. It can be forecasted, mitigated, delayed up to a certain point, to facilitate the resumption of economic activity; but to cancel them, in spite of a variety of techniques, still nobody has been able"[15]. Repeated economic cycles of 7-11 years, including the phase of recovery, recession and crisis, depression, were also first discovered by C. Juglar and named as "Juglar Cycle" in his honor based on suggestion of another famous economist J. Schumpeter. The phases of the economic cycle formulated by

---

[13] Greenspan A., "The Age of Turbulence: Adventures in a New World", M., 2009, Publishing House., «Alpina Business Books» (in Russian language), p., 92

[14] Tugan-Baranovsky M., Periodic Industrial Crises, M., 2008, Directimedia Publishing (in Russian language), p., 21.

[15] Juglar C. Des Crises Commercialeset de leur retour periodique en France, en Angleterreet aux Etats-Unis, Paris, 1862, Guillaumin.

C. Juglar are found practically in all economic schools, beginning with Karl Marx, neo-Marxists, G.M. Keynes to modern representatives of the neo-Keynesian, neoclassical and institutional lines of economic thought.

However, for understanding the nature of economic crises, along with medium-term Juglar cycles it is very important to bear in mind that there are also long-term economic cycles that largely determine the dynamics and duration of medium-term cycles, structural changes in the socio-economic structure of society. In economic science, serious attention is paid to long-term economic cycles, which were investigated by economists of the first half of the twentieth century (Й. ВанГелдерен, М. А. Бунятин, С. деВольф), however they are addressed in the most complete form in the works of the famous Russian economist N.D. Kondratieff. In recent years, the theory of Kondratieff's waves has found further development in the works of many modern economists, in particular: Mandel E. («Late Capitalism», 1975), Dickson D. («Technology and Cycles of Boom and Bust», 1983), Goldstein J. («Long Cycles: Prosperity and War in the Modern Age», 1988), Berend I. T. («Economic Fluctuation Revisited», 2002), Jourdon Ph. («La monnaie unique europeenne et son lien au development economique et social coordonne: uneanalysecliometrique», 2008).

N.D. Kondratieff, based on a statistical analysis of the most important indicators' dynamics for the US, UK and French economies (prices, interest on capital, nominal wages, foreign trade volume, a number of production indicators) identified long-term economic cycles (about 50-60 years), during which deep structural changes took place in the economy and social life and specific character of macroeconomic indicators and features of Juglar's medium-term cycles development were noticed. N.D. Kondratieff identified three cycles in the works of the latest economists (Table1).

Table 1

Long economic cycles identified by
N.D.Kondratieff and modern economists

Sequence number of a long wave	Phases of a long wave	Period	Technological structure
I	Ascending	End of 1780's – beginning of 1790's. – 1810-1817	Textile industry and textile machinery
	Descending	1810-1817 – 1844-1851	
II	Ascending	1844-1851– 1870-1875	Railways, coal and steel
	Descending	1870-1875– 1890-1896	
III	Ascending	1890-1896 – 1914-1920	Electricity, chemistry and heavy engineering
	Descending	1914-1929 – 1939-1950	
IV	Ascending	1939-1950 – 1968-1974	Car, oil, artificial materials, electronics
	Descending	1968-1974 – 1984-1991	
V	Ascending	1984-1991 – 2005-2008	Microelectronics, personal computers, telecommunications, biotechnology
	Descending	2005-2008 – ...	

Sources: Kondratyev N., "Big cycles of conjuncture and foresight theory.",M., 2002, Publishing House., «Ekonomika» (in Russian language); Ayres R.U., Did the Fifth K-Wave Begin in 1990-1992? Has it been Aborted by Globalization? Kondratieff Waves, Warfare and World Security/Ed. By T. C. Devezas/ Amsterdam, 2006, IOS Press; Jourdon Ph., La monnaie unique europeenneet son lien au development economiqueet social coordonne: uneanalysecliometrique, These, Montpellier, 2008, Universite Montpellier; Papenhausen Ch., Causal Mechanisms of Long Waves, Futures 40.

In his theory of long economic cycles, N.D.Kondratieff proceeded from the fact that the driving force behind economic development was represented by capital investments (primarily long-term ones), which were necessary for creation of basic capital goods that have been existing for decades and requiring considerable time and costs for their creation (the largest buildings, railways, channels, communication lines and so on). N.D. Kondratieff in building long-term cycles of economic development also relied on the methodology of medium-term cycles of reproduction of Karl Marx: "If Karl Marx argued that the material basis of periodically recurring crises or average cycles in each decade was material wear and tear, change and expansion of production tools in the form of machines and workers during 10 years at average, it can be assumed that the material basis of large cycles is wear and tear, as well as change and expansion of major material goods requiring long period and excessive costs for their production"[16].

When reviewing the upward wave of the economic cycle, N.D. Kondratiev noted that it was characterized by the renewal and expansion of the basic capital goods, radical changes and the rearrangement of the main productive forces of society. To implement large-scale investments, a considerable capital is needed, the accumulation of which reaches a significant size by the time of the beginning of the upward wave, and in subsequent years the rate of capital accumulation must exceed the investment rate. In this phase of the cycle, capital is not in a dispersed state, but is concentrated in the disposal of powerful business centers, facilitated by the banking and financial systems. At the same time, there is an abundance of "free" and cheap capital.

In addition to the availability of significant capital ready for investment, the beginning of the upward wave of the economic cycle is characterized by a high degree of technological innovation: "for about two decades, before the beginning of the upward wave of a large cycle, there is a revival in the sphere of technical inventions. Prior to beginning and at the very start of the upswing wave, a wide application of these inventions in the sphere of industrial practice is observed, connected with the reorganization of production relations"[17].

The presence of significant cheap and free capital and technological changes in production leads to the fact that large-scale investments in production and infrastructure, causing a radical change in the conditions of production, become quite cost-effective, and therefore inevitable. Begins a period of relatively grandiose new construction, the widespread use of accumulated technical inventions and creation of new productive forces. At the same time,

---

[16]   Kondratyev N., "Big cycles of conjuncture and foresight theory.",M., 2002, Publishing House., «Ekonomika» (in Russian language), p., 390.

[17]   Kondratyev N., "Big cycles of conjuncture and foresight theory.",M., 2002, Publishing House., «Ekonomika» (in Russian language), p., 374.

the upward wave is accompanied by an intensification of the struggle for new markets, which leads to increased tensions in international political relations with growing likelihood of military conflicts. The upward wave also leads to significant socio-political changes due to the pressure of the developing productive forces on obsolete production relations inhibiting development.

Significant investments lead gradually to a decrease in capital and an increase in demand for it. The demand curve for capital begins to approach the accumulation curve and then exceeds it, which leads to a rise in the cost of capital, a trend that can be strengthened by domestic and foreign policy factors (for example, an increase in public debt due to increased military and social spending may also increase the demand for capital).

As a result, prerequisites are formed for a general break in the conjuncture curve to decline, the downward wave of the economic cycle begins to develop, which is characterized by the search for ways to reduce the cost of production and new technological inventions that contribute to this cheapening. Simultaneously, due to the decrease in demand for excessively expensive capital, the price growth is suspended and conditions are created to reduce its value.

Later, in the course of a downward wave, gradually, factors that increase accumulation of capital become stronger and "the curve of the capital accumulation rate significantly exceeds the investment curve. Capital is getting cheaper. Thus conditions are created that are favorable for recovery"[18].

The theory of Kondratieff's long waves (K-waves) has been confirmed in the studies of many modern economists. For example, E. Mandel analyzed the world trade growth rates for the period from 1820 to 1967 and came to the conclusion that during the upward phases, the average annual growth rate of world trade as a whole was significantly higher than during the adjacent phases. K-waves were confirmed by D. Gordon for the dynamics of world production per capita, as well as by T. Kushinsky for the dynamics of world industrial production. At the same time, it should be noted that a number of researchers, in particular K. Barr and K. Eklund, expressed doubts

---

[18] Kondratyev N., "Big cycles of conjuncture and foresight theory.",M., 2002, Publishing House., «Ekonomika» (in Russian language), p., 394.

about the methodology for calculating the Kondratieff cycles. Nevertheless, most researchers, including many prominent economists, for example, J. Schumpeter, used long cycles to analyze and forecast the economic situation.

The crisis of 2007-2009 (as well as the devastating crises of 1929-1933 and 1971-1973) just happened during the transition from an upward to a downward phase of a long cycle, which to some extent explains its depth and negative consequences. As shown by historical experience, the structural reorganization of the economy and the social sphere, which takes place during the crisis and post-crisis period, is going to be of a large scale and a new economic model of development with a high degree of probability will begin to form, just as in the 1930's of 20th century, when the "new course" of F.D. Roosevelt was implemented and a transition to a neoliberal economy started in the late 70's - early 80's.

Along with long-term economic cycles there are medium-term ones (in recent decades, their duration was about 7-8 years), which were already described by K. Juglar, and the reasons of which are addressed by each economic school.

"The savior of capitalism" J.M. Keynes in analyzing economic cycles and crises has focused on the issue of aggregate social demand, which depends on the propensity of the population to consume (usually income growth outstrips consumption growth) and the rate of return on capital, which is largely related to the level of interest rates on loans (the higher the loan rate, the lower the rate of profit and the greater the propensity of entrepreneurs to keep money not in production, but in liquid form). When speaking about the key cause of economic crises, J.M. Keynes noted that "the main explanation of the crisis should be sought not in the growth of interest, but in the sudden drop in the marginal efficiency of capital"[19]. In addition, the marginal efficiency of capital essentially depends on the expected return on investment in the future. At the stage of economic recovery, investments bring satisfactory income for businesses, but as the current profit and the constant growth of commodity stocks decrease, expectations begin to deteriorate, eventually "when in a market dominated by excessive optimism and excessive purchases, panic

---

[19] Keynes J.M., "The General Theory of Employment, Interest and Money" (anthology of classic economy), M., Publishing House., «Ekonov», 1993 (in Russian language);, 1993, p., 381.

begins, it acquires a sudden and even catastrophic force"[20]. Regulation of the volume of investments and aggregate demand, according to J.M. Keynes, are capable to become an antidote to the devastating crises of the laissez-faire era: "Thus, there are sufficient grounds for simultaneous actions in two directions - increasing investment, and increasing consumption to a level that the existing propensity to consume not only would correspond to increased investment, but also was even higher"[21]. J.M. Keynes advocated both direct public investment and state responsibility in creating a favorable investment climate, moderate inflation and stimulating economic growth and maximum employment. At the same time, the state should actively manage macroeconomic processes using tools of forecasting, regulation and planning.

The scientific concept of JM Keynes became the theoretical basis for the economic policy of a number of western countries in the 30's-60's of 20th century. One can notice the similarity of the economic prescriptions of J.M. Keynes and the anti-crisis measures of the administration of F.D. Roosevelt, as well as the economic and social policy pursued in post-war Western Europe. It should be noted that the socio-economic policies of developed countries in the second half of the 40's-60's of 20th century were very effective, which was reflected in the course of economic cycles: high rates of economic growth in the long stage of recovery were combined with a short and insignificant recession, which gave rise to many economists to talk even about the 25-year period of economic prosperity. Later, the theory of J.M. Keynes was developed in the works of economists of the neo-Keynesian school, in particular by R. Clauer, E. Hansen, A. Leijonhufvud, P. Davidson, A. Coddington, J. Robinson and L. Pazinetti.

Despite the weakening of the position of the Keynesian school in the 70's-90's in connection with the transition of developed countries to the neoliberal economic model in recent years, both scientifically and in practice, there is considerable interest in this economic concept. The long-term stimulation of consumer demand due to credit resources in the last decade before the crisis of 2007-2009, practically zero interest rates on loans from the central bank of developed countries and increase in direct state investments in the crisis and post-crisis period largely coincided with Keynesian recipes. It seems that in the

---

[20]   Ibid, p., 381

[21]   Ibid, p., 388.

context of a large-scale crisis interest in the anti-crisis tools of the Keynesian school will remain at a high level, the accumulated scientific potential of this school may well be involved in the formation of a new model of economic growth.

An alternative to Keynesianism was the economic theory of supply (A. Laffer), the conclusions and proposals of which have been applied by conservative governments of developed countries since the late 70's of 20th century. Stagflation in the 1970's (the combination of galloping inflation with a decline in production) raised the question of the inefficiency of the prevailing Keynesian model of economic development, although critics of this model held back about such inflation factors as explosive growth in oil prices. In general, the question was raised about the ineffectiveness of significant state intervention in the economy, including such aspects as high level of taxation and public spending, especially social, high weight in the public sector economy, the negative impact of state regulation on the level of entrepreneurial activity. In fact, the authors of this concept saw the causes of crises as ineffective state intervention in the economy and the social sphere.

The theory of the supply economy, like other neoclassical directions of economic thought, transfers the micro-level principles of entities' operations to the macro level. According to authors of this theory, the level of using resources in the economy is connected with the supply of capital and labor. The supply of capital in this theory is related to the level of savings that is determined by the choice between consumption today and in the future, and the supply of labor is a choice between leisure and work. At the same time, the key question is how the policy of the state influences the supply of labor and capital. High taxation and social costs distort the relative attractiveness of labor with respect to leisure and the relative attractiveness of savings in comparison with consumption. The reduction in income tax, in particular on income from deposits and dividends, leads to an increase in the propensity to save, increases the supply of loan capital, which leads to a decrease in the interest rate and stimulation of business activity. The reduction in corporate income tax leads to an increase in the level of dividends paid and, consequently, to the growth of the market value of the business and additional opportunities to raise funds in the market, which creates the conditions for increasing investment activity. The reduction in the rates of taxes on labor income helps to increase the supply of labor force. As a result, an increase in the rate of accumulation and an acceleration of economic growth are achieved.

In general, the recipes on tax reduction by the authors of this scientific school were actively used by the administrations of R. Reagan, George H.W. Bush and George W. Bush, which on the one hand, according to some economists, contributed to the emergence from the crisis of 1979-1982, but on the other hand led to a significant loss of tax revenue and the growth of public debt. As noted by the famous American Economist G. Mankiw, "Almost all professional economists, including those who supported Reagan's tax cuts, saw that such statements were too optimistic. Lowering the tax burden may encourage people to work harder, and to some extent these additional efforts of workers can compensate for direct effects of tax cuts, but there was no convincing evidence that these additional conditions would be sufficient to increase tax collection amid a reduction in tax rates ... "[22].It is also worth recalling that on the eve of the reduction in tax rates by the Bush administration in 2003, the *American Nonpartisan Economic Policy Institute* published a statement by 10 Nobel laureates in economics who opposed tax cuts.

In general, this theory raises the actual issue of the optimal level of taxation, which is very important for ensuring sustainable economic growth. When forming a new economic model of growth, it is important to include a constant monitoring of the aggregate level of taxation, which should be optimal both from the perspective of stimulating the economic initiative and in terms of ensuring the sustainability of public finances and maintaining conditions for the reproduction of labor resources.

Another alternative to Keynesianism was the monetarist theory (M. Friedman, C. Brunner, A. Melzer, D. Leidler, R. Selden, F. Keigan). Representatives of this area of scientific thought place the money supply, as well as control over its magnitude and dynamics, at the center of the study of economic cycles, especially in the long term. Market economy, according to their version, is stable with respect to some optimal level of production, which does not exclude the natural level of unemployment. Optimal level of production is

---

[22]   Moore Stephen, Think Twice About Gregory Mankiw, National Review, 2003, Feb., 28.

achieved through the operation of the price mechanism, which is an effective way to allocate resources. The change in the money supply through the effect of cash balances leads to a change in spending and nominal incomes, which in the short term affects the level of prices and output, and in the long run it only affects the level of prices. The stability of the economy is connected with maintaining a stable relationship between the mass of money in circulation and the most important macroeconomic indicators. The main goal of the government's economic policy is to maintain a stable price level and monetary circulation. For this, it is necessary to maintain a moderate growth in the money supply, determined by the ratio of the long-term growth rate of production and the speed of circulation of money. At the same time, active intervention in economic processes and short-term adjustment of the economy can destabilize the economic situation and lead to a crisis. Thus, control over the size of the money supply and the level of prices and minimization of state intervention in economic processes represent the quintessence of monetarist theory.

Monetarist prescriptions for maintaining economic stability along with the ideas of the supply economy became the theoretical basis for the neo-liberal economic model that was formed in developed countries in the 1980's of 20th century and existed with little or no major changes before the global crisis of 2007-2009. To a certain extent, the monetarist recipes looked quite effective in the 1980's and to a lesser extent in the 1990's, but according to a number of economists and politicians, ultimately the decline in the role of the state in the economy and the ineffectiveness of passive monetary policy led to the last systemic crisis.

Despite the collapse of the economic concept of development proposed by the monetarists, importance of a number of their recommendations for sustainable economic development should be noted. It is primarily about the need to control inflation and maintain a stable price level, which is very important for attracting long-term investments, maintaining economic and social stability.

Representatives of *The Austrian Economic School* (the founders K. Menger, O. von Böhm-Bawerk, at a later time - L. von Mises, H. Hazlitt, M. Rothbard, F. von Hayek) had their own view of the nature of the crises. In their study of the economy, they focus on studying the psychological characteristics of consumer behavior, the structure of capital and its temporal variability. At the same time, scientists of this direction emphasize the subjective approach to research and fundamentally refuse to use economic-mathematical models as imperfect in terms of reflecting real economic processes. The key point of the Austrian school research was the problem of coherence of actions of economic entities in the spatial and temporal aspects. At the same time, prices represent an effective information and communication system designed to solve this problem. Based on previous studies of the Austrian school economists, F. von Hayek formulated a modern view of this direction on the nature of the economic cycle and crises. In his opinion, intertemporal coordination in the economy and equalization of supply and demand of resources used at various stages of the production process occur if prices, as information signals, adequately reflect people's preferences. However, people's preferences are constantly in the process of change, which affects the economic equilibrium, understood as a process in time. Changes in preferences lead to economic cycles, as the process of adapting the structure of production and capital to such changes takes time and involves a number of limitations. Equilibrium can also be violated by other factors, for example, as a result of the influence of regulators on bank interest and money supply, which can lead to deformation of the price system, cause inadequate changes in the structure of production and even provoke a crisis. In a polemic with J.M. Keynes, F. von Hayek spoke extremely negatively about the possibility of inflationary lubrication of the economy, which distorts the price structure and leads to imbalances in the economy. In this regard, in accordance with the views of representatives of the Austrian school, the political neutrality of the Central Bank is very important, and since, in the opinion of F. von Hayek, in the modern world it is illusory enough, he even proposed the denationalization of money - the provision on a competitive basis of the rights of private financial Institutions to issue good payment instruments, in contrast to not very good ones, issued by the monopolist state.[23]

It seems that in this economic concept there are also many aspects that may be important in the construction of a new economic model of the post-crisis world economy. Primarily these are understanding of the analysis of driving motives of economic agents, caution in the application of formal macroeconomic models and careful deliberations of intervention in the

[23]   Hayek F., Denationalization of Money, L., 1976.

monetary sphere and unsuccessful actions in this area, according to many economists, can really provoke a crisis.

Undoubtedly, an important milestone in the study of the nature of economic cycles and crises was the concept of overproduction crises proposed by K. Marx, which is covered in this or that perspective throughout his fundamental work - *Capital*. Theoretically, potential probability of a crisis arises from a transition from an in-kind exchange to a money exchange, since there is a gap in time between selling and buying, and this creates the possibility of an economic crisis, while the credit development increases this time gap.

When analyzing the economic cycle, K. Marx noted that at the stage of recovery there are incentives for capital accumulation, a growing demand for labor, a reduction in unemployment and a rise in wages and a decrease in the rate of profit. Then there is overproduction of goods, the fall in the rate of profit reaches such a point that the incentives for the capital accumulation cease to function, and investments stop. Then a sharp reduction in demand, primarily for investment, is noticed and unemployment increases dramatically (the "reserve army of labor"), real wages are falling, prices are falling and accumulated capital reserves are depreciating. In turn, the reduction in wages and the depreciation of inventories increase the profit margin, which again leads to the accumulation of capital, the beginning of recovery. An important point was the statement of K. Marx on the cyclical and the systemic nature of economic crises. It should be noted that Marx also foresaw the systemic upheavals of capitalism, stemming from the contradiction between the social nature of production and the private nature of the appropriation of its results.

Later, after the revolutions in the first half of the 20th century, Marx's economic theory became the basis of the socioeconomic policy of the USSR, China, Cuba, a number of countries in Eastern Europe, Asia and Africa. Socialist and social democratic parties that came to power in a number of western countries also formally recognized most of Marx's economic theory, although it was largely revised and modernized. The concept of K. Marx always becomes popular during periods of deep crises, and with some certainty it is possible to predict its renaissance at certain extent in modern conditions, although the experience of practical implementation of this concept in the 20th century in a number of countries created a powerful vaccine against ideological and formal application. At the same time, one cannot help but admit that deepening the problems of poorly regulated market economy, which is becoming less and less social and attractive, again puts on the agenda the search for effective alternatives to avoid the growth and deepening of contradictions in the social and economic sphere.

The causes of crises were also raised by representatives of the American institutional school. According to the famous American economist J.K. Galbraith in the modern economy with an oligopoly, "the self-propelled force of competition is a chimera". In modern conditions, the ability of the economy to self-regulate depends on balancing the forces of monopolies - sellers and monopolies buyers. In a number of cases, countervailing forces do not cope with the situation, and a crisis arises. In this case, the intervention of the state, also acting as one of the balancing forces, comes to the scene. Along with business and the state, the third main counterbalancing force of the economy is represented by trade unions as monopolies for the sale of labor. In our opinion, this structuring of the forces acting in the economy reflects the real situation in developed countries and could be taken into account when forming a new economic model. In addition, in the emerging market economies, the role of these three main counterbalancing forces has not yet been fully formed. For example, trade unions are still largely a formal institution and not a real economic force, which puts on the agenda further development of all economic and social institutions of the market economy.

Supporters of the asymmetric information theory (K. Arrow, J. Akerlof) see the reasons for the crises emergence in possessing varying degrees of information by economic contractors (buyer and seller, creditor and debtor, etc.) about transaction. As a result, for example, theoretically, a bank cannot have the level of information about a debtor that is available to the latter. In these conditions, banks can inadequately assess credit risks, raise interest rates on loans taking into account all potential risks, which will repel credit for potentially reliable borrowers and attract unreliable customers.

The issue of economic crises and cycles was also studied in the historical economic school (F. List, G. Shmoller, M. Weber, V. Sombart). In a polemics with M. Weber, who saw the source of capitalistic development in Protestant ethics, V. Sombart singled out various historical types of entrepreneurs, noting that different types of entrepreneurs are in demand in different phases of the economic cycle (at the boom stage - "conquerors", at the stage of recession - "organizers"). V. Sombart somewhat deviates from the concept of the economic cycle, considered, for example, by K. Marx, and replaces it with the concept of conjuncture. The rhythmic movement of developed capitalism is determined by the desire for entrepreneurship, while the expectation of profit leads to speculative upsurge, which primarily covers the inorganic goods of durable use (railways, vehicles, income houses, electric power equipment). For the expanded production of these goods, an expanded production of production means (machinery and structural materials) is necessary, which V. Sombart defined as "the secondary benefits of a conjuncture recovery." As a result of expanding production of both types of goods, large enterprises emerge, into which monetary capital flows more and more easily. At the same time, the attached "property capital" (raw materials, auxiliary materials) is increasing, and the number of hired workers is rapidly growing. However, such an impulsive development of production encounters disproportions, of which the major one, according to W. Sombart, is between the sizes of production in the industries based on the inorganic basis, and in the industries that process agrarian products and lag behind by growth rate. This disproportionality is combined with another one - between the abundance of fixed capital and the lack of money. As a result, the continuous growth of production turnover outstrips the possibilities of lending and in the long run a large number of enterprises are unable to meet their liabilities. From this moment begins a backward movement in the demand chain. According to V. Sombart, both the periods of upsurge and the periods of recession are necessary, because thanks to them both sides of capitalism speculative-grasping and calculating-organizational are developing. The period of recovery is connected with the "popularization of the capitalist spirit", the economic outburst, the stock-speculation not only of entrepreneurs, but of broad sections of the population. The period of decline is characterized by an internal improvement of the capitalist system, technical and organizational innovations, the transition of the management of economic life from "conquerors" to "organizers."

When speaking about the views of historical school economists as a whole, one can note a rather important opinion about the need of accounting and analysis in economic policy of country's national development, including historical, geographical, cultural, ethical factors, only on the basis of which, according to G. Shmoller, "the building of a certain national economic system can be erected."

One of the factors causing the global crisis of 2007-2009 was excessive credit expansion of financial institutions (credit boom), which makes it necessary to consider the theory of the crises emergence due to credit expansion. However, first of all, researchers face the problem of identifying a credit boom.

Researchers K. Azaridis and L. Kaas in the study "Self-fulfilling credit cycles", actively discussed among economists, wrote that the dynamics of sentiment in the credit market plays an important role in determining the behavior of the economy. Shocks arising in the credit system can lead to fluctuations in the real economy (self-fulfilling fluctuations in the credit markets). The expectation of a recession leads to a decrease in lending, which in turn leads to a fall in asset prices and a slowdown in economic activity[24].

The causes of the credit boom (when the level of lending to the economy is growing more rapidly than the average statistical level), according to some researchers, are rooted in the growing price of assets. If assets grow in price, then the value of collateral also increases. Loans disbursed under the growing security are becoming quite attractive for financial institutions. As a result, the level of lending increases with the growing value of collateral.

Another theory on the credit boom origin and its impact on the emergence of crises was proposed by the well-known researcher of the crises nature - H. Minsky in his work "Theory of Financial Instability" (Financial Instability Hypothesis, 1984). According to his hypothesis, a long period of economic prosperity inevitably leads to a crisis due to the fact that at the initial stage of economic growth hedging debtors dominate, which can pay both the principal amount of the loan and carry out interest payments. Then, speculative debtors appear on the market, able to pay only interest. Closer to the end of the economic recovery, the so-called Ponzi-debtors begin to predominate in the market, which can pay their debts only with the growth of asset prices. This inevitably leads to a financial crisis.

According to economist Taylor, the first signal of the financial crisis is on-lending, which at any time may be prone to contraction, and the credit market participants' expectations can play a big role in this. For example, if debtors

---

[24] Kaas L., Azariadis K., Self-folfilling credit cycles, www.bis.org, Central Bank Research Hab., 24/10/2012

expect squeezing in lending, then their initiative of default will increase, leading to an increase in the aggregate level of defaults and credit squeeze.

Another reason for credit booms is the policy of central banks. History shows that the policy of very low refinancing rates leads to the emergence of a bubble in the asset market and the subsequent credit boom. So, in the early 2000's the Fed kept rates at 1%, which, according to many economists, led to a sharp rise in house prices and a credit boom. This process became poorly managed, the money supply grew rapidly until the crisis of 2007-2009 began even though the rate was adjusted (obviously, with a long delay).

The causes of credit booms and the crises they cause are also in the field of herding behavior of banks, information distribution, poor quality of credit risk management, lowered lending standards, provision of state guarantees and behavior of debtors.

Many economists, including G. Zhimenez note that after periods of rapid credit growth, there are periods of defaults and bank losses on loans, which is associated with a decrease in lending standards during credit expansion, which attracts debtors with a higher level of risk to the bank for loans and leads to an increase in the risk level of banks' loan portfolios and losses[25]. There is ample evidence that at the peak of the economic boom, banks are funding even projects with a negative NPV.

The data of economists' research is confirmed by statistics, according to which currency crises closely correlate with credit booms in 50% of cases, and banking ones - in 15%. At the same time, credit booms, as a rule, are observed after financial reforms. Recessions, complicated by the previous credit boom, are more acute than ordinary recessions, which is noted, in particular, by the economist O. Jorda in the study "When credit bites back"[26]. The stronger the growth of lending to the economy, the more painful and longer the recession will be.

---

[25]   Gabriel Jim'enez and Jes'usSaurina, Credit cycles, Credit risk and Prudential regulation, 2006, Banco de Espana.

[26]   Jorda O., When credit bites back, Federal Reserve Bank of San Francisko Working Paper, Nov., 2011.

Other researchers in analyzing the causes of crises focus not so much on the credit boom, as on the growth of assets (bubbles in the asset market) or their decline. In the 1980's, after financial liberalization in many countries, an increase in asset prices, including stocks and real estate, was noticed in the west. Researchers Borio, Kennedy and Prous in the article "Exploring aggregate asset price fluctuations across countries" note that property prices have a very strong impact on the economic cycle (unlike share prices, whose influence is weaker and not always directly related to the economic cycle). An example of the US in the late 2000's and Japan in the 1990's can be noted, when real estate bubbles led to a severe crisis and a period of stagnation.

The fall in asset prices is also very dangerous for the economy and the banking system, as noted by the famous economist I. Fisher as early as in 1931. According to his research, the fall in asset prices during the Great Depression led to the effect of deflation of debts and massive bankruptcy of banks, entailed by an even greater fall in asset prices. Most debtors began to pay off their debts, which led to deflation. J.M. Keynes also noted at that time that the fall in asset prices led to lower lending by banks to the population, and as a result, economic activity declined in the country.

The above studies on the impact of credit booms (the dynamics of asset prices) on the economic cycle make it necessary to consider these dangerous destabilizing phenomena when developing a new economic policy.

Thus, we gave the main views of economists on the nature of economic cycles and crises. There are also more exotic versions, for example, the influence of solar activity on socio-economic processes, but we found it possible to limit ourselves to mainstream theories. Of course, in each of the above versions there is a significant rational kernel that can be used to form a new economic model.

1.3. World crisis of 2007-2009: stages of development and social and economic consequences

The last global economic crisis that began to unfold in 2006-2007 and ended in 2009 according to the official version of international financial institutions (although politicians and economists often believe that it has not been overcome yet), was characterized by the deepest decline in economic activity and the highest level of unemployment in developed countries since the Great Depression, the unprecedented magnitude of losses in the financial and banking sectors of the economy and the equally large level of state support for these sectors, the protracted nature of development, the ever-present threat of emergence of "new wave" of the crisis and a serious deterioration in public finances.

In order to understand the nature of this crisis and make recommendations on the formation of a more sustainable economic model, it is necessary to consider the stages of the crisis development, the escalation of the collapse of individual markets and institutions into a world economic pandemic, which is still not completely overcome.

The global crisis that started in 2007, like the previous crises, represents one of the medium and long phases of economic cycles. If we consider it from the perspective of Kondratieff's long waves, it falls just for the period of transition from ascending phase to descending one of the long-term economic cycle[27], which is always characterized by very deep and destructive consequences of the crises, representing the beginning of formation of a new economic development model. By using this crisis as an example, we can clearly see all the stages of the business cycle, including the pre-crisis boom of speculative nature. After the economic "dot-com" crisis of 2000-2002, the world economy as a whole, and the economies of developed countries showed rather high growth rates (Table 2). However, already in 2006, GDP growth rate in the US economy began to slow down, which continued in 2007, and in 2008 it went negative. In a number of developed countries, for example, Germany, Italy, France and Canada, the slowdown in GDP growth rates was already noted in 2007. In 2008, many developed countries experienced negative growth rates, and in 2009 in almost all developed states and many developing economies a significant recession occurred (Table 2).

---

[27]   Jourdon Ph., La monnaie unique europeenneet son lien au development economiqueet social coordonne: uneanalysecliometrique, These, Montpellier, 2008, Universite Montpellier; Papenhausen Ch. Causal Mechanisms of Long Waves, Futures 40.

Table 2

Annual GDP growth rate, %

	1995-2005	2006	2007	2008	2009	2010	2011	2012	2013	2014	2015	2016
World economy	**3,9**	**5,5**	**5,6**	**3,0**	**-0,1**	**5,4**	**4,2**	**3,5**	**3,4**	**3,5**	**3,4**	**3,1**
Developed countries	**2,8**	**3,0**	**2,7**	**0,1**	**-3,4**	**3,1**	**1,7**	**1,2**	**1,3**	**20**	**2,2**	**1,7**
USA	3,3	2,7	1,8	-0,3	-2,8	2,5	1,6	2,2	1,7	2,4	2,6	1,6
Japan	1,0	1,7	2,2	-1,0	-5,5	4,7	-0,5	1,7	1,6	-0,1	0,6	
Canada	3,3	2,6	2,0	1,0	-3,0	3,1	3,1	1,8	2,5	2,6	0,9	1,4
Great Britain	3,4	2,5	2,6	-0,6	-4,3	1,9	1,5	1,3	1,9	3,1	2,2	1,8
Eurozone countries	**2,1**	**3,2**	**3,0**	**0,4**	**-4,5**	**2,1**	**1,6**	**-0,9**	**-0,3**	**1,2**	**2,1**	**1,7**
Germany	1,2	3,9	3,4	0,8	-5,6	4,0	3,7	0,7	0,6	1,6	1,5	1,8
France	2,3	2,4	2,4	0,2	-2,9	2,0	2,1	0,2	0,6	0,6	1,3	1,2
Italy	1,4	2,0	1,5	-1,1	-5,5	1,7	0,6	-2,8	-1,7	0,1	0,8	0,9
European countries with the developing and transitional economy	**4,0**	**6,5**	**5,6**	**3,1**	**-3,0**	**4,6**	**6,6**	**2,4**	**4,9**	**3,9**	**4,7**	**3,0**
Post-Soviet States	**4,2**	**8,9**	**9,0**	**5,3**	**-6,4**	**4,7**	**4,6**	**3,5**	**2,1**	**1,1**	**-2,2**	**0,4**
Russia	3,8	8,2	8,5	5,3	-7,8	4,5	4,1	3,5	1,3	0,7	-2,8	-0,3
Ukraine	2,8	7,6	8,2	2,2	-15,1	0,3	5,5	0,2	0,0	-6,6	-9,8	2,3
Belarus	6,9	10,0	8,6	10,2	0,2	7,8	5,4	1,7	1,0	1,8	-3,8	-3,0
Kazakhstan	6,4	10,7	8,9	3,3	1,2	7,3	7,5	5,0	6,0	4,3	1,2	1,1
Georgia	6,5	9,4	12,6	2,4	-3,7	6,3	7,2	6,4	3,4	4,6	2,9	2,7
Developing Asia	**6,9**	**10,1**	**11,2**	**7,2**	**7,5**	**9,6**	**7,9**	**7,0**	**7,0**	**6,8**	**6,7**	**6,4**
China	9,2	12,7	14,2	9,6	9,2	10,6	9,5	7,9	7,8	7,3	6,9	6,7
India	6,4	9,3	9,8	3,9	8,5	10,3	6,6	5,5	6,5	7,2	7,9	6,8
Countries in Latin America	**2,9**	**5,6**	**5,9**	**4,0**	**-1,8**	**6,1**	**4,7**	**3,0**	**2,9**	**1,2**	**0,1**	**-1,0**
Brazil	2,4	4,0	6,1	5,1	-0,1	7,5	4,0	1,9	3,0	0,5	-3,8	-3,6
Argentina	2,3	8,1	9,0	4,1	-5,9	10,1	6,0	-1,0	2,4	-2,5	2,7	-2,3
Countries in the Middle East and North Africa	**5,0**	**5,9**	**5,6**	**4,8**	**1,4**	**4,8**	**4,4**	**5,4**	**2,4**	**2,8**	**2,7**	**3,9**
Sub-Saharan Africa	**5**	**6,3**	**7,1**	**5,9**	**3,9**	**7,0**	**5,0**	**4,3**	**5,3**	**5,1**	**3,4**	**1,4**

Source: *IMF, World Economic Outlook databases, April 2017,* www.imf.org

The dynamics of the economic cycle (the upswing, followed by a recession) can be clearly seen in other important macroeconomic indicators. So, if in 2005 the growth rate of the world trade volume was 7.8%, in 2006 - 9.3% and in 2007 - 8.1%, in 2008 it equaled- 3.1% and in 2009 - negative 10.5%. The level of savings in the world economy in 2007 reached 25.5% of world GDP, in 2008 - 25.0% of GDP, and in 2009 - 23.1% of GDP. The volume of global investment in 2007 was 25.1%, in 2008 - 25.1% of GDP, and in 2009 it equaled 23.0% of GDP[28].

The phases of the economic cycle can even more clearly be seen based on an example of developed countries (Fig.1).

Figure 1.

Dynamics of the main macroeconomic indicators of developed countries, 2004-2016 (%)

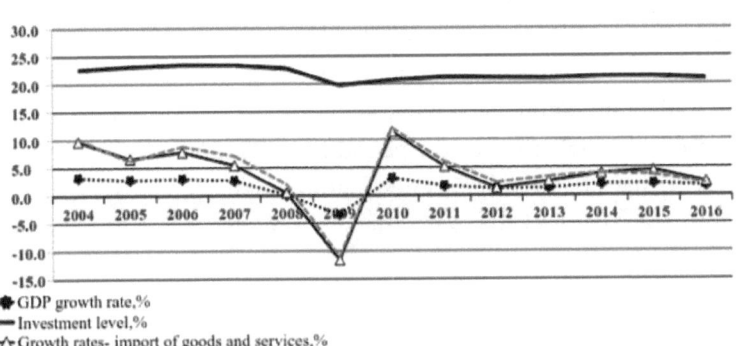

♦ GDP growth rate,%
— Investment level,%
☆ Growth rates- import of goods and services,%

Source: *IMF, World Economic Outlook databases, April 2017,* www.imf.org

In the US economy, whose influence on the world economic processes remains dominant (like the influence of the English economy in the 19th century), we can also clearly observe the overheating of the economic conjuncture and the inflation of various bubbles, especially of the mortgage. Indeed, the liberal monetary policy pursued in the US (and also in a number of other developed

---

28   IMF, World Economic Outlook databases, April 2017, www.imf.org

countries) contributed to the inflating of credit and mortgage bubbles. In the US, the Federal Reserve rate on federal funds was reduced from 6.5% in January 2001 to 1% in June 2003, reaching its lowest level in half of a century. In 2003, it remained at 1%, and then began to slowly increase to 5.25% in 2006. When speaking about the reasons of such low rates for centralized loans, the former head of the Federal Reserve A. Greenspan wrote about the global surplus of savings[29], while many analysts, in particular the American Economist J. Taylor, noted the deliberate monetary expansion[30].

Following the lowering of rates for US federal funds, there was an almost synchronous reduction in mortgage rates, which is especially noticeable in mortgage loans with a floating interest rate (ARM, Adjustable-rate mortgage). However, after the growth in rates for federal funds that began in 2004, there was a corresponding increase in rates for mortgage loans with a floating rate, the share of which in all subprime mortgage loans reached 90%[31] in 2006. Such an increase in interest rates, according to many economists, became the trigger of the mortgage crisis.

Monetary policy of the authorities aimed at stimulating lending definitely achieved its goal: both the total amount of loans extended by banks and other institutions to various borrowers, and the size of mortgage loans have steadily increased (data on commercial bank loans are presented in Table 3). It can be seen from the table that for the period from 2003 to 2007, the volume of all extended loans increased 1.5 times, loans to industry and trade - 1.7 times while mortgage loans - 1.6 times.

[29] Greenspan A., The Crisis, 2nd draft., Manuscript, 2010.
[30] Taylor J., Monetary Policy, Economic Policy, and the Financial Crisis: An Empirical Analysis of What Went Wrong, In Friedman, 2011.
[31] Zandi M., Financial Shock: A 360-Degree Look at the Subprime Mortgage Implosion, And Now to Avoid the Next Financial Crisis, N. J., FT Press, 2008.

Table 3

Dynamics of Deposit Secured Loans Provided by US Commercial Banks, 2003-2014 (as of the end of the year), Billion Dollars

	2003	2004	2005	2006	2007	2008	2009	2010	2011	2012	2013	2014	2015
Total loans:	4 432	4 910	5 385	5 984	6 629	6 841	6 499	6 597	6 721	7 045	7 243	7 633	8173
Industry and trade	870	908	1020	1 140	1 369	1 416	1 150	1 121	1 276	1 438	1 506	1 651	1779
Secured by immovable property	2 273	2 623	2 986	3 432	3 676	3 842	3 823	3 650	3 550	3 607	3 597	3 700	3921
Credit losses	77	74	69	69	89	157	214	218	179	152	127	113	109

Source: *Federal Deposit Insurance Corporation. Bank Data and Statistics. Loans and Leases FDIC-insured Commercial Banks US and Other Areas, www.fdic.gov*

Low interest rates on mortgage loans were combined with other fundamental measures to stimulate the housing market. Therefore, the Clinton administration set as its goal to increase the share of homeowners from 65 to 67.5% of the population. In accordance with this decision, the United States Department of Housing and Urban Development decided that the share of issued for low and medium income borrowers mortgages redeemed by the *Federal National Mortgage Association* ("*Fannie Mae*") and the *Federal Home Loan Mortgage Corporation* ("*Freddie Mac*"), should increase. In 1997 *Fannie Mae* began to buy back the mortgages the down payment for which was only 3%. To implement the slogan "property-based society" it was decided during the George Bush administration that these companies should buy back the mortgages requiring no down payment[32]. Moreover, *Fannie Mae, Freddie Mac* and the *Federal Home Loan Bank System* were active actors in the subprime mortgages market purchasing by 2007 MBS (mortgage-backed security) worth USD 1049 billion and PLMBS (private-label MBS) worth USD 308 billion[33].

---

[32]   Wallison P., Housing Initiatives and Other Policy Factors, In Friedman, 2011.

[33]   Friedman J., Kraus V., "Man-made financial crisis. Systemic risks and failure ofregulation" (translated from English), M., Publishing House., «YRISEN» и «Mysl», 2012 (in Russian language); p., 31.

Furthermore, in the years preceding the crisis, the market of securities secured to some extent by mortgage on real estate (MBS, CDO, PLMBS etc.) had been actively developing. The volume of such securities in circulation is estimated at about USD 7 trillion. In the portfolio of commercial banks, the volume of such securities amounted to USD 1325 billion, while in the portfolio of state corporations *Fannie Mae* and *Freddie Mac* - USD 1049 billion. The volume of the securities owned by investment banks made up USD 303 billion, hedge funds - USD 125 billion, insurance companies - USD 1,070 billion and foreign investors - USD 1,171 billion[34]. There are also larger-scale estimates of the volume of securitized debt and other bubbles in the asset market. As early as 2005, *Morgan Stanley*, an investment bank, issued a report "Global Economy: Bubbles around Us", in which the volume of market bubbles is estimated at half of global GDP.

As a result, in 2006, the share of Americans owning their own dwelling houses reached 69%, which is an increase of 4 percentage points over 10 years; at the same time, in the same period, the number of houses in which their owners lived, rose from 68 million to 75 million[35].

The role of speculative capital had become increasingly felt in the real estate market. According to the National Association of Realtors, in 2005, speculative investors accounted for 28% of homes (usually their share did not exceed 10%). As A. Greenspan points out, they turned into a market force, which increased the turnover of existing residential property by one third[36].

At the same time, despite the obvious overheating of the economy, there was no noticeable price increase, which usually serves as a sign of an upcoming crisis. A. Greenspan, the former Chairman of the Federal Reserve Board of the United States, considered this situation to be a puzzle, but the rapid growth of prices in the financial and real estate market rather than in the consumer market should be taken into account, which was typical for the 1929-1933 crisis as well.

---

[34] ibid, p.,31

[35] Jonson S., Kwak J., 13 Bankers: The Wall Street Takeovers and the Next Financial Meltdown, NY., Pantheon, 2010.

[36] Greenspan A., "The Age of Turbulence: Adventures in a New World", M., 2009, Publishing House., «Alpina Business Books» (in Russian language);p., 230.

Meanwhile officials did not notice emerging problems. For example, A. Greenspan notes that "strangely enough, but I did not expect at all that the financial system would not be able to effectively protect itself from inflating the bubble of euphoria. We at the Fed always counted on the ability of banks to avoid the most unpleasant risks"[37]. As a result, "by the spring 2006, the financial system, with its extraordinary dependence on credit leverage - and its blind belief that prices will continue to rise - was fully prepared for the emergence of a universal scale disaster. Euphoria, which began in the residential real estate market, embraced the whole financial system, giving rise to many enthusiasts ready to take on new risks, and a handful of skeptics, who raised alarm, but nobody listened to them... So in spring 2006, the housing market began evening, and house prices, which in the previous decade doubled in real terms, stopped growing"[38]. Due to a number of factors, in the first place, the growth of interest rates on mortgages, poorer debt servicing by low-income borrowers, the drop in incomes of the population, including borrowers, due to the growth of consumer good prices, changes in the mood of speculative investors, the demand for residential property in 2006 started to decrease significantly. From March 2006 to March 2008 sales of single-family homes, both new and existing ones, declined by a third[39].

The first financial problems emerged in the so-called "shadow banking institutions", which were engaged in banking operations, including lending and investment, but were not actually regulated (such institutions were engaged in quite teeming activities in the years preceding the crisis). There was a huge discrepancy between the terms of borrowing and lending of most of these organizations. Taking money for a short time, they invested them for a long time in illiquid assets.

According to the IMF, the share of overdue payments on subprime mortgages issued in 2000 (before the boom) began to grow starting from 2005, when its

[37]   Greenspan A., "The Age of Turbulence: Adventures in a New World", M., 2009, Publishing House., «Alpina Business Books» (in Russian language);p., 494.

[38]   Roubini N., "Crisis Economics: A Crash Course in the Future of Finance", M., EKSMO, 2011 (in Russian language); c., 106.

[39]   Greenspan A., "The Age of Turbulence: Adventures in a New World", M., 2009, Publishing House., «Alpina Business Books» (in Russian language);p., 487.

average value reached 25% of the outstanding mortgage balance[40]. The share of overdue payments for subprime mortgage loans issued in 2006 reached 25% already in a year. The increase in borrowers' defaults on subprime loans immediately affected the financial state of shadow banks, as they were also deprived of support from major banks and could not rely on loans from the Fed.

The first company to go bankrupt in the mortgage lending market was *Merit Financial*, a brokerage firm, which according to eyewitnesses, issued loans in 15 minutes. By the end of 2006, 10 credit brokers had become bankrupt, while by the end of March 2007 more than 50. *New Century Financial*, the second-largest subprime lender, was declared bankrupt on April 2, 2007. It is interesting that at this time, problems in the US mortgage market were considered exclusively as a temporary local phenomenon, rather than a beginning of a worldwide pandemic.

The ABX index was an important indicator of the state of the mortgage securities market. *Markit Group*, a British company, began to calculate this index in spring 2007 based on the monitoring of the market prices of the CDS basket used to insure risks associated with default on mortgage-backed securities. The index immediately went into a free fall mode and all market participants could see the depth of losses on assets that had recently been considered first-class. The riskiest mortgage securities lost 80% of their value during 2007; considered the most reliable, tranches with "AAA" ratings lost 10% of their value by July 2007.

In summer 2007, two hedge funds created under the auspices of *Bear Sterns* collapsed. They had used short-term loans from individual and institutional investors as a source of funding and invested them in mortgage-backed securities. When problems arose in the real estate market, creditor banks required that the hedge funds return the funds issued to them otherwise threatening to start large-scale sales of mortgage-backed securities that were pledged for loans. Because of investors' shaken confidence, it was obvious that the sale of mortgage-backed securities could exacerbate the problem.

---

[40] IMF, Global Financial Stability Report: Containing Systemic Risks and Restoring Financial Soundness, April 2008, p., 6.

Therefore, *Bear Sterns* poured additional funds into the hedge funds, however, this did not save the bank from bankruptcy.

In July 2007, problems in the US mortgage market affected European and other foreign investors (from hedge funds to governments) who owned in one form or another a variety of mortgage-related financial instruments. In Germany in July 2007, *Commerzbank*, a banking concern, IKB, a bank, and the Allianz holding reported the amount of their investments in mortgage-backed securities and the estimated decrease in their annual profit. Three German investment funds – *Postbank, Bank of Saxony and Deutsche Bank* - made the similar statements in August.

At this time, the rating agencies were reviewing their extremely high estimates of mortgage lenders and structured products. There was a sharp increase in volatility in the stock market, which exacerbated the financial problems of many investors. *American Home Mortgage*, the mortgage giant, went bankrupt in the US.

As in any acute phase of the crisis, the situation on the interbank market started deteriorating. Banks cut or closed credit limits. As a result, in August 2008, the difference between the LIBOR rate and European central bank rates soared from 10 to 70 points. The situation developed in such a way that "every bank in Europe and the United States wanted to get a loan, but no bank would not lend money, except that at a hefty interest rate"[41]. In particular, on August 9, 2007, *BNP Paribas*, a French bank, suspended trade on its mutual funds, which led to the collapse of short-term interbank markets for several hours in the whole world. Panic was observed among depositors, in particular, a massive withdrawal of deposits started in *Northern Rock*, a British bank. *Aegis Mortgage*, a US bank, applied for protection against creditors.

In these conditions, on 9 August 2007 the European Central Bank provided EUR 94.8 billion or banks to support liquidity. In the following days, the ECB and other world central banks poured into the banking sector further EUR 300 billion to maintain liquidity. Central banks also started reducing refinancing rates in order to improve liquidity in the financial sector and

---

[41] Roubini N., "Crisis Economics: A Crash Course in the Future of Finance", M., EKSMO, 2011 (in Russian language); p., 115.

stimulate economic activity. In particular, on September 18, 2007, the Fed lowered the discount rate from 5.25 to 4.75%, on October 31 - to 4.5%, on December 11 - to 4.25%. Moreover, the Fed made it easier for banks to access their discount window, but with the proviso that every bank that applies for help could be perceived by the Fed as weak and on the brink of collapse. *The Bank of England* provided financial support of EUR 25 billion for *Northern Bank.*

Having spread to the financial markets of developed countries, after August 2007 the crisis started to have a negative impact on the nonfinancial sector of the economy. A. Greenspan described the situation as "tug-of-war between healthy non-financial sectors and sick financial systems[42]. In addition, the situation was complicated by rising energy prices. In January 2008, for the first time oil prices exceeded USD 100 per barrel. Speculative capital, which moved from the mortgage and financial markets to raw materials, quickly "turned up" oil prices in July 2008 to USD 147 per barrel. But then oil prices started declining sharply reaching USD 36 per barrel in December 2008.

In nonfinancial sectors of the economy the first blow was made to the construction and related industries. In 2007, the US construction industry lost 125,000 jobs, while housing construction fell by more than a third (from USD 676 billion to USD 414 billion in annual terms). Sales of building materials decreased by 13%[43]. In December 2007, the US economy officially entered a recession.

With many of the world's largest financial institutions facing losses and problems with liquidity, in autumn 2007, a global character of the crisis became obvious. Banks like *Merrill Lynch, Citigroup,* and *HSBC* found themselves in a difficult financial situation.

Rating agencies started to drop sharply ratings of issuers and structured products. At the same time, the securitized securities market was actually frozen in autumn 2007. Moreover, all market participants suspected their counterparties of being addicted to financial risky products, but no one knew

---

[42] Greenspan A., "The Age of Turbulence: Adventures in a New World", M., 2009, Publishing House., «Alpina Business Books» (in Russian language);p., 487.

[43] Wesbury B., It is Not as Bad as You Think, NY., Hoboken, John Wiley, 2010, p, 108.

for sure the extent to which a particular bank, investment company or fund was involved in such investments. Information asymmetry reached its peak, as "the financial system was completely opaque, and most of the transactions of its participants - for example, with credit default swaps - were carried out outside the regulated stock exchanges. It was more and more like a wide minefield. Several mines have been already activated, but most of them were still waiting for a suitable opportunity"[44].

The end of 2007 witnessed a large number of bankruptcies; losses on tranches rated "AAA", which were previously considered safe, became a reality. The fall in prices for mortgage-backed securities provoked a similar decline in prices of other securities, including shares, corporate and municipal bonds. This situation was largely explained by the fact that "during periods of large-scale crises like those experienced in 2007-2009, all securities begin to correlate, as investors and all institutions of the securities market were forced to sell high-quality assets in order to generate liquidity"[45]. The prices of traditional banking assets, including car loans, student loans and other forms of consumer loans, also fell.

Almost for the whole year (from November 2007 to October 2008) stock indices showed a declining trend. In particular, the S&P 500 index fell by 30%, the MSCI World index, which shows the dynamics in the developed countries' stock markets, decreased by 32.3%, and the index of the developing market of MSCI Emerging Markets - by 40.5%. In October 6-10, 2008 US trading floors saw a historically maximum drop of indices. The Financial Times compared the fall of the stock market on Friday October 10, 2008 with a collapse of October 10, 1938[46]. The stock market decline in October 2008 was the record one for the US over the past 20 years, and the collapse of the Japanese market - for the entire history of the country.

---

[44] Roubini N., "Crisis Economics: A Crash Course in the Future of Finance", M., EKSMO, 2011 (in Russian language); p., 116.

[45] Poszar Z., at al., Shadow Banking, Federal Reserve Bank of New York Staff Report 458, July 2010.

[46] Long View: Heed the Harsh lessons of history to find value, The Financial Times, 2008, October 10.

The current situation required more decisive measures from the monetary authorities. In December 2007, the US government developed a package of anti-crisis measures.

It is interesting that the crises of 2007-2009 and 1929-1932 have one more detail in common: some time after the development of the crisis (in 2007 and 1929) a period came when it seemed that anti-crisis measures that had been applied proved to be effective, that the scale of the disaster was relatively small and recovery was close. This was the case in 1930 as well, when US President G. Hoover said that "the worst is behind us - and if we continue making joint efforts, we will quickly recover," and in 2008, when US Treasury Secretary H. Paulson announced that "the worst is left behind".

Indeed, the injection of liquidity from the Fed and other central banks, the creation of the Fed in conjunction with the ECB and the Bank of England, the system of the Term Auction Facility (TAF), further lowering of interest rates (the Fed lowered it twice in January 2008, twice in March, and also in April, as a result, the rate fell to 2%), the decline in lending activity of banks and attracting investors from Asia to the financial sector (*Citigroup* received USD 7.5 billion from the fund in Abu Dhabi, *UBS* - USD 11 billion from Singapore state fund and a group of private investors from the Middle East, *Morgan Stanley* – USD 5 billion from Chinese investors, *Merrill Lynch* – USD 5 billion from Singapore investors) created the illusion of recovery.

However, the depth of the crisis, especially the size of the "toxic assets" of the financial sector was so great that injections of hundreds of billions of dollars would not prevent it, other scale of expenses was required, which became clear a few months later. Moreover, the crisis had become increasingly evident in the industrial and service sectors.

Thus, in February 2008 in Germany, a state-owned *KfW bank*, declared that due to the scale of the financial losses it was no longer able to support *IKB*, the key bank for the German economy, as a result, the bank was supported from the budget funds. In Great Britain, *Northern Rock*, a major bank, was saved only through nationalization. In March, *Bear Sterns*, the largest mortgage lender, announced that it needs urgent financing, which the Fed and *JPMorgan Chase* agreed to allocate. On March 16, 2008, the bank was bought by *JPMorgan Chase* for USD 236.2 million (USD 2 per share, while on March 14 the cost of per share was USD 30). By no means was the fall in the share price of *Bear Sterns* the only case witnessed in the first half of 2008, the rates of shares in European and American banks as well as American mortgage agencies *Freddie Mac* and *Fannie Mae* steadily declined.

In September 2008, the crisis seriously worsened, which to some extent was due to the bankruptcy of *Lehman Brothers*, the major systemically important American bank, the debts of which amounted to USD 613 billion. According to many analysts, the bankruptcy of this bank had become the line behind which the development of the crisis became like avalanche and global in nature.

By the same time, 200 non-bank mortgage lenders had ceased operation in the United States. Insurance companies, ranging from small ones like *Ambas* and *ACA*, to such a giant as *AIG*, found themselves in a critical financial situation, largely due to insurance of mortgage-backed securities CDO through a credit default swap mechanism (worth several trillion dollars). Rating agencies began to lower the ratings of insurance companies, which did not allow them to provide high ratings to insured structured products and municipal bonds, which led to the failure of municipal bond placement. As a result, serious budget problems arose, for example, in California.

In summer 2008, the financial condition of mortgage agencies *Freddie Mac* and *Fannie Mae*, which owned or guaranteed mortgage loans worth USD 5.3 trillion, worsened dramatically. By September 2008, shares of these mortgage giants depreciated by 85% and 82% respectively. As a result, the US government was forced to nationalize them in September 2008.

Washington Mutual, the country's largest savings and loan bank, went bankrupt (with the insured deposits worth USD 143 million). Only the acquisition of this institution by *JPMorgan Chase* for USD 1.9 billion prevented the largest possible payments to depositors in the history of the United States.

Faced with serious financial problems, another core US bank, *Merrill Lynch*, was saved only thanks to its purchase by *Bank of America* for USD 43.5 billion. English bank *Lloyds TSB* agreed to take over *HBOS*, the largest mortgage bank of Great Britain. Under pressure of financial problems *Bank of Wachovia* was forced to agree to a merger with *Wells Fargo*. In October, the largest US bank *Citigroup* was rescued by the US monetary authorities. *Goldman Sachs* and *Morgan Stanley* were reorganized and became bank holding companies, which helped them seek financial support from the Fed. At the same time, these banks in their new form came under more stringent regulation. Thus, within a few months all five of the largest investment banks were either reorganized or liquidated, which, according to unanimous opinion of analysts, meant a drastic change in the US financial system.

Following the banks and insurance companies, other financial institutions, in particular, monetary funds, also started experiencing problems. The flight of depositors from monetary funds began with *Reserve Primary Fund*, which, as it turned out, secretly invested the money of depositors in toxic securities. The US government was forced to declare guarantees for all existing money market funds whose volume of transactions was estimated at USD 4 trillion. The crisis from the money market spread to the corporate securities market, as a result of which the largest corporations began to experience an acute need for liquidity. It was then that the Fed decided to help not only financial institutions but also those enterprises that operated in other fields.

In order to prevent panic among depositors, the US monetary authorities raised the ceiling on deposit guarantees. To prevent the outflow of other types of creditors, on October 14, 2008, the US *Federal Deposit Insurance Corporation* (FDIC) made a decision on guarantees for new preference debt obligations (bonds) of regulated financial institutions, including banks and bank holding companies. Such a measure allowed regulated financial institutions to prolong debt obligations of USD 360 billion over the next six months at low interest rates. The American experience of state guarantees on the debt obligations of financial institutions was adopted by many European countries. In addition, in the US government credit lines were opened not only to banks but to corporations and investment companies, for example, *General Motors* and *GE Capital*.

A number of politicians expected that the US mortgage crisis would not seriously affect the European and developing countries. However, in autumn 2008, many European banks, in particular, *Hypo Real Estate, Dexia, Fortis, Bradford & Bingley,* began to experience serious problems. As a result, Britain had to almost completely nationalize the banking system. It was not just a matter of the situation in the US mortgage and financial markets, but also that "other states have long pursued policies that inflated their own speculative bubbles, and therefore they were vulnerable to a crisis"[47]. The deterioration of the financial condition of European banks led to credit squeeze, which immediately affected other sectors of the economy.

Globally, in autumn 2008, the crisis deepened due to a sharp drop in commodity prices, in particular, oil and metals. In October, the turnover of trade, both external and internal, began to fall. A number of the largest retail chains were in a critical situation.

As a result, in 2008 a number of countries experienced a decline in production. For example, in Denmark it amounted to 0.8%, Estonia - 4.2%, Greece - 0.2%, Luxembourg - 0.7%, the US - 0.3%. In 2008, the unemployment level increased in the US, Great Britain, Spain, Italy, Ireland, Iceland, Estonia and New Zealand. In 2008, the world trade growth rate made up only 3.1% (compared to 8% in 2007).

However, during this period, the monetary authorities made serious efforts to stabilize the situation. Thus, the US adopted the Paulson's plan, which provided for the allocation of USD 700 billion to fight the crisis. At the G-20 meeting in November 2008, Washington adopted policy statements, in particular, on the intention to reform the world financial system. At the same time, the national currency was devalued in many countries, which adversely affected the living standards of the population.

In 2009 the crisis further developed on a global scale. The collapse of *Lehman Brothers* led to the actual freezing of the credit market, including interbank lending and trade finance. Banks stopped even issuing letters of credit and providing guarantees, which had a rather negative impact on world trade. World trade fell by 10.6% in 2009. Exports from developed countries fell by 11.6%, while from developing countries by 7.9%. Import from developed countries decreased by 12.1%, while from developing countries by 8.3%[48].

---

[47]   Roubini N., "Crisis Economics: A Crash Course in the Future of Finance", M., EKSMO, 2011 (in Russian language); p., 136.

[48]   IMF, World Economic Outlook, April 2013, www.imf.org

There was a significant drop in exports in several countries: 45% in Singapore and Japan, 30% in China and Germany[49].

In 2009, due to falling demand and decrease in oil and other commodity prices, the economic situation in some developing countries and economies in transition deteriorated sharply. The situation was aggravated by a massive outflow of capital from emerging markets. As a result of the combination of such factors as the outflow of "hot capital" and the drop in exported goods prices, the economic situation had become quite acute in a number of these countries. As N. Roubini noted, "Hungary, Iceland, Belarus, Ukraine and Latvia turned with their outstretched hand to the International Monetary Fund. All three Baltic republics suffered from a dizzying increase in the unemployment rate and watched their banking sector roll into the abyss".

In 2009, the world GDP growth rate equaled to zero, the GDP of developed countries decreased by 3.4%, including in the US by 2.8%, France - 2.9%, the UK - 4.3%, Germany - 5.6%, Japan and Italy - 5.5%, Denmark - 5.1%, Iceland - 4.7%, Finland - 8.3% and Estonia - 14.7%. The decline in production was also noted in many developing countries and economies in transition: it reached in Bulgaria - 5%, Romania - 7.1%, Hungary - 6.6%, Russia -7.8% and Ukraine - 15.1%[50]. At the same time, the unemployment rate rose sharply, reaching 9.3% in the US, 7.5% in Great Britain, 9.5% in France, 7.7% in Germany, 7.8% in Italy and 8.3% in Canada[51].

At the same time, in 2009 the monetary authorities continued to implement anti-crisis measures. Thus, in an effort to maintain liquidity and stimulate growth in the economy and the financial sector the Fed, the European Central Bank, the Bank of England, the Bank of Japan, the Bank of Canada and some other central banks reduced interest rates to almost zero. The Fed launched a number of new refinancing instruments, in particular, *PDCF* - the provision of overnight loans to primary dealers with which the Fed made a deal in the open market. The other tool was *TSLF* - lending medium-term securities to banks and Fed dealer partners in exchange for illiquid securities of these organizations. The Fed also used tools such as *CPFF*, a Commercial Paper

---

[49] Baldwin R.,TalyoniD., The Great Trade Collapse and Trade Imbalances, VoxEu. org, 27 November, 2009.

[50] IMF, World Economic Outlook, October 2015, www.imf.org

[51] IMF, World Economic Outlook, October 2015, www.imf.org

Funding Facility, *MMIFF*, the Money Market Investor Funding Facility and *AMLF*, the Asset-Backed Commercial Paper Money Market Mutual Fund Liquidity Facility.

Moreover, central banks launched a large-scale quantitative easing program (Quantitative easing, QE). In March 2009, the Fed announced its intention to redeem long-term treasury bills of more than USD 300 billion, buy mortgage-backed securities worth more than USD 1 trillion and mortgage agencies' debt obligations of USD 55 billion. Moreover, USD 1 trillion was directed to the implementation of the *TALF* (Term Asset-Backed Securities Loan Facility) program. The measures implemented prevented the collapse of the financial system and even resuscitated the mortgage market, but as a result of such operations, the balance of the Fed increased from USD 900 billion to 2.4 trillion from 2007 to 2009. The assets accumulated during the crisis, including potentially hazardous assets acquired from *Bear Sterns* and *AIG*, accounted for a big share of this amount. Moreover, as noted by N. Roubini, "the Fed holds a significant number of no less dangerous assets through a specially created corporation known as Maiden Lane I, II and III, each of which is secretly managed by a structure called Black Rock Financial Management"[52]. The quantitative easing policy (QE1, QE2, QE3) continued in the following years until 2014.

In the future, focusing on the main macroeconomic indicators, primarily employment, in October 2014 the US Fed decided to completely stop the quantitative easing program QE3. Following the meeting of the *Federal Open Market Committee* held on 28-29 October 2014, the following statement was issued: "The Committee believes that since the beginning of the current asset purchase program, there has been a significant improvement in the state of the US labor market. Moreover, the Committee also believes that the economy has sufficient dynamics for further progress towards maximum employment in the context of maintaining price stability. In accordance with this assessment, the committee decided to complete the asset purchase program this month. Based on current estimates, the committee expects that it will be appropriate to maintain interest rates in the range of 0 to 0.25% for a long period after the completion of the asset purchase program this month,

---

52   Roubini N., "Crisis Economics: A Crash Course in the Future of Finance", M., EKSMO, 2011 (in Russian language); p., 178.

especially if the projected inflation rate remains below the target of 2% and with the condition that long-term inflation expectations will remain stable."[53]

In the United States, the adoption of the *Dodd-Frank* law in 2010 was an important stage in the fight against the crisis and movement towards a more sustainable economy. It was designed to reduce systemic risks in the financial sector, provide additional protection for consumers of financial services and modernize the regulation of the activities of core financial institutions.

Anti-crisis programs were adopted and implemented in other countries, both in developed and developing ones. These programs had a lot in common (recapitalization of the banking sector, support for its liquidity, and stimulation of economic growth) but their volumes and details vary greatly by country.

Thus, in the UK, the *Bank of England* in 2008-2009 also pursued a policy of quantitative easing, sending GBP 150 billion for the redemption of government and corporate bonds. In the UK, measures were taken to stimulate economic activity, in particular, the value-added tax was reduced from 17.5% to 15%, the tax credit for investment was doubled (up to 40%), and tax deferral for corporations were introduced. The largest banks such as *Northern Rock* and *Bradford & Bingley*, as well as *Royal Bank of Scotland* and *Lloyds Banking Group* were nationalized. The government bought out from banks troubled assets worth GBP 50 billion total, provided guarantees on interbank loans for GBP 250 billion and issued GBP 10 billion in loan to small and medium businesses. In February 2009, a new law on banks was adopted, significantly expanding the powers of the *Bank of England* in the field of regulation and regulating procedures for helping problem banks. The Financial Markets Regulator (The Autorite des marchés financiers) initiated the revision of the system of regulation of banks' activities towards more stringent and transparent rules. The issuers of securities were obliged to disclose more information, stricter requirements were imposed on branches and subsidiaries of foreign banks. GBP 1.5 billion was allocated from the budget for the construction 20 thousand new affordable houses in two years. Moreover, various benefits for borrowers of mortgage loans were introduced, for example, a three-month grace period for repayment of principal, an extended grace period (up to 6

---

[53]   Board of Governors of the Federal Reserve System. Press Release. Release Date: October 24, 2014, www. Federalreserve.gov

months) for mortgage payments, a deferral of interest payments of up to two years for unemployed people or persons with a deteriorated financial situation. For the operational management of the economy in times of crisis, special institutions were set up: The National Economic Council, the Infrastructure Commission, the financial investment management agency (for assets that have become state property).

In Australia a USD 26 billion package of measures stimulating the economy was adopted, USD 6 billion worth of mortgage securities were purchased, state guarantees were introduced to return 100% of all deposits and bonds of commercial banks (for a period of 5 years).

In Austria, banks were recapitalized by USD 20 billion, state guarantees were introduced for the return of 100% of all depositors' deposits (including SME) and for new bank bonds and interbank loans.

In Argentina USD 21.5-billion program was adopted to create jobs in the construction industry, which called for an increase in the number of employed people from 362 to 770 thousand. The program was financed from nationalized pension funds. *Aerolineas Argentinas*, the largest airline, and *Austral*, its subsidiary, were nationalized. Tax incentives were introduced for the reinvested capital of compatriots.

In Brazil, a sovereign wealth fund (USD 6 billion) was set up to mitigate the crisis consequences, in particular, to make investments in the real sector of the economy. The two major state-owned banks were entitled to acquire shares of troubled banks.

In Hungary, a USD 1.5 billion program was adopted to recapitalize banks. Guarantees were provided for refinancing debt obligations of USD 1.5 billion and for SME - USD 3.4 billion. A business support program was approved for a total amount of HUF 560 billion, including HUF 140 billion in soft loans to SME for the replenishment of their working capital. The state guarantee for deposits increased from HUF 6 million to HUF 13 million.

Germany adopted a law on the implementation of measures to support the financial market, aimed at economic growth, protection of jobs, and restoration of confidence in financial institutions. Measures were taken to further guarantee the deposits of the population. The rules for valuing assets and preparing a balance sheet were amended. The *Financial Stabilization Fund* of EUR 100 billion was set up. It was announced that the federal government had provided guarantees for interbank loans of EUR 400 billion. Direct government financial assistance was provided to a number of banks, in particular, to *Hypo Real Estate, Commerzbank, The Bavarian Land Bank* and *The Bank of the Northern Lands*. Measures were applied to improve the supervision of the financial market, in particular, the supervision functions were concentrated in the German Federal Bank. To support the real sector of the economy, programs were adopted to fund job security (EUR 2.6 billion in 2009 and EUR 5.7 billion in 2010), make investments in the development of transport infrastructure (EUR 1 billion in 2009 and 2010); additional costs were incurred for structural regional policy and *KfW* capital increase (EUR 0.3 billion in 2009 and EUR 0.4 billion in 2010); additional federal investments were made, including the construction of schools and kindergartens (EUR 3 billion in 2009 and EUR 12 billion in 2010). Tax incentives were provided to promote economic growth, in particular, income tax was lowered, child allowances were raised, the rates of deductions for medical insurance were reduced, and children's benefits for the unemployed with children aged 6-13 years were increased.

Greece adopted a program to provide EUR 5 billion for bank recapitalization and guarantees of EUR 15 billion for bank debt obligations.

Denmark recapitalized banks by USD 13.4 billion and opened a credit line of USD 20 billion for banks. A salary ceiling for bank managers was introduced and banks were prohibited from paying dividends to shareholders, buying back and exchanging their own shares or conducting additional emissions for two years. A USD 5.1 billion insurance fund of credit institutions was set up, a guarantee was introduced for 100% of deposits, interbank loans, new and existing bank debt obligations.

India adopted a USD 4 billion economic support program, which included additional government spending, encouraging bank lending and lowering excise taxes. The program also called for the issuance of government bonds worth USD 6 billion for the implementation of infrastructure projects. The base interest rate was lowered from 7.5% to 6.5%, while mandatory reserve requirements for banks, from 5.5% to 5%.

In Ireland, the government invested EUR 5.5 billion in three major banks: EUR 2 billion in *Bank of Ireland* and *Allied Irish Banks* each (the state became the owner of 25% of shares) and EUR 1.5 billion in *Anglo Irish Bank* (the state became the owner of 75% of shares). A EUR 400-billion program was implemented to purchase assets and provide guarantees for interbank deposits and new debt obligations. Moreover, the guarantee was provided for 100% of bank deposits of private depositors.

Iceland nationalized major banks.

Italy adopted the law on urgent measures to guarantee the stability of the credit system, which provided for the recapitalization of banks. The Ministry of Economy and Finances was authorized to approve and guarantee an increase in the capital of those banks whose capital, according to the Bank of Italy, was insufficient. Such banks had to adopt a stabilization plan, which was subject to approval by the Bank of Italy. They could receive loans from the Bank of Italy through a simplified scheme. The law called for the introduction of temporary external management and special administration in problem banks. The ceiling of guaranteed deposits increased to EUR 103.3 thousand. Moreover, state guarantees for banks' new debt with a maturity of fewer than five years were introduced, government securities were temporary exchanged for bank assets or counter obligations of banks, guarantees were provided for the contracts made by Italian market participants with foreign banks. The Ministry of Economy and Finances obtained the right to purchase financial instruments issued by Italian banks. The Bank of Italy was to assess the bank's capital and the characteristics of the financial instruments issued in this case. Moreover, this state-backed banks had to support SME with credits in the same amount over the next three years under the same conditions as in the previous two years, facilitate the work of guarantee funds for SME, support the liquidity of government creditors through discounting amounts owed for the respective operations, suspend payment of mortgage debt (at least for 12 months at no extra cost) for borrowers who lost their jobs, adopt the code of conduct, which would contain questions related to the payment of compensation to the top management.

In Canada, insured mortgage loans of USD 20 billion and securities worth USD 61 billion secured by a pool of mortgage loans were redeemed. The state guarantee program was adopted for new debt obligations of USD 179 billion. Funds allocated for infrastructure development were doubled to USD 6 billion, of which USD 3.2 billion went to the development of infrastructure of provinces, territories and municipalities, USD 1.6 billion was spent on repairs and construction of colleges and universities, while USD 813 million was spent on the implementation of environmental projects.

China reduced reserve requirements for commercial banks, provided USD 20 billion for the recapitalization of the *Agricultural Bank of China*, adopted a major program for the development of infrastructure and energy-saving technologies, applied measures to increase employment, especially in SME (in particular, the regulatory rules encouraged banks to lend mainly to those sectors of the economy), introduced tax incentives for exporters and abolished personal income taxes on deposits in banks and took major steps to stimulate domestic demand.

Kazakhstan allocated USD 4 billion for the support of the agro-industrial complex and USD 1 billion for SME. USD 4 billion was allocated for the recapitalization of the four largest system-forming banks. The state interests in these banks are represented by the *National Welfare Fund Samruk-Kazyna*. The distressed assets fund was assigned the task of buying out and managing dubious assets from banks. USD 5 billion was allocated for the implementation of mortgage programs, while for innovative, infrastructure and industrial programs - USD 1 billion. *Samruk-Kazyna* also placed USD 2 billion in deposits with two largest banks - *Kazkommertsbank* and *People's Bank of Kazakhstan*. These funds were used to maintain the liquidity of these banks and lend to the real sector of the economy.

In Luxembourg, the banks were recapitalized by EUR 2.9 billion, a guarantee was provided for deposits amounting to up to EUR 100 thousand.

In Norway, government bonds worth EUR 46 billion were repurchased. The government proposed to create two funds (financial and bond) with a total capital of USD 14.8 billion to increase the capital of the banking sector and purchase corporate bonds. A state guarantee was introduced to cover deposits of up to EUR 227 thousand. Banks were given the opportunity to receive government securities from the Bank of Norway in exchange for refinancing bonds with the central bank as part of swap deals. Also the Bank of Norway announced its readiness to extend loans for up to two years at a fixed interest rate for small banks.

In Poland, state guarantees for bank deposits were increased from EUR 22.5 to EUR 50 thousand, measures were taken to stimulate the acquisition of new cars.

In Portugal, banks were recapitalized by EUR 4 billion and credit institutions that were close to bankruptcy were nationalized. State guarantees were provided for deposits of up to EUR 100 thousand and for all banking transactions for a maximum amount of EUR 20 billion.

In Slovakia, state guarantees were provided for 100% of bank deposits. The Slovak banks, which received financial assistance from the state, decided to reduce interest rates on mortgage loans for borrowers experiencing financial difficulties.

In Taiwan, infrastructure projects worth USD 2 billion were implemented, taxes were cut by USD 4 billion and state guarantees for interbank loans were provided.

In Finland, a EUR 4 billion program was implemented for the recapitalization of banks, state guarantees were provided for new debt obligations of EUR 50 billion and a package of measures was adopted to stimulate economy.

In France, state guarantees were provided for interbank loans of EUR 320 billion in total, and the banking sector was recapitalized by EUR 40 billion. A special refinancing company managed by the French Banking Commission and the state holding company (for recapitalizing banks) were founded to implement these goals. A number of French banks were granted loans at a rate of 4% per annum. Financial assistance was provided to the major banks, in particular, *Credit Agricole* received EUR 3 billion, *BNP Paribas* – EUR 2.55 billion and *SocieteGenerale* – EUR 1.7 billion. A state strategic investment fund of EUR 20 billion was set up to provide state support for business, in particular, to purchase stakes in strategic enterprises to protect these enterprises from takeover by foreign companies, and to divert funds from the financial sector to industry. A special agency was set up to monitor the situation in the credit market and to assist enterprises in obtaining loans;

a special local tax on fixed assets that constrained the investment process was abolished. A comprehensive anti-crisis plan to stimulate the economy was adopted. The key areas of the plan were: assistance in providing liquidity for companies in the form of tax holidays and tax credits, the provision of a special tax credit for investments in fixed assets, R&D for a total of EUR 11.4 billion, financing of state investment programs, provision of social and housing programs, twofold increase in the number of non-interest-bearing housing loans (the volume of financing EUR 11.1 billion), provision of funds for major state-owned companies in particular, for *Électricité de France, Gaz de France*, etc. for the modernization of railway, energy infrastructure and postal service (EUR 4 billion). Measures were also taken to provide social support to the population in times of crisis, in particular, the income tax on low incomes was partially abolished, a social investment fund of EUR 2.5-3 billion was set up at the suggestion of the trade unions, recommendations were made to banks to revise the terms of servicing citizens who found themselves in a difficult financial situation.

The Czech Republic adopted a EUR 2.44 billion plan to stimulate economy. The plan called for tax cuts, investments in infrastructure and ecology and provision of loans to automakers and small businesses.

Anti-crisis measures were implemented at the international level as well. An important stage was the G-20 summit held in London on April 2, 2009, at which the Action Plan for Overcoming the Crisis was adopted, in particular, the IMF resources were increased to USD 750.

The increased financial capacity allowed the IMF to increase the scale of anti-crisis measures, in particular, to support 14 countries (including Ukraine, Hungary and Pakistan) under the *Stand-By Arrangements* (SBA). These loans were accompanied by conditions of carrying out economic reforms. More advanced countries in terms of reform, for example, Poland and Mexico, received support in the form of flexible credit lines. To some extent, the Fed also acted as an international lender, signing swap agreements with central banks of other countries (for example, USD 30-billion agreement with Mexico) on the purchase of foreign currency by dollars with subsequent repurchase.

Anti-crisis measures taken in 2008-2009 by national governments and international financial organizations, including huge injections of liquidity into the financial sector, helped mitigate the crisis consequences. In 2010, most countries experienced economic growth (Table 2).

However, the rapid increase in government spending associated with overcoming the crisis led to a noticeable increase in the budget deficit in many countries, including in the most developed economies (Table 4). Many countries have not managed yet to fully overcome the problem of imbalance in public finances.

Table 4

State Budget Deficit in a Number of Stats, % of GDP

	2005	2006	2007	2008	2009	2010	2011	2012	2013	2014	2015	2016
USA	-3,1	-2,0	-2,9	-6,7	-13,2	-10,9	-9,6	-7,9	-4,4	-4,0	-3,5	-4,4
Japan	-4,4	-3,0	-2,8	-4.1	-9,8	-9,2	-9,1	-8,3	-7,6	-5,4	-3,5	-4,2
Great Britain	-2,9	-2,8	-2,7	-5,3	-10,2	-9,5	-7,5	-7,7	-5,6	-5,7	-4,4	-3,1
Germany	-3,4	-1,7	0,2	-0,2	-3,2	-4,2	-1,0	0,0	-0,2	0,3	0,7	0,8
France	-3,2	-2,3	-2,5	-3,2	-7,2	-6,8	-5,1	-4,8	-4,1	-4,0	-3,5	-3,3
Italy	-4,2	-3,6	-1,5	-2,7	-5,3	-4,3	-3,7	-2,9	-2,9	-3,0	-2,7	-2,4
Canada	1,6	1,8	1,8	0,2	-3,9	-4,8	-3,3	-2,5	-1,5	0,0	-1,1	-2,0
Spain	1,2	2,2	2,0	-4,4	-11,0	-9,4	-9,6	-10,5	-7,0	-6,0	-5,2	-4,6
Ireland	1,6	2,8	0,3	-7,0	-13,8	-32,1	-12,6	-8,0	-5,7	-3,7	-1,9	-0,9
Greece	-6,2	-6,0	-6,7	-10,2	-15,1	-11,2	-10,2	-6,5	-3,7	-4,0	-3,4	0,0
Portugal	-6,2	-4,3	-3,0	-3,8	-9,8	-11,2	-7,4	-5,7	-4,8	-7,2	-4,4	-2,3

Source: IMF. World Economic Outlook, April 2017, www.imf.org

An increase in budget deficit led in turn to an increase in a state debt, the amount of which reached a critical level in a number of countries (Table 5).

Table 5

Size of State Debts of a Number of Countries, % of GDP

	2005	2006	2007	2008	2009	2010	2011	2012	2013	2014	2015	2016
USA	65,3	64,2	64,7	73,6	87,0	95,7	99,9	103,4	105,4	105,2	105,6	107,4
Japan	184,9	184,3	183,4	191,3	208,6	215,9	230,6	236,6	240,5	242,1	238,0	239,2
Great Britain	40,1	41,0	42,0	50,2	64,5	76,0	81,6	85,1	86,2	88,1	89,0	89,2
Germany	67,0	66,5	63,5	65,1	72,6	81,0	78,7	79,9	77,5	74,9	71,2	67,7
France	67,0	64,2	64,2	67,9	78,8	81,2	85,0	89,4	92,3	95,6	97,1	
Italy	101,9	102,6	99,8	102,4	112,5	115,4	116,5	123,4	129,0	131,7	132,0	132,6
Canada	70,9	70,1	66,8	87,8	79,3	81,1	81,5	84,8	85,8	85,4	91,6	92,3
Spain	42,3	38,9	35,5	39,4	52,7	60,1	69,5	85,7	95,4	100,4	99,8	99,2
Ireland	26,1	23,6	23,9	42,4	61,7	86,3	109,6	119,6	119,6	105,4	78,7	76,4
Greece	107,4	103,6	103,1	109,4	126,8	146,3	172,1	160,0	178,0	181,0	179,4	181,3
Portugal	60,9	61,6	68,4	71,7	83,6	96,2	111,4	126,2	129,0	130,6	129,0	130,3

Source: *IMF. World Economic Outlook, April 2017, www.imf.org*

The economic growth that started in 2009 proved unsustainable; in 2011-2013 many countries experienced a slowdown in growth rates and even a recession (very similar to the cyclical development of the Great Depression of the 1930s). In September 2011, the world stock markets experienced a significant drop in stock prices and for the week from September 19 to 23, markets lost USD 3.4 trillion of capitalization. Speaking at a press conference in St. Petersburg on September 30, 2011, C. A. Pissaride, a Nobel Prize laureate in economics, clearly stated that the world economy was still in a recession that began in 2008. In his opinion, the crisis began from the financial sector and has now resulted in problems with debts, rather than investments, as usual[54]. At the end of the first half of 2012, the five largest US banks reported the worst financial results for the half year since the crisis. Moreover, 320 banks went bankrupt in the United States in 2010-2012.

---

[54]   NEWS.ru. 30 September 2011.

In 2017, the world economy looks good in the short term, but there are negative factors that threaten growth in the medium term, in particular, increasing income inequality and low growth in labor productivity, which is noted in the World Economic Outlook of the IMF[55](April 2017). Global risks as terrorism, local conflicts, the growth of political and social instability in many countries should not be forgotten either. In general, in 2016, the growth rate of the world economy amounted to 3.1%, which is somewhat lower indicator than in 2015 (3.4%), but in 2017 global economic growth is projected at 3.5%. In 2017, a slight acceleration of GDP growth is expected in both developed and developing countries.

1.4. Dangerous Triad of Deregulation, Financial Innovations and Speculative Nature of Business

The crisis of 2007-2009 was caused by a number of macroeconomic, institutional and socio-political factors. Undoubtedly, it has some similarities with previous crises, however, like any crisis, it has its own specific characteristics, including special conditions for the emergence and development, in particular, excessive money supply, long-term and large-scale credit expansion, a revolution in financial technologies.

Economists and politicians provide a lot of versions of the emergence of the latest crisis. Depending on the views of these experts, different factors dominate in crisis emergence. Thus, experts with conservative views focus on ineffective policies of monetary authorities and credit institutions, in particular, low interest rates in 2001-2005, weaker loan issuance standards, the confidence of major banks that the state will support them in any situation. Liberal researchers, in turn, emphasize systemic problems, in particular, the deregulation of the financial sphere, moral hazard and "irrational euphoria" of investors.

Nevertheless, most researchers of the crisis point out the problem of ineffective regulation of markets and institutions. In our opinion, the regulatory system plays an extremely important role in the prevention and correction of the emerging imbalances in the market economy, which has been proved by the long experience of the use of regulatory tools, in particular, in overcoming the

---

55   IMF. World Economic Outlook, April 2017: Gaining Momentum?

disastrous crisis of the 30's in the 20th century. A long period of sustainable economic development from the second half of the 1940's to about the early 1970's can be also largely explained by an effective system of economic regulation (which, of course, was successful in specific historical conditions and, certainly, cannot be mechanically copied in some other situation).

However, in the 70's of the 20th century the question of changing the doctrine of socio-economic development came to the agenda of developed countries both ideologically and in practice. This included a significant role of the state in the economy and the social sphere, systemic and fairly stringent regulatory rules for the behavior of economic agents, a significant role of institutions designed to serve as a counterbalance to the unfettered market forces (it is possible to note here regulatory institutions, state organizations acting on the market as economic agents, trade unions etc.).

Discussions about the change of economic focuses in politics arose amidst stagflation (a combination of inflation and economic recession) in the 1970's, which, to a certain extent, was caused by a decline in business performance, primarily in state-controlled industries, a fairly high level of public spending, especially social spending and a high level of taxes that hampered investment activity. Adverse external influences, in particular, a sharp rise in oil prices increased inflation. The collapse of the Bretton Woods system in 1971-1973 also destabilized the currency circulation in developed countries and contributed to the development of inflationary processes. Considering the changing economic situation, the economic model, which was quite effective for 25 years, undoubtedly needed to be developed and improved. In the scientific and political circles of the time, the idea of a drastic change to the economic course is becoming increasingly popular. Indeed, the era of serious crises that threatened the existence of the economic system passed, which created opportunities for significant maneuvers and experiments. P. Krugman, a famous economist, describes the situation in the scientific world quite clearly: "Approximately in 1970, apparently people similar to Voltaire's Dr. Pangloss, who assured us that we live in the best of all possible worlds, started studying financial markets. Conversations about the irrationality of investors, the soap bubbles of the financial market, destructive speculation practically disappeared from the scientific discussions"[56]. Instead of a macroeconomic Keynesian model, proponents of an efficient market proposed the CAPM (Capital Asset Pricing Model) for the assessment of not only assets but also derivatives and other financial instruments. As a result, "the elegance and apparent practicality of the new theory led to a series of Nobel Prizes to its creators ... Quiet professors from business schools could become and became "stratospheric specialists" on Wall Street, receiving appropriate payments"[57]. The basis for a new economic policy was the research of a monetarist school, in particular, M. Friedman's article "Theoretical Framework for Monetary Analysis" published in 1970. At this time, ideas such as A. Laffer's supply-side approach also became quite popular in the ruling circles. However, it is now clear that "their own project failed. It turned out that the new models did not explain the key facts that were peculiar to recessions"[58].

Nevertheless, in those times these scientific ideas were strongly supported by conservative intellectual and political circles, which began to come to power in virtually all developed countries in the late 70's - early 80's (the victory of the Tory party led by Margaret Thatcher in Great Britain's parliamentary elections in 1979 marked the beginning of the triumph of the conservative wave). Under the J. Carter administration and especially under President R. Reagan the United States launched active measures to dismantle the existing regulation system.

In the late 70's - early 80's deregulation in the United States began with the activities of airlines, road freight transport operators and the oil & gas industry. Soon it was extended to the financial sphere, in particular, depository institutions' activities were deregulated and prohibitions and restrictions on the payment of interest on deposits were lifted. In 1982, the *Garn-St. Germain Act* was adopted. It aimed to deregulate the credit activity of depository institutions. The removal of restrictions on bank interest rates stimulated the issuance of risky loans, which ultimately led to a large-scale crisis in the sector of deposit institutions in the US in the 80's.

---

[56] Krugman P., "The Way Out of the Slump!",M., «Azbuka-Attykus», 2013 (in Russian language);p., 143.

[57] Krugman P., "The Way Out of the Slump!", M., «Azbuka-Attykus», 2013 (in Russian language);p 146

[58] Krugman P., "The Way Out of the Slump!", M., «Azbuka-Attykus», 2013 (in Russian language);p., 149

This period also witnessed radical changes in the tax sphere. In 1981 the maximum level of taxes was reduced from 70% to 50%, while in 1986 - to 28%. Spending on social programs was reduced. The differentiation in income of the population increased. The share of the national income attributable to 5% of the richest Americans rose from 16.5% to 18.3%, while the share of the poorest 20% declined from 4.2% to 3.8%. At the same time, state spending on defense sharply increased, which led to an unprecedented increase in public debt under the Reagan administration (from USD 997 billion to USD 2.85 trillion).

Deregulation in the 80's-90's covered more and more new industries and became the focus of programs and speeches of conservative politicians. In this regard, the Congressional Oversight Panel report on the oversight of *Troubled Asset Relief Program* (TARP) is interesting: "... the failure of regulation, which caused a new crisis, is basically a philosophical rather than a structural one"[59].

The policy of deregulation continued during the administration of President Bill Clinton, which "dealt the last blow to the guidelines of the Great Depression, abolishing the restrictions of the *Glass-Steagall Act* that separated commercial and investment banks"[60].

The *Glass-Steagall Act* was the cornerstone of the anti-crisis measures adopted in the 30's of the 20th century in the US. In particular, it banned commercial banks from dealing with securities and companies operating on the securities market from carrying out banking operations. Moreover, combining positions in commercial banks and investment companies was banned. At the same time, a state deposit insurance system was set up and the membership of the Fed participating banks was expanded.

However, in the 80's and 90's of the 20th century abolishing the *Glass-Steagall Act*, which hampered the development of the risky and speculative business, topped the agenda. However, even before its complete abolishment, the

---

[59] Stiglitz J., "On the Reform of the International Monetary and Financial System: Lessons from the Global Crisis". Report of the UN Financial Mechanism Commission, M., «MezhdunarodnyeOtnosheniya"», 2012 (in Russian language);, p., 128.

[60] Krugman P., "The Way Out of the Slump!",M., «Azbuka-Attykus», 2013 (in Russian language);p 99.

separation of the banking and investment business contained in the Act became "the victim of thousands of small wounds inflicted on it"[61]. Starting from the late 80's the Fed allowed commercial banks to trade in certain securities. Initially, however, banks could receive no more than 10% of all profits from trading in securities but in 1996 this limit increased to 25%. In 1997, there was a precedent of the purchase of a company operating on the securities market by *Bankers Trust*, a commercial bank. The number of such banks increased during the following years. In addition, the line between the traditional banking and investment business was constantly blurred through the adoption of respective judicial decisions and the interpretation of its norms by the US Controller of Foreign Exchange and the Fed. In particular, the provision of the *Glass-Steagall Act* that did not recognize a transaction with securities as a result of which the assets were transformed into securities, but the holder of this paper had the same rights with respect to assets that before transformation, was interpreted in favor of the bank operations with securitized securities.

In the late 90's a number of economists and politicians begin to criticize the remaining provisions of the *Glass-Steagall Act* as obsolete, weakening the competitive positions of American business. The mood was clearly reflected by Senator-Democrat Charles E. Schumer, who announced on November 4, 1999 in connection with the discussion of the Financial Services Modernization Act: "This act is of vital importance for the future of our country. Unless we pass the act now, we can find out that London, Frankfurt or even Shanghai have become the financial capitals of the world. This will have very serious consequences for whole America, where the financial services market is the most important area, where the need for new jobs is growing most rapidly, where our technology is ahead of anyone else, where our capital dominates the whole world... Unless this is done, after three years with the development of technology we will find out that most American companies leave the country and transfer their business to those countries whose legislation allows doing all these things"[62].

---

[61] Roubini N., "Crisis Economics: A Crash Course in the Future of Finance", M., EKSMO, 2011 (in Russian language); p., 88.

[62] Semilyutina N., "The US law on modernizing financial services" 1999., «Depositarium», 1999, № 10 (in Russian language);

Proposals for the repeal of the *Glass-Steagall Act* received a broad public response, and its catalyst was the "merger of Travelers and Citicorp, which resulted in combining commercial banking, insurance services and underwriting securities under one roof. This caused serious problems because such a financial "hippopotamus" contradicted the laws effective at that time"[63].

As a result, in 1999, the USA adopted the *Financial Services Modernization Act* (the *Gramm–Leach–Bliley Act*) designed to fundamentally change the rules of the game in the financial sector. So the law allowed the banking holdings to be transformed into financial holding companies that could own both commercial banks, and investment banks and insurance companies. With the approval of the Fed, investment banks and insurance companies could create financial holding companies. Commercial banks obtained the right to be transformed into limited universal banks, which could engage in commercial and investment banking, insurance, non-financial transactions. The adoption of this law marked the beginning of a rapid growth in the number of financial holding companies. In 2005, on the eve of the crisis in the US, there were 469 such organizations with total assets of USD 8 trillion.

In practice, the *Gramm–Leach–Bliley Act* dramatically increased systemic risks in the financial sector of the economy. In addition, in 2004, five of the largest US investment banks came up with the initiative to ease restrictions on borrowing for them. The request of the investment business giants was unanimously supported by the members of the *Securities and Exchange Commission*, although according to one of the commission members: "we told them ... that if something goes wrong, it will lead to terrible disorder"[64]. As a result, on the eve of the "terrible disorder" investment banks increased their credit leverage (the ratio of the value of assets to capital) to 25 to 1 and even higher (while for ordinary commercial banks the limit was set at 12.5 to 1).

The Financial Services Modernization Act allowed banks to become active participants in the securitized securities market, which inflated a bubble in the financial market, on the one hand, and sharply increased the potential risks for banks and other financial institutions, on the other.

---

[63] Roubini N., "Crisis Economics: A Crash Course in the Future of Finance", M., EKSMO, 2011 (in Russian language); p., 88.

[64] Roubini N., "Crisis Economics: A Crash Course in the Future of Finance", M., EKSMO, 2011 (in Russian language); p., 90.

The 2007-2009 crisis exposed all the pitfalls of deregulation and, in particular, the provisions of the *Gramm–Leach–Bliley Act*. This law was criticized quite sharply by T. Cooley, a Professor of Economics and Dean of New York University Stern School of Business. The latter noted that the adoption of the law led to "the emergence of a completely new source of instability: a systemic risk for financial markets due to the complex conditions and interaction of these financial conglomerates. As a result, the current situation has led to the collapse, and the violation of the system has proved to be so destabilizing. There comes a point of time when regulation, as the concept of evolution, loses its effectiveness. The key problem that we face today is related to the fact that these innovations have given rise to companies that are much more difficult to regulate - and to restore in case of collapse"[65].

Already during the crisis, U.S. officials, in particular, Federal Reserve Chairman Ben Bernanke, pointed out the need to amend this law: "Provisions of the *Gramm-Leach-Bliley Act* limit the ability of the Federal Reserve, as consolidated supervisor, to examine, obtain reports from, or take actions with respect to subsidiaries that are supervised by other agencies... We hope that the Congress will consider revising the provisions of *Gramm-Leach-Bliley* to help ensure that consolidated supervisors have the necessary tools and authorities to monitor and address safety and soundness concerns in all parts of an organization"[66].

Along with deregulation, the pre-crisis period also saw a lack of regulation or insufficient regulation of institutions and markets.

In recent decades, especially in the pre-crisis years, the market for derivatives had rapidly developed (Table 6). Although derivatives were historically associated with trading, and later, currency operations, since the 80's of the 20th century they have been based on transactions with securities, credit transactions, structured financial products and other complex financial tools.

---

[65]   Maslov O, "World Crisis 2007-2009: Who is to blame? Weekly Independent Analytical Review", www. polit.nnov.ru (in Russian language;

[66]   Bernanke B., "Lessons of the Financial Crisis for Banking Supervision", Speech of the Chairman of the Board of Governors of the Federal Reserve Systemat the Federal Reserve Bank of Chicago Conference on Bank Structure and Competition, Chicago,May 7, 2009., www.fedspeak.ru (in Russian language);

There was a tendency to reduce the volume of issued derivatives in 2014-2016 but it is early to talk about whether this tendency will be kept or not.

Table 6

**Dynamics of Issued Derivative Financial Instruments
(in trillion US dollars)**

	2004	2005	2006	2007	2008	2009	2010	2011	2012	2013	2014	2015	20
Total Derivatives, including	259	299	418	586	598	604	601	648	636	711	628	552	5
Credit Default Swaps	6,4	13,9	28,7	58,2	41,9	32,7	29,9	28,6	25,1	21	16,4	14,6	1

Source: Bank for International Settlements. Statistics. Derivatives Statistics, www.bis.org/statistics

As a result, "similarly to a system of interconnected vessels, each element of the market is in some way linked with the others, although it is increasingly difficult to trace the true connections between them ... Dealers are not even able to calculate profitability of their own transactions. In order to be able to trade their "structured products" financial jugglers need programs for assessing value and risk, which they are forced to blindly believe".[67]Not surprisingly, the excessive interest in operations with derivatives in the 90's led to serious financial problems at the *Frankfurt Iron and Steel Works, Procter & Gamble Corporation*, the major Japanese bank *Daiwa*, the German insurance companies *Gothaer, Colonia,* and *HannoverscheRueckversicherungs AG,* the British bank *Barings,* and Orange County in California.

In the US, during the pre-crisis period, the market of credit default swaps (CDS) - a special type of derivatives, designed to protect its buyers from the counterparty's default - was also developing rapidly. Besides, in 2000, an amendment to the Law "On Financial Modernization" completely freed credit-default swaps and "off-exchange" derivative instruments from regulation.

---

[67] Martin H..Schumann X.., "Trap of globalization: an attack on prosperity and democracy".,M., Publishing House., «Alpina», 2001 (in Russian language); p., 124.

Such operations were almost completely deregulated in other countries as well. Consequently, "the explosion of derivatives trading not only increased the risks in the financial sector, but also paralyzed the security systems that have been forming for decades".[68]

Operations with "over-the-counter" derivative instruments, as a rule, were not only deregulated, but also non-transparent, as banks and financial companies did their best to keep details of such transactions in secret. Such lack of transparency played the role of a catalyst of the last crisis. Moreover, being confident of the low risk of these instruments large financial players (e.g.: insurance company AIG), accumulated such liabilities in huge amounts and furthermore, did not create the necessary reserves.

In the pre-crisis years, record high growth rate was characteristic not only to derivatives, but also some other financial instruments, namely - debt securities. In the world's leading economy, the United States, the volume of debt securities issued also grew at an unprecedented pace, increasing from $ 18,372 billion in 2002 to $ 28,608 billion in 2007, i.e. nearly 1.6 times. Such a rapid growth of financial markets increased systemic risks in the economy and accumulated a critical mass leading to the crisis.

It must be noted that the deregulation policy was carried out not only in the United States, but also in other countries. For example, during the period from 1995 to 2001, the UK adopted 48 legal acts on deregulation. A special body responsible for assessing the state regulation measures – the Regulatory Impact Unit (RIU) was established within the Secretariat of the Cabinet of Ministers. This body was commissioned to analyze the entire range of state regulation measures in various areas of the society's activities. The RIU also had to make recommendations on deregulation. In 1999, in line with the deregulation policy, the UK established another institution - the Public Sector Team (PST), whose main tasks included: official assessment of the extent to which the state regulation affected various types of public activities; identification of administrative and bureaucratic procedures that hampered the development and functioning of various activities; study and analysis of the current legislation and draft laws in order to develop programs for further

---

[68]   Martin H..Schumann X.., "Trap of globalization: an attack on prosperity and democracy".,M., Publishing House., «Alpina», 2001 (in Russian language); p., 125.

sociological research and surveys. Besides, the PST was also tasked with developing recommendations on the deregulation of economic and social activities in accordance with the law adopted in 1994 – the *Deregulation and Contracting out Act* (Section 5) and the law on reforming the system of state regulation adopted on April 10, 2001 – the *Regulatory Reform Act*, 2001.

In the pre-crisis years, deregulation and lack of regulation took place on the background of a revolution in financial and banking technologies, when new products were constantly appearing in this sector, designed, according to their authors, to minimize and distribute risks among various counterparties, attract creditors and investors, and increase profitability of operations.

Thus, the first mortgage securities appeared in 1970's, when the Government National Mortgage Association of the United States pooled all mortgages it had and issued mortgage-backed securities. This, of course, was a revolution in the banking sector, because now banks could immediately regain granted loan amounts (or their part) by selling such bonds to investors. In their turn, the investors received part of the income from credit payments. The practice of pooling low-liquid or illiquid assets into packages (pools) and transforming them into more liquid assets, e.g. mortgage securities (securitization), quickly became widespread in the financial sphere. Issuers and buyers of new financial instruments were government mortgage agents *Freddie Mac* and *Fannie Mae*, investment banks, brokerage companies and even developers.

Even though the first mortgage securities appeared in the 70's and 80's, the explosive growth of this market was observed in the 90's. To some extent, this was due to the lessons that bankers learned from the crisis of 1600 American savings institutions in the 1980's, as their bankruptcy was directly related to the "bad" loans that were on their balance sheet. The traditional banking approach to "create and hold" loans turned out to be too risky in certain circumstances, and the financiers offered to replace it with the new "create and sell" principle. Issued securities were restructured ("cut") in different tranches, each of which had its own rating from AAA to B, assigned by the rating agency. Payments made to investors with regard to these tranches were subordinated depending on the order of their issuance and rating.

In addition, derivative instruments, such as CDOs (collateralized debt obligations), have been issued on the basis of mortgage-backed security pools.

Lack of transparency in the process of forming such pools and tranches contributed to an increase in the risk level of investments made in such instruments. Thus, according to a number of researchers already in 2003 "CDOs mainly consisted of mezzanine tranche fragments of subprime or alternative (Alt-A) mortgage pools that had an increased probability of default."[69]

Later on, in addition to the mortgage loans to individuals, securitized mortgage loans were also issued for the purchase of commercial real estate as well as for various types of consumer loans such as auto loans, credit card loans, student loans, and so on. By the time when the crisis stuck, securitization scale has grown so much that it covered aircraft lease agreements, income from forests and natural resources, revenues of public organizations and municipal governments, etc. At the same time, the "banks or companies issuing the securities had practically little or no interest to pay due attention to assessing the likelihood of receiving the income based on the securities. Investment banks that acted as midwives at the moment when the security pools were created, were not interested in carrying out serious checks either: they cared only about selling the credits converted into securities and thus remove them from their balance sheets"[70].

Interestingly, potentially risky subprime mortgages that had nominal credit ratings (e.g.: BBB) and were used in the securitization schemes, were transformed into mortgage-backed securities with the same rating and then cut into tranches. After this, the senior tranche, which could be comprised of up to 80% of all securities included into the pool, acquired AAA rating. Thus, the designers of these financial products turned "toxic" assets into illusory, reliable securities.

Then, financial technologists stepped even further: some CDO papers were combined with other CDOs, and then divided into parts (so-called "CDO in square"). The CDO in cube (CDO from CDO, made from third CDOs) was also circulated on the market. There were also so-called "synthetic CDOs", consisting of credit default swaps for basic CDOs.

---

[69] Bass K., Testimony before Subcommittee on Capital Markets, Insurance, and Government Sponsored Enterprises, 2007.

[70] Roubini N., "Crisis Economics: A Crash Course in the Future of Finance", M., EKSMO, 2011 (in Russian language); p., 78.

The increasingly complex financial products could be evaluated only using mathematical models that were based on optimistic expectations and, of course, could not take into account real risks that existed along the entire chain of structured products, created through the above mentioned opaque process. As a result, we received a "completely opaque and impenetrable financial system that was fully ripe for a crisis".[71]The scope of such opaque products was also quite impressive: in 2008, the US financial market traded mortgage securities worth $ 6,594 billion, including: bonds of mortgage agencies *Freddie Mac* and *Fannie Mae* worth $ 4,363 billion; tranches of *PLMBS* with AAA rating, worth $ 1636 billion; CDO tranches with AAA rating, worth $ 475 billion; and mezzanine tranches of *PLMBS* and CDO, worth $ 120 billion.[72]At the same time, mortgage securities accounted for a significant portion of the aggregate portfolio of debt securities of banks. In the US this indicator was 48%, in Great Britain - 29%, in other European countries - 24%, while in Asian states - 32%.[73]

Besides financial markets, where individual products and segments were virtually unregulated (e.g.: OTC derivatives), the problem of inadequate regulation also encompassed the market economy institutions. During the financial boom, so-called "shadow banks" (i.e. financial institutions that essentially performed banking operations but were not subject to adequate regulation) were formed and developed without official authorization by the state. Such institutions had various forms and names: non-bank mortgage lenders, structural investment companies, investment banks, broker-dealers, money market funds, hedge funds, private equity funds, etc. These institutions, like banks, mainly attracted money on market for a short time, but invested them for a longer period. At the same time, lack of regulation of these institutions created great temptations for excessively risky policies. Besides, unlike ordinary banks, they did not have direct access to the credits of the Federal Reserve System, which means that in case of serious problems

---

[71] Roubini N., "Crisis Economics: A Crash Course in the Future of Finance", M., EKSMO, 2011 (in Russian language); p., 80.

[72] Friedman J., Kraus V., "Man-made financial crisis. Systemic risks and failure of regulation" (translated from English), M., Publishing House., «YRISEN» и «Mysl», 2012 (in Russian language); p., 31.

[73] Friedman J., Kraus V., "Man-made financial crisis. Systemic risks and failure of regulation" (translated from English), M., Publishing House., «YRISEN» и «Mysl», 2012 (in Russian language); p., 64.

they could not rely on quick and sufficient support from the "lender of the last resort". It is true that during the last crisis such support was provided to a number of these institutions, in particular to money market funds, but this was associated with the emerging threat of the collapse of the entire financial system.

The activities of other important institutions in the financial market - rating agencies - can also serve as an example of under-regulation, complicated by the privileged status of several major rating agencies. After a rapid development of the securities market in the 1920's soon followed by the outbreak of the Great Depression, all economic counterparts were in great need of independent professional risk assessments of issuers and financial products. Since 1936 in the United States, this role was gradually assigned to the so-called "big three" rating agencies (Moody's, S&P and Fitch).

In 1975, the US Securities and Exchange Commission created the nationally recognized statistical rating organization, comprising of seven rating agencies, including the "Big Three". Soon, as a result of several mergers, the only members in the list of this organization were the rating agencies from the "big three" (in recent years, however, the list has been slightly expanded). The then Securities Commission adopted regulations that required issuers and sellers of bonds to have their financial products necessarily rated by one of the three largest rating agencies. As a result, "taking into account the fact that since 1975 no competitor has been allowed to benefit from the mistakes of the three rating agencies, it is not surprising that these agencies have made mistakes".[74]

In addition, in the 80's there was a change in the rating agencies' model of receiving income. If initially investors received information about the financial status of issuers and then assigned ratings based on this information, now the rating agencies began to generate their income at the expense of issuers and sellers of financial products, which in general led to a conflict of interests, i.e. "created conditions for massive abuses. Banks were able to negotiate with

---

[74] Friedman J., Kraus V., "Man-made financial crisis. Systemic risks and failure of regulation" (translated from English), M., Publishing House., «YRISEN» и «Mysl», 2012 (in Russian language); p., 175.

rating agencies on buying higher valuations. An agency that issued bank note's ratings that did not suit the customers, was in danger of getting bankrupt".[75]

Subsequently, rating agencies began offering consulting services to customers (issuers, sellers of financial instruments) on what the design and look of a financial product should be in order to get the highest rating of the same agency.

Moreover, shortly before the crisis, the importance of rating evaluations increased, as they became an integral element of regulatory documents, both at the international level (the Basel II Agreement) and at the national level. In the United States, the special role of their ratings was secured, in particular, in the regulatory document "P-Rule" (Final Rule on Risk-Based Capital Guidelines, 2001). These regulatory documents contained a procedure for calculating the adequacy of bank's capital based on weighing the risk degree of assets taking into account the ratings. The regulatory instruction stated that "investors rely on ratings when making investment decisions. This circumstance has a disciplining effect of the market nature on rating agencies and ensures credibility and prestige of their ratings."

On the other hand, the markets' reliance on ratings gives assurance to the agencies that their ratings can be considered as the main factor determining the weighted risk factors during calculation of the weighted number of assets used to estimate capital adequacy rates".[76]As a result of this role of rating agencies in the regulatory system, they themselves were basically outside the state supervision. The methods and procedures applied by the agencies for assigning, revising, and annulling ratings, possible conflicts of interest of rating agencies, sources of their income, level of professionalism and quality of their management systems - all these important parameters were practically not regulated. Therefore, it is not surprising that under such conditions e.g. the rating agency Moody's has not revised its "basic statistical hypotheses for the valuation of financial instruments, in particular, mortgage bonds ever since 2002 and until the crisis."[77]

---

[75] Roubini N., "Crisis Economics: A Crash Course in the Future of Finance", M., EKSMO, 2011 (in Russian language); p., 227.

[76] 66 Fed. Reg. 59614 (November 29, 2001).

[77] Jones S., How Moody's Faltered, Financial Times, October 17, 2008.

As for the shortcomings in the regulatory system, it can also be noted that in fact, in the pre-crisis period, the asset risk assessment system applied in the United States and other countries for calculation of capital adequacy, actually stimulated banks to invest in mortgage securities, rather than in other types of assets, such as loans to industrial enterprises. For example, in accordance with the regulator's methodology, *PLMBS* mortgage securities with ratings from BB to BBB had 100% investment risk (like standard loans to enterprises), papers rated A - 50%, while papers rated from AA to AAA - 20%. Regulators created a situation where "P-Rule actually punished those banks that did not invest in the securities that were issued against liquid assets (ABS) and had high ratings, because, according to this Rule, the banks needed to have 400% more equity for giving loans to commercial companies or individuals than for purchasing ABSs with AA or AAA ratings".[78] According to many researchers[79], this imperfection of the regulatory rules (which did not change even with the evident bloat of the mortgage market bubble) played a very important role in the emergence of the crisis.

An important factor in the emergence of the crisis was the changing nature of the economy – a growing shift from a regulated economy with the dominance of the real sector to the economy where the share of poorly regulated or not regulated speculative operations was constantly increasing. Thus, in recent years, the role of the financial sector has steadily increased in the economies of developed countries. In the last 15 years the share of financial services in the GDP structure has increased in the UK from 13.3% to 28.5%, in the USA - from 17% to 25%, in Germany - from 14% to 28%. The growth of financial markets significantly outpaced the growth of the real sector of the economy. This trend is well illustrated by the example of the world's leading economy, the United States, where the growth rates of financial markets, in particular the debt securities market, significantly outpaced the growth rate

---

[78]   Friedman J., Kraus V., "Man-made financial crisis. Systemic risks and failure ofregulation" (translated from English), M., Publishing House., «YRISEN» и «Mysl», 2012 (in Russian language); p., 123.

[79]   Kling A., The Unintended Consequences of International Bank Capital Standards, Mercatus on Policy 44, 2009, April; Acharya V., Richardson M., Restoring Financial Stability: How to Repair a Failed System, New York University Stern School of Business, 2009; Wallison P., Cause and Effect: Government Policies and the Financial Crisis, Critical Review 21 (2-3). p., 365-376

of the economy as a whole. At the same time, it should be noted that in recent years the situation has radically changed.

In addition, the development of speculative operations, primarily currency transactions and portfolio investment, was facilitated by the lifting of restrictions on cross-border capital flows. As early as in 1970, the USA, Canada, Germany and Switzerland abolished control over the movement of capital. In 1979, Great Britain and Japan removed the last restrictions. Soon, the liberalization of capital flows spread almost everywhere.

However, already in the 90's the movement of speculative capital began to have a destabilizing effect on the economy of individual countries. There are well-known examples when the actions of currency and financial speculators led to a sharp depreciation of currencies (for example, devaluation of the pound sterling and the Italian lira in 1992) or a collapse in stock markets e.g.: in the countries of Southeast Asia in the late 90's. As a result, the situation developed in a deregulated global economy allowed "global currency and securities traders to direct a continuously growing flow of free capital and thereby bring welfare or misfortune to entire countries, which they did, largely avoiding state control".[80]

In the period preceding the crisis, the problem of moral abuse, especially in the financial sphere, also became widespread. Besides, it perfectly fit into the dominant speculative and deregulated nature of economic development. Managers of banks and financial companies, as well as mortgage brokers seemed not to notice the risks of investing in the rapidly growing financial pyramid of structured products, since such operations brought quick and significant revenue, which allowed them to pay super-high incomes to the managers and traders of these companies. At that, a significant part of the income was paid in the form of bonuses. In 2006, the average size of bonuses in the five largest US investment banks reached 60% of all compensation payments, and the number of bonuses on the eve of the crisis also reached

---

[80] Martin H.,Schumann X.., "Trap of globalization: an attack on prosperity and democracy".,M., Publishing House., «Alpina», 2001 (in Russian language); p., 74.

unprecedented amounts: in 2005 they amounted to 25 billion dollars, in 2006 - 36 billion dollars, and in 2007 - 38 billion dollars.[81]

The devastating impact that the current system of management's financial incentives had on the final results of financial institutions was analyzed by many researchers, in particular in the works of R. Posner and R. Rajan. One of the explanations of the moral abuse problems in companies is the theory of the "principal agent problem", according to which agents (managers) of enterprises are better informed about the real situation in the company and can use this information for their personal purposes. The problem becomes especially acute in case of financial companies, especially those with a large volume of transactions, where management and traders can make many risky transactions on a daily basis in order to earn the maximum possible premium. It is especially convenient to carry out such operations in companies that have a complex and diversified structure and where the authorization scale of traders is rather high. Vivid examples of such structures are investment banks and funds, financial holdings, and large insurance companies. The collapse of the insurance company *AIG* "can be considered as the most vivid example of risks related to moral abuse, which demonstrates seriousness of the problems caused by "principal-agent" and information asymmetry. In the *AIG* case, the actions of a small group of employees from the company's London office not only brought a huge corporation to its knees, but nearly destroyed the whole global financial system".[82]

After reviewing the factors that led to the crisis, such as deregulation, financial innovations, speculation and moral abuse, it is necessary to note that the crisis was developing on the background of ever-increasing globalization, which undoubtedly influenced both its origin and development. Features of the influence of globalization on the emergence and development of the crisis of 2007-2009 are described in the next section.

---

[81] Roubini N., "Crisis Economics: A Crash Course in the Future of Finance", M., EKSMO, 2011 (in Russian language); p., 82.

[82] Roubini N., "Crisis Economics: A Crash Course in the Future of Finance", M., EKSMO, 2011 (in Russian language); p., 84.

1.5. Development of the Global Economy and World Crisis

Globalization of the economy and social sphere, which has been steadily increasing in recent years, undoubtedly influenced the emergence and character of the global crisis of 2007-2009.

Globalization, often defined as a process of worldwide economic, political, and cultural integration and unification, has become a notable trend of the world development in the 80's. In the 90's and 2000's its influence on the world processes has become determinative. In the context of globalization, the world economy, which was a combination of national economies linked to each other by means of a system of the worldwide division of labor, has turned into a world market which was functioning based on trans-nationalization, regionalization, and partial restriction of national sovereignty. During the globalization process a new economic space was formed in which the sector structure, information and technology exchange and production location were determined taking into account the world market condition. A well-known financier J. Soros defines globalization as "the development of global financial markets and growth of transnational corporations' power as well as their influence on national economies ... most of the negative characteristics attributed to globalization by public opinion - including introduction of market values in the areas where they have traditionally been absent - are based in the above-mentioned "parameters"."[83]

Globalization is inseparably linked with the increase in the degree of freedom of movement of capital, goods, services, labor, and information.

The free, virtually unlimited flow of capital is perhaps the key element of the system of global economic relations, since it has largely changed the face of the world economy in recent years. Withdrawal of restrictions on the movement of capital in most countries in the 80's and 90's led to a sharp increase in the scale and speed of capital transfer. This was also facilitated by the revolution in financial and information technologies and formation of world financial markets working around the clock in real time.

---

[83] Soros G., "On Globalization", M., «Eksmo», 2004 (in Russian language); p., 15.

Statistical data on the increase of capital flows (especially private) in the pre-crisis years is impressive. According to the IMF, global capital flows that fluctuated within 2-6% of the world GDP in 1970-1995, reached 15% in 2005-2007. In 2006, in absolute terms, they amounted to 7.2 trillion USD, having increased threefold in comparison with 1995.[84]

Like any other capital, international investments flowed to the markets of those countries where the rate of return was the highest. Naturally, a high profit rate (and, therefore, a higher risk) existed in the markets of developing countries, where direct investments found cheap raw materials and labor, low or concessional taxation, and weak state control combined with corruption. Portfolio investments were made in poorly organized and poorly regulated financial markets, which also brought super profits. Therefore, in the pre-crisis years, especially on the eve of the crisis, private capital, primarily prone to risky and speculative operations, uncontrollably reached out for the markets of developing countries (Table 7).

Table 7

Dynamics of Private Capital Flows at Markets of Developing Countries (billion USD, 2002-2009)

	2002-2004 (Average)	2005	2006	2007	2008	2009
Total Net Private Investment	168,8	312,2	308,6	691,0	278,8	320,9
Including:						
Direct Investments	167,7	277,3	301,1	439,3	479,8	334,5
Portfolio Investments	20,3	36,7	-30,7	106,7	70,2	90,4
Other Investments	-19,1	-1,8	38,2	144,9	-130,8	-104,0

Source: IMF, World Economic Outlook, April 2017, www.imf.org

With the onset of the crisis (2008), "hot" foreign investments (portfolio and other) left the markets of developing countries as suddenly as they entered them, causing their sharp destabilization.

---

[84]   IMF, Globalization and the Crisis (2005 – present), www.imf.org

In the pre-crisis years, direct foreign investments in the economies of developing countries increased noticeably, bringing with them new production and technology. Many large companies started to transfer production from the Western countries to developing countries. This contributed to very high rates of economic growth in developing countries, especially in Asia. On the eve of the crisis, capital investments made in the economy of Asian countries dominated in the total structure of private direct foreign investments in developing countries, reaching USD 166.4 billion in 2007 (Figure 2).

Figure 2

The Structure of Private Direct Foreign Investments in Developing Countries (by regions, 2007)

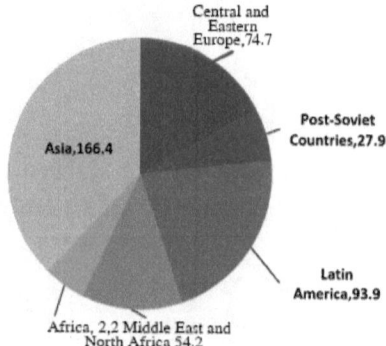

Source: *IMF, World Economic Outlook, April 2017, www.imf.org*

Among developing countries China was the leader in attracting foreign direct investment since 1993. As early as in 2001, there were 202,000 enterprises with foreign investment in China, where every tenth Chinese worked. These enterprises provided 50% of China's exports. By 2013, the number of such enterprises increased to 442,000. The vast majority of the largest transnational corporations have invested in the Chinese economy. To a great extent, this was due to China's attractiveness for investors, in particular, the scale of its market, availability of free economic zones, cheap labor, and political and economic stability.

Indeed, China had an unlimited reserve of labor. So, according to a study of costs in the textile industry, the cost of labor in China in the early 2000's was only 30 cents an hour, while in neighboring Taiwan - $5, and in the US - 10.3 dollars. Not surprisingly, in the 90's in China, 70% of enterprises with foreign capital were involved in labor-intensive production. Foreign investors also pursued the long-term goal of entering the vast Chinese market, which was easier to do in the form of direct foreign investment. Foreign investment was also facilitated by a preferential taxation regime and rather simple procedures for registration of enterprises with foreign participation.

At the same time, China became the largest exporter to the markets of developed countries, supplying relatively cheap products, since Chinese exporters in essence enjoyed subsidies in the form of cheap capital, land, labor and energy. Growth of export opportunities of China was promoted by the understated exchange rate of the Yuan to the dollar, being also a kind of subsidy to the export sector of the country. In general, the volume of China's foreign trade increased from USD 20.6 billion in 1978 to USD 2.3 trillion dollars in 2008.

At the same time, a significant part of the received foreign exchange earnings was invested in foreign assets, in particular, in US securities. It can be said that this was a kind of secret agreement, which allowed all involved parties to receive benefits, although at the same time had negative consequences. A famous American Financier L. Summers called such a situation a "financial clinch", because "neither side can make a move without upsetting the existing balance. China cannot stop buying US debt, because otherwise it will lose its largest market. The United States, in turn, cannot continue to build protectionist barriers, as this can force China to moderate its current financial prodigality".[85]

At the same time, it is obvious that the growth of output and export of certain Chinese products to the markets of developed countries did not contribute to the development of the real sector of the economy in these countries. The increased role of the financial sector (including through excessive capital inflows from developing countries) also exacerbated macroeconomic

---

[85] Roubini N., "Crisis Economics: A Crash Course in the Future of Finance", M., EKSMO, 2011 (in Russian language); p..., 291.

imbalances. The intensified process of the withdrawal of enterprises from the real sector of the economy from the US and other Western countries to developing countries occurred against the backdrop of hypertrophied development of some sectors, such as housing construction, which heavily depended on consumer demand, lending, and the state of financial institutions. The excessive development of the financial market and banking services sector further increased disproportions and systemic risks.

However, before the crisis erupted, the tactical benefits of cooperation outweighed the fear of potential threats. With the emergence of the crisis, the situation began to change. A well-known researcher of the crisis Professor R. Rajan from the University of Chicago Booth School of Business stated that "in the government offices in Washington one can now hear accusations of dishonest trade the disparity of which seems obvious, with the unemployment rate in the US reaching 10% and the level of Chinese economic growth also reaching 10%. In Congress, calls for the establishment of trade barriers in one form or another become louder and louder, which, perhaps, will not abate even if the Yuan starts to strengthen again".[86]

After China, India and Brazil also demonstrated the best dynamics in terms of inflow of foreign direct investment. The volume of foreign direct investment in the economy of India increased after 1991, when reforms aimed at liberalizing the economic life were carried out. Thus private companies were given access to such industries as aircraft construction, air transport, shipbuilding, smelting of cast iron steel and nonferrous metals, production and distribution of electricity etc. At the same time, income tax rates were reduced, restrictions on the import of raw materials and capital equipment were removed and most enterprises received the right to attract foreign investments. Customs duties were significantly decreased. In 1991, the rupee devaluation stimulated development of exports. Rupee became partially convertible currency. As a result, in 1991-2008 the total amount of direct foreign investment reached $ 74.3 billion. The structure of India's exports also changed: if before the reforms it was dominated by textile products and jewelry, later on India became the largest exporter of high-tech software and pharmaceutical products.

---

[86] Rajan R., "Rift lines. Hidden cracks, still threatening the global economy", M., Publishing House of the Gaydar Institute, 2011 (in Russian language); pp., 396-397.

The Brazilian economy became attractive for the direct foreign investment as a result of the government policy of openness and stabilization (Real Madrid Plan), which included a national privatization program, the amendments of constitutional provisions related to economic activity, and flexibility of the legislative order with regard to foreign capital. Initially, direct foreign investments, mostly coming from the European countries, were linked with the privatization process going on in the Brazilian economy and mainly concentrated in the sectors of services, telecommunications, energy and finance. However, later on, especially after the arrival of transnational corporations, foreign investments penetrated the manufacturing, automobile, electrical, and food industries. As a result, in 2011, the volume of foreign investment in the Brazilian economy reached 50.5 billion dollars, and its economy ranked the sixth in the world in terms of GDP.

In the course of these tectonic changes, new economic centers emerged in the world economy. Starting from the late 80's and early 90's, the economic role of Asian tigers (China, India, South Korea, Taiwan, Singapore, and Hong Kong) increased. Since the early 2000s, the economic role of a group of the South American countries (Argentina, Brazil, and Mexico) as well as a number of other countries (e.g.: South Africa), increased dramatically.

All this led to a high level of investment and increased economic growth in a number of developing countries, while developed countries increasingly lagged behind the new economic centers in terms of investment, GDP growth and exports. Thus, in 1999-2006, the level of investment in developed countries was, on average, 21.1% of GDP (including 19.9% in the United States, 17.3% in the United Kingdom, and 21.1% in the euro zone), while in the developing Asian economies it reached 33.3%.

This difference is especially evident when comparing developed countries with rapidly developing Asian countries (Table 8).

Table 8

GDP Growth Rates in Developed Countries and Developing Asian Economies, in 1995-2015

	1995-2005	2006	2007	2008	2009	2010	2011	2012	2013	2014	2015	2016
The World Economy	**3.9**	**5.5**	**5.6**	**3.0**	**-0.1**	**5.4**	**4,2**	**3.5**	**3.4**	**3.5**	**3.4**	**3.1**
Developed Countries	**2.8**	**3.0**	**2.7**	**0.1**	**-3.4**	**3.1**	**1.7**	**1.2**	**1.3**	**2.0**	**2.2**	**1.7**
USA	3.3	2.7	1.8	-0.3	-2.8	2.5	1.6	2.2	1.7	2.4	2.6	1.6
Japan	1.0	1.4	1.7	-1.1	-5.5	4,2	-0.1	1.5	2.0	0.3	1.2	1.0
Canada	3.3	2.6	2.1	1.0	-3.0	3.1	3.1	1.8	2.5	2.6	0.9	1.4
UK	3.4	2.5	2.6	-0.6	-4.3	1.9	1.5	1.3	1.9	3.1	2.2	1.8
Euro Zone Countries	**2.1**	**3.2**	**3.0**	**0.4**	**-4.5**	**2.1**	**1.6**	**-0.9**	**-0.3**	**1.2**	**2.1**	**1.7**
Germany	1.2	3.9	3.4	0.8	-5.6	4.0	3.7	0.7	0.6	1.6	1.5	1.8
France	2.3	2.4	2.4	0.2	-2.9	2.0	2.1	0.2	0.6	0.6	1.3	1.2
Italy	1.4	2.0	1.5	-1.1	-5.5	1.7	0.6	-2.8	-1.7	0.1	0.8	0.9
Developing Asian Countries	**6.9**	**10.1**	**11.2**	**7.2**	**7.5**	**9.6**	**7.9**	**7.0**	**7.0**	**6.8**	**6.7**	**6.4**
China	9.2	12.7	14.2	9.6	9.2	10.6	9.5	7.9	7.8	7.3	6.9	6.7
India	6.4	9.3	9.8	3.9	8,5	10.3	6.6	5.5	6.5	7.2	7.9	6.8

Source: *IMF, World Economic Outlook databases, April 2017, www.imf.org*

In the pre-crisis years, along with direct investments, the world economy was flooded with hot speculative money in the form of portfolio investments. They quickly formed "bubbles" in the financial markets of developing countries, but then left them very quickly after receiving super high profits. Such capital reversals provoked crises in those developing economies that had a significant budget deficit and where the obligations of economic agents and governments were denominated in foreign currency, while export earnings heavily depended on the world prices. As a result, the strongest systemic crises struck Mexico in 1994, South Korea, Thailand, Malaysia, and Indonesia - in 1997, Russia,

Ukraine, Kazakhstan, Brazil, Ecuador, and Pakistan - in 1998-1999, Turkey and Argentina - in 2001.

Disproportions and "bubbles" in the economies of developing countries were formed not only as a result of flows of "hot" money, but also due to significant borrowings in foreign currency on foreign markets. For example, in the Eastern European countries with transition economies and in the former Soviet Union, which actively borrowed money from the banks of developed countries and attracted foreign investors (from 2002 to 2006, the amount of loans attracted from foreign sources increased by 60% annually), the in the situation developed in a very dramatic scenario time of the crisis. As a result, "the crisis hit countries as diverse as Romania, Bulgaria, Croatia, Russia, and especially the Baltic States - Latvia, Estonia and Lithuania - Hungary and Ukraine, all of them were victims of a sharp reversal of capital flows, because willful investors fled from risky markets - in other words, from developing countries - to safer harbors".[87]

No less destructive role was played by the massive cash flow moving from developing countries (China, the Gulf countries) to the financial markets of developed countries. Excessive liquidity in the financial markets, which was significantly promoted by the developing exporting countries, contributed to the formation of various "bubbles", such as mortgage securities.

Growing disparity between the trade and current account balances of developed and developing countries was another serious problem of the global economy. Enhanced divergence between capital flows and goods continuously exacerbated this situation. As a result, a number of countries (usually those with a significantly export-oriented economy) constantly had a positive current account balance, and at the same time there was a group of countries with chronic deficit of the trade and current account balances.

In general, in the pre-crisis years the developed countries had a chronic trade balance deficit (on average, in 2000-2007 it was 185.2 billion dollars) because weakening of the real sector of the economy outstripped the growth rate of imports compared to exports. At the same time, some developed countries,

---

[87] Roubini N., "Crisis Economics: A Crash Course in the Future of Finance", M., EKSMO, 2011 (in Russian language); p.., 153.

such as Germany and Japan, had a positive trade balance. In 2008, Germany had trade surplus of 224 billion dollars. It was also preserved in the following years. However, the excessive orientation of these economies on exports has led to the situation where "the super-efficient manufacturing sector existed in parallel with an agonizing sector of services: focus on foreign demand was preserved, while domestic demand remained undeveloped".[88]

The US is the leader among the developed countries in terms of trade deficit: in 2007 it reached $ 700 billion. In addition to the deficit of the US trade balance, the current account deficit has also been present for a long time, one of the reasons of which is capital import. In the 1990's the current account deficit in the US was largely due to foreign investment in US stocks (which in 2000 reached $ 300 billion). After the collapse of the market of high-tech companies' shares, foreign investment intensively flowed into the US debt obligations and mortgage-backed securities. As a result, the American economy faced a situation where "non-residents now actually own about half of US Treasury bills and bonds (with the exception of those which are on the balance of the Federal Reserve System)".[89]

In general, on the eve of the crisis in 2006, the current account deficit was observed in the vast majority of developed countries, in particular, it accounted for 5.8% of GDP in the United States, 2.8% of GDP in Great Britain, 0.6% of GDP in France, 9% of GDP in Spain, 1.5% of GDP in Italy, 11.4% of GDP in Greece, and 5.3% of GDP in Australia. At the same time, many transition and developing economies had a positive current account balance, for example, China - 8.5% of GDP, Indonesia - 2.6% of GDP, Malaysia - 16.1% of GDP, Russia - 9.3% of GDP, Azerbaijan - 17.6% of GDP, Uzbekistan - 9.2% of GDP, Argentina - 3.4% of GDP, Brazil - 1.3% of GDP, Chile - 4.6% of GDP, Saudi Arabia - 26.3% of GDP, and Qatar - 15.5% of GDP.[90]

Thus, increased globalization intensified the uneven and unstable development of the world economy and promoted formation of new economic centers that often suffered from destructive crises. At the same time, disparities

[88]   Rajan R., "Rift lines. Hidden cracks, still threatening the global economy", M., Publishing House of the Gaydar Institute, 2011 (in Russian language);p., 122.

[89]   Roubini N., "Crisis Economics: A Crash Course in the Future of Finance", M., EKSMO, 2011 (in Russian language); p..., 298.

[90]   IMF, World Economic Outlook databases, April 2017, www.imf.org

accumulated in the economies of developed countries and the structure of the economy changed. Such large-scale economic changes could not be accompanied by the corresponding institutional changes. Indeed, in the years leading up to the world crisis, a few global and regional organizations were formed, while the activities of the previous ones underwent significant changes.

Strengthening the influence of developing countries on global economic and political processes led to the emergence of a group of G20 countries, the inaugural conference of which was held on December 15-16, 1999 in Berlin. The group was created as a result of an initiative of the finance ministers of the G-7 countries to conduct a dialogue with developing countries on key issues of economic and financial policy. In the conditions of an erupting crisis, summits of ministers and leaders of the G-20 countries became regular.

Thus, on November 14-15, 2008, the anti-crisis summit of G20 countries was held in Washington, during which agreements were reached on cooperation in key areas for mitigation of the crisis consequences, general principles of reforming international financial institutions and measures to prevent crises in the future.

At the London Summit of G-20 (April 2, 2009) an action plan was adopted to overcome the crisis, and statements were made on strengthening the financial system and channeling resources through international financial organizations. Decisions were made to significantly increase the IMF resources (up to $ 750 billion), to allocate $ 100 billion to the International Development Bank for lending purposes, to support trade finance in the amount up to $ 250 billion, to direct the proceeds from the agreed sale of IMF gold for financing the poorest countries on preferential terms. Also, a new *Financial Stability Board* with an expanded mandate was created, which became the successor to the *Financial Stability Forum*.

The Summit in Pittsburgh on September 24-25, 2009, was largely devoted to banking issues and creation of a coordinated action system for all G20 participants in the field of the economic policy. At the summit in Toronto on June 26-27, 2010, developed countries decided to reduce the budget deficit by half by 2013. Currency policy issues of leading economic powers, in particular the United States and China, were discussed at the Summit in

Seoul on November 11-12, 2010. Measures to prevent the crisis and control over banking activities were considered at a summit in Cannes on November 3-4, 2011. At the Mexican summit in Los Cabos on June 18-19, 2012, the European debt crisis was discussed. The IMF reserves were increased by 450 billion dollars. At the St. Petersburg Summit on September 5-6, 2013, the main attention was paid to ensuring economic growth and financial stability, stimulating investment and creating jobs.

The summit that took place in Brisbane on November 15-16, 2014, determined the most important task of increasing world GDP by at least 2 additional percent (in absolute terms of $ 2 trillion) by 2018 and thus create millions of jobs. To achieve this goal, it is planned to develop trade and investment and to create an international infrastructure center.

As a result of the summit, an anti-corruption plan for 2015-2016 was also approved, envisaging measures to ensure transparency of business ownership, which will allow to combat bribery, tax evasion and money laundering. The document also speaks of the need to reflect in the legislation the concept of "beneficial owner". The G20 countries undertook the obligation to start an automatic exchange of tax information by the end of 2018.

At the same time, the communique notes that the world economy still faces risks associated with geopolitical instability. "The global economy remains vulnerable to shocks; financial instability persists" - the document says.

The summit in Antalya on November 15-16, 2015, paid considerable attention to the struggle against international terrorism.

The Hangzhou Summit that took place on September 4-5, 2016, adopted a few important documents such as *Blueprint on Innovative Growth*, *G20 Action Plan for the New Industrial Revolution*, and *Hangzhou Plan of Action*, which outlines a strategy for ensuring universal and sustainable growth, as well as the G20 initiative on development and cooperation in the digital economy.

In the last two decades, integration processes that were important for the world economy took place in Europe. The European Union, created in 1957 in the form of the EEC, has undergone significant qualitative and quantitative changes.

In the economic sphere, the basic EU principles were free movement of capital, goods, services and population within the union, which was in the mainstream of global changes. In 1995, the EU expanded with new memberships of countries such as Sweden, Finland and Austria. In 2004 there was a significant expansion of the EU in which the countries of Southern and Eastern Europe (the Baltic countries, Poland, the Czech Republic, Slovakia, Hungary, Slovenia, Malta, and Cyprus) became members. In 2007, Bulgaria and Romania, while in 2013 - Croatia became members. Thus, now this regional organization includes 28 states with 500 million inhabitants, producing 23% of the world's GDP.

Adoption of the *Maastricht Agreements* legally initiated creation of the EU in the modern sense. Since that moment, the responsibility for monetary policy has been entrusted to the European system of central banks within the national banks and the European Central Bank. In accordance with the *Maastricht Agreements*, all countries that joined the European Monetary Union had to meet certain criteria, in particular, their state budget deficit should not exceed 3% of GDP, while the public debt should not exceed 60% of GDP. In addition, the state had to participate in the mechanism of exchange rates for two years and maintain the exchange rate of the national currency in the specified range, while the inflation rate should not exceed 1.5% of the average of the three EU member countries with the most stable prices. At the same time, long-term interest rates on government bonds should not exceed the average value of corresponding rates in the countries with the lowest inflation by more than 2%.

Unfortunately, in future, the criteria established by the *Maastricht Agreements* were not respected in due measure by all the EU participants, which aggravated the problems of these countries during the global crisis of 2007-2009.

Creation of the European Monetary Union and the introduction of the single currency - euro in 1999 was an important qualitative change within the EU. Currently, most EU countries (17) are part of the Eurozone, although during the global crisis in European countries, the positions of euro-skeptics, who favor weakening of integration processes, especially in the monetary and political spheres, have strengthened.

87

In the EU, many political, legal and financial institutions were created, in particular, *The European Commission, The Council of the European Union, The European Council, The Court of the European Union, The European Court of Auditors* and *The European Central Bank.*

In 2012, in order to further strengthen the economy of the Eurozone, the leaders of the EU countries proposed to create a banking union. The first stage in the formation of the banking union was the decision to establish a single supervisory mechanism on the basis of the ECB.

In November 2014, Frankfurt hosted the grand opening and launch of the Single ECB supervisory mechanism, which would take control of more than 120 banks in the euro area. The Head of the European Council Herman van Rompuy called this event "a revolution in European financial architecture". A single oversight mechanism was part of a large-scale euro zone project to establish a banking union and one of the most important steps in promotion of this project. Its primary goal is to protect taxpayers, who suffered the most during the bank restructuring process. At the same time, the mechanism protects depositors of banks: deposits worth over 100 thousand euros are insured and will not be affected during reorganization or liquidation of a bank. Introduction of this institute will increase the confidence of depositors and creditors in the European financial institutions. Before the official launch of mechanism, the ECB conducted stress tests of euro-zone banks during one year and according to the results of which 24 banks had capital deficit.

In general, the integration processes in Europe allowed the EU countries to create a certain protective mechanism in the face of increasing globalization. However, the accumulated imbalances in the economy and social sphere, primarily the high level of public debt, weak growth in labor productivity, decrease in export competitiveness, and an aging population make European countries vulnerable to the global economy, especially in the context of the global crisis. In addition, the EU has a serious differentiation of countries in terms of economic development and financial stability. While "Germany and some other countries over the past decade have reduced their financial imbalances and increased the competitiveness of their exports through corporate restructuring, the reverse situation was observed in Italy, Spain,

Greece and Portugal, where financial imbalances remained significant, and growth rates of wages outpaced productivity growth."[91]

The fastest growing economies of the world - Brazil, Russia, India, China, South Africa, have combined to form the BRICS group of countries (Brazil, Russia, India, China, South Africa), which has also become a very notable event in recent years.

Initially, the term "countries of the BRICS group" (BRICS) was used in the analytical report of the investment bank *Goldman Sachs*. The 2005 report noted that these countries are the most dynamic in economic development and by 2050 their aggregate GDP will exceed the corresponding indicator of G8 countries. The report also predicted that within a decade the number of people with an annual income above 3 thousand dollars will reach 800 million, and the number of people with an annual income over $15,000 will exceed 200 million. Such changes in income mean that the middle class and consumer demand for expensive goods and services will grow significantly.

In September 2008, UNCTAD published a report according to which the BRICS countries are among the five countries considered by transnational corporations to be most attractive for investment.

At a time when the BRICS countries became the object of research of international financial organizations, they had not yet coordinated their activities and the term BRICS was used only by analysts. However, the regular summits of ministers and leaders of these countries soon began to take place. Thus, the first brief meeting of the heads of state took place on July 9, 2008 in Toyako-Onsen (Japan), at which it was decided to hold a full-scale summit in 2009.

The first BRICS summit was held in Yekaterinburg on June 16, 2009. It adopted, in particular, a joint statement on global food security. At the second summit in Brasilia on April 15-16, 2010, a number of interstate agreements were signed and issues such as overcoming the consequences of the crisis and creating a new financial order (including the rights of the BRICS countries, for greater influence in international financial institutions) were touched

---

[91]   Roubini N., "Crisis Economics: A Crash Course in the Future of Finance", M., EKSMO, 2011 (in Russian language); p..., 321.

upon. At the third summit in Sanya (China) on April 13-14, 2011, issues of mutual cooperation and comprehensive reform of the United Nations were raised. The fourth summit that took place in New Delhi on March 15-16, 2012, was devoted to the problems of the global economy, anti-crisis measures, the possibility of creating a joint bank and the mechanisms for convergence of its stock exchanges. The fifth summit was held in Durban (South Africa) on March 26-27, 2013. Following that summit, the *Etequin Declaration and the Etequin Plan of Action* were promulgated. The declaration assesses the current world political and economic situation and reflects common approaches of the BRICS countries on topical issues of multilateral cooperation. The Action Plan concretizes the work of the BRICS for the coming year and also includes new promising areas of cooperation. Agreements on cooperation in the field of "green economy", joint financing of infrastructure projects in Africa and the *Declaration on the establishment of the BRICS Business Council* were signed. It also announced the signing of the *Declaration on the Establishment of the Consortium of Experts Centers of the BRICS Countries* and publication of a joint statistical bulletin of the BRICS countries.

At the Sixth Summit of the Heads of BRICS states (July 15-16, 2014, Fortaleza and Brasilia), agreements were signed to establish a new development bank and to create a pool of conventional foreign exchange reserves of the BRICS countries. The limit of the authorized capital of the development bank was set at $100 billion. The agreement on the pool of conditional currencies (BRICS Reserve Fund) provided for financial assistance to the member countries where necessary.

In the context of globalization, international financial institutions were also developing. In general, the world has a sufficiently developed system of international financial institutions, including the *IMF*, the *World Bank*, and the *Bank for International Settlements*, as well as the *World Trade Organization* (WTO), the *International Labor Organization* (ILO), and the *Food and Agriculture Organization* (FAO). In post-war development of the world economy and social sphere, these institutions played a noticeably positive role, despite some failures. It is difficult not to agree that "although the system has never functioned as originally conceived, its internal logic remains highly attractive; until the early 1970's, the mechanisms that were not fully realized, provided support for the post-war recovery and the "golden age" of economic growth inspired by Keynesian ideas."[92]

The Basel Committee on Banking Regulation and Supervision under the *Bank for International Settlements* played a significant role in regulation and supervision in the banking sector both at the national and international levels. The main task of the committee is introduction of uniform standards in the field of banking regulation, for which it develops directives and recommendations for regulatory bodies of member states that are not binding, but, in most cases, are reflected in the national legislations of the member states. Development of directives and recommendations is carried out in cooperation with banks and regulatory agencies around the world and therefore they are also used in countries that are not the committee members.

The Basel Committee recommended three fundamental documents (agreements) in the field of regulation and supervision. *The Basel I Agreement* (1988) provided for the division of the bank's capital for regulatory purposes into two categories - first and second tier capital and classification of all the bank assets into five groups, depending on the risk degree. *The Basel II Agreement* (2004) provided for minimum capital requirements, supervisory procedures and market discipline. *The Basel III Agreement* (2010) established new capital and liquidity requirements, including additional capital buffers.

The system of prudential banking norms introduced in many countries on the initiative of the Basel Committee, played a significant role in building commercial risk management systems by commercial banks. At the same time, similarly to the activities of other international financial institutions, the recommendations of the Basel Committee to a certain extent lagged behind the rapid changes in the financial sphere and the globalization level of the economy. Some provisions of these recommendations did not fully take into account the real risk level of banks' investments, e.g. investments in mortgage securities highly rated by international rating agencies.

---

[92] Stiglitz J., "On the Reform of the International Monetary and Financial System: Lessons from the Global Crisis". Report of the UN Financial Mechanism Commission, M., «MezhdunarodnyeOtnosheniya"», 2012 (in Russian language);pp., 219-220.

In general, despite all the positive impact on the global economic processes, the international financial institutions did not fully correspond to the level of problems and risks. This became especially evident on the eve and during the global crisis. The situation is explained by the fact that "serious shortcomings in the powers, policies, use of resources and management of these institutions limited their ability to take adequate measures to prevent a crisis and overcome its consequences and had a negative impact on their mission of ensuring sustainable development. The IMF's ability to maintain the stability of the global economy was undermined by significantly greater resources and volatility of globally integrated private financial institutions."[93]

Thus, globalization has created certain opportunities for the economic development of a number of countries, but at the same time increased economic and social instability of many countries and contributed to the development of the global crisis on such a scale and in such an acute form. Based on the nature of the modern economy, it is not enough to take efforts to create sustainable economic growth only at the national level. Along with national and regional economic and social reform programs, efforts are required to radically change the role and functions of reforming international financial institutions, unifying and harmonizing tax and customs legislation and regulation and supervision system as well as synchronizing economic policies at the international level. Certain steps in this direction have been made, but they do not yet meet the challenges of the time.

---

[93] Stiglitz J., "On the Reform of the International Monetary and Financial System: Lessons from the Global Crisis". Report of the UN Financial Mechanism Commission, M., «MezhdunarodnyeOtnosheniya"», 2012 (in Russian language);, p., 225-226.

CHAPTER 2
Anti-crisis measures: issues of efficiency and sufficiency

2.1. Maintenance of liquidity in the economy and financial sector: achievements and problems

Economic crises, as a rule, are accompanied by liquidity problems in the economy in general, and in the financial sector in particular. During the boom, a significant number of risky assets accumulates on the banks' balance sheets, which, when the market collapses, becomes illiquid, "toxic." At the same time, banks are under increased pressure from creditors and investors seeking to return the invested funds as soon as possible. Such problems negatively affect the banking liquidity, cause its shortage, can lead to the suspension of banking operations and the bankruptcy of credit institutions. The bankruptcy of a single bank, especially a large one, can result in a series of bankruptcies, since, as another financial guru of the 19th century, W. Bagehot noted, "the ruin of one of these great banks would greatly impair the credit of all"[94]. The dramatic development of many crises in the 19th century, and especially the catastrophic Great Depression of the 1930's visually demonstrates the acute problems with liquidity in financial institutions, "an instant suspicion

---

[94] BagehotW., LombardStreet: adescriptionofthemoneymarket, p., 249, www. Book-lib.com

of the whole system"[95], massive bankruptcies of credit organizations, which further deepened and aggravated the course of the crisis. To a large extent, such an acute development of the crisis of 1929-1933, in the opinion of most economists, was associated with insufficient actions by the monetary authorities to maintain the liquidity of the banking sector. In particular, monetarists who had a great influence on many modern representatives of monetary authorities believed that "the inaction and incompetence of the FRS not only failed to prevent the impending disaster, but also contributed to its onset"[96].

Undoubtedly, the negative experience of the Great Depression and the recommendations of well-known scientists dealing with the crises problems, led to the fact that in the post-war period the role of monetary authorities in ensuring stable development of the economy significantly increased. At the same time, post-war crises were not large-scale, which allowed central banks to limit themselves to relatively small and short-term injections of liquidity into the financial sector. However, already during the crisis of technology companies in the US at the turn of the millennium, the Fed significantly reduced loan rates and implemented a large-scale injection of liquidity, which soon "contributed to the formation of a 'new' bubble in the real estate market of the United States and then of many other countries"[97].

The crisis that erupted in 2007-2009 was so large that it could entail the collapse of the financial system and the chaos in the economy. The monetary authorities of the developed countries, which had the negative experience of the Great Depression in their luggage, quickly began to implement unprecedented measures to maintain liquidity (first financial institutions, and then corporations). These measures included both the provision of loans in various forms and for different periods, as well as the issuance of loans under guarantees and debt obligations.

Credits provided by monetary authorities to financial institutions represented the first measure of assistance in the conditions of the developing crisis.

---

[95] ibid.

[96] Roubini N., "Crisis Economics: A Crash Course in the Future of Finance", M., EKSMO, 2011 (in Russian language); p., 157.

[97] Roubini N., "Crisis Economics: A Crash Course in the Future of Finance", M., EKSMO, 2011 (in Russian language); p.39.

Since the crisis emerged and took the most ambitious forms in the American economy, it was there that the most significant anti-crisis measures were implemented, including in the form of lending to financial institutions (and later corporations). In the context of the crisis, "the Fed decided to go directly to the market, abandoning the usual mechanism of injecting liquidity - by reducing the "overnight" rate of federal funds - and issuing loans directly to needy financial institutions. Thus, the FRS became the quintessence of the last instance creditor, providing unprecedented access to liquidity for the broadest range of participants in the most diverse segments of the financial system"[98]. Thus, the program of loan auctions, *Term Auction Facility* (TAF), was launched in the US in December 2007, providing for loans for 28 and 84 days against a wide set of securities (operated until March 2010). According to this program, the Fed had committed to hold regular loan auctions (every two weeks) with a fixed amount of liquidity (initially it was $20 billion, then it was $30 billion, and later $50 billion). The average rate at these auctions was lower than the discount window rate. An important feature of these auctions was the anonymity of their participants (unlike the discount window, which allowed them not to advertise financial institutions for their liquidity needs.) Demand at the first auction on December 17, 2007 amounted to $61.5 billion, significantly exceeding the supply ($20 billion). In the future, high demand from borrowers persisted, which confirmed the high relevance of this refinancing instrument among US borrowers.

In March 2008, the US adopted a program of urgent credit auctions of securities (*Term Securities Lending Facility*, TSFL). A special feature of this program was the crediting of primary dealers for a period of 28 days not in cash, but with treasury obligations (secured by other securities). The list of securities accepted for collateral was significantly expanded. In addition to securities of mortgage agencies, it included commercial mortgage securities (rated at least AAA). The Fed set a limit on such operations at the level of $200 billion. The first auction was held on March 27, 2008 and the sum of the offered treasury obligations was $75 billion.

At the same time, in March 2008, the *Primary Dealer Credit Facility* (PDCF) program was launched, providing for overnight loans secured by reliable

---

[98] Roubini N., "Crisis Economics: A Crash Course in the Future of Finance", M., EKSMO, 2011 (in Russian language); p.169.

securities. In 2008, the program covered 20 large primary dealers, many of which were not banks. As part of this program, the Fed widened access to the discount window, allowing new participants, and expanded the list of securities accepted as collateral for loans. The list included, for example, various derivatives from mortgage loans.

Simultaneously, the Federal Reserve started a special program of operations in the open market in the form of a single tranche (*Open Market Operations Program*), designed to simplify the procedure for providing mortgage-backed securities by the borrower as a collateral and to extend the loan term from the usual *Open Market Operations Program* period to 28 days.

In November 2008, the program for lending against futures covered by assets (*Term Asset-Backed Securities Loan Facility*, TALF) was introduced. The program provided for loans of up to $200 billion against securities backed by automobiles, educational and other loans, as well as against securities backed by a pool of mortgages. Later, under President Obama's administration, the volume of the program was increased to USD 1 trillion.

In December 2008, short-term loans were provided to the industrial giants *General Motors* ($13.4 billion) and Chrysler ($4 billion). Direct credit support by the state to the corporate sector has to some extent become a revolutionary innovation for the United States.

To extend mortgage refinancing and stimulate lending, the *Fraud Enforcement and Recovery Act* was passed in May 2009. The law significantly expanded the powers of the Federal Deposit Insurance Corporation and the National Board of Credit Unions in this matter.

Also in the United States, programs such as the *Commercial Paper Financing Program* (CPFF), *Money Market Investors' Program* (MMMF), *Liquidity Fund of Asset-Backed Commercial Paper* and *Money Market and Mutual Investment Funds* (AMLF) were implemented. In order to maintain liquidity in September 2008, the Fed entered into swap agreements with central banks in a number of countries, in particular with the European Central Bank (ECB). These agreements provided for the provision of dollar liquidity abroad through the expansion of swap transactions limits.

Support for the liquidity of financial institutions and enterprises in the form of loans was offered in other countries as well. In Hungary, for example, repo transactions with the ECB were carried out to maintain liquidity, providing swap loans in euros for one day to reduce pressure on the interbank lending market (totaling $6.5 billion). The Central Bank of Hungary has allocated commercial banks a loan of 5 billion euros for six months.

In Germany, the liquidity of the money market was provided, in particular, through the *Financial Market Stabilization Fund*, as well as in the form of direct financial support to a number of banks, in particular, *Hypo Real Estate, Commerzbank, BayernLB* and *Nordbank*.

Denmark received from the ECB access to a credit line for 12 billion dollars. The country's monetary authorities have opened a credit line to commercial banks for 20 billion dollars.

In Italy, in accordance with the decree-law "Urgent measures to guarantee the stability of the credit system" of October 9, 2008, measures were introduced to maintain liquidity, in particular, the rules for obtaining loans from the central bank were simplified.

In Kazakhstan, the liquidity of financial institutions was supported by placing the funds of the *National Welfare Fund Samruk-Kazyna* in the amount of $2 billion on deposits in two largest commercial banks - *Kazkommertsbank* and *Halyk Bank*.

In Norway, banks were able to obtain loans of up to 120 million euros from the central bank at a fixed rate for up to two years.

In France, loans to 13 banks valued at 23 billion euros at a rate of 4% were channeled through the state holding company to recapitalize banks.

In Sweden, a plan was developed by the government for the financial sector of the country in the amount of 152.2 billion euros (local banks will have the opportunity to borrow from the Central Bank up to 164 million euros). Monetary authorities assisted in maintaining the liquidity of the banking sector in the amount of $6 billion. At the same time, the government received the right to purchase additional shares of banks on existing market terms. The

Swedish Stabilization Fund was created, through which the banking sector was provided with a total of 152 billion euros.

Direct lending to banks and enterprises is certainly a quick and powerful tool in a crisis, but it leads to an increase in the money supply, potentially contributing to an increase in inflation and / or the emergence of bubbles in financial markets. Therefore, from the perspective of maintaining macroeconomic stability, the provision of guarantees by the monetary authorities or their financial agents for loans or debentures (for example, issued or issued bonds) of banks, mortgage agencies and enterprises is the preferred means of maintaining liquidity.

In the United States, in particular, in October 2008, a *Temporary Liquidity Guarantee Program* (TLGP) was adopted, providing for offering state guarantees for newly issued liabilities of banks and insurance companies through the *Federal Deposit Insurance Corporation*, as well as for unlimited insurance of interest-free bank deposits. The program was extended twice and ended on December 31, 2010. During the program period, the maximum amount of guaranteed debt reached $345.8 billion. In general, the funds received by FDIC within the program framework exceeded the payments[99]. Also, state insurance of assets of money market funds was introduced and insurance compensation for deposits increased from 100 to 250 thousand dollars.

State guarantees have become an active anti-crisis tool in many countries. So in Australia, state guarantees were introduced for all bank debt obligations and deposits of private investors. A large-scale program of state guarantees (for 75 billion euros) for new debt obligations and interbank loans was adopted in Austria. In the UK, government guarantees were provided on interbank loans ($250 billion) and loans to small and medium-sized enterprises ($10 billion). In Hungary, guarantees were extended to refinance debt obligations ($1.5 billion), business loans ($3.4 billion) and the value of insured deposits was increased from 6 to 13 million forints.

In Germany, the federal government guarantees on interbank loans reached 400 billion euros. Greece also introduced guarantees for all deposits and

---

[99] Federal Deposit Insurance Corporation. Regulation & Examination. Temporary Liquidity Guarantee Program, www.fdic.gov

interbank loans. The Danish Monetary Authority provided guarantees for interbank loans, new and existing debt obligations. Large-scale programs of state guarantees were adopted in Ireland, in particular, the value of the program of guarantees for interbank loans and new debt reached 400 billion euros, and the volume of guarantees for deposits - 100 billion euros.

In Italy, in October 2008, state guarantees were provided for new debts of commercial banks with a maturity (payment) of less than 5 years, as well as under contracts concluded by Italian market participants with foreign banks. The value of the insured deposits was raised to 103.3 thousand euros.

The monetary authorities of Canada have allocated 179 billion dollars for the purpose of guaranteeing new debt obligations. In Norway, the guaranteed level of deposit refund reached 227 thousand euros. In Portugal, the state guarantees for all banking operations were introduced, and the amount of insured deposits was increased from 25 to 100 thousand euros. In Finland, the government allocated 50 billion euros for guarantees on new debt obligations. In France, 320 billion euros were allocated to guarantee interbank loans, a special institution was established for this purpose - a refinancing company, owned by banks (66% of capital) and the state (34%). In Sweden, the amount of state guarantees for new debt obligations reached 191 billion euros. In South Korea, the government guaranteed external debt obligations of banks issued from October 20, 2008 to June 2009 with a maturity of up to 3 years (the number of guarantees was $ 100 billion).

Another fairly common form of maintaining liquidity during the crisis was the redemption of distressed assets. Unlike the provision of loans (which properly must be repaid in due time, and with interest), asset redemption is essentially the financing and subsidization of recipients of such assistance (usually financial institutions). The state in the person of authorized institutions in this case actually provides financial assistance to credit institutions, since illiquid "toxic" assets (which resulted from excessive speculation and growing bubbles, poor risk management, moral abuse) are bought or replaced by highly liquid assets, for example, government bonds. The state, while acquiring such "bad" assets, runs the risk of never selling them or selling with a very high discount in an indefinite time. Thus, in this case, losses of financial institutions from the inefficient allocation of funds are compensated at the expense of the budget or the central bank.

During the last crisis, the monetary authorities of many countries applied this form of maintaining liquidity. So in the United States in September 2008, the program for the purchase of asset-backed commercial securities of the money market funds (AMLF), aimed at increasing the liquidity of money market mutual funds, was launched by the Federal Reserve System to provide funds to banks for redemption from mutual funds (according to the amortization cost). Moreover, in accordance with the *Emergency Economic Stability Act* (EESA) in October 2008, the *Assistance Program for Problem Assets* (TARP) for $700 billion was adopted, and the Program for the purchase of short-term commercial papers from companies with a high rating (*Commercial Paper Funding Program*, CPFF) was launched in October 2008. At the same time, the FRS began to buy short-term market instruments with a maturity period of less than 90 days in order to support the participants of the money market in accordance with the *Money Market Investor Funding Facility* (MMIFF).

In November 2008, *Fannie Mae, Freddie Mac* and federal banks repurchased $100 billion in housing loans, as well as mortgage-backed securities of these agencies for an additional $500 billion. In March 2009, in accordance with the *Treasury Purchase Program*, the Fed redeemed the US Treasury's long-term commitments of $300 billion.

In other countries, the state also bought out distressed assets. For example, in Australia, securities backed with housing mortgage loans totaling $6 billion were redeemed. In the UK, in March 2009, a program was adopted for the purchase of pools of mortgage loans and government bonds, as well as other assets worth 75 billion pounds sterling, and in May 2009 it was increased to 125 billion pounds. Subsequent decisions on the repurchase of distressed assets were made at monthly meetings of the Bank of England's Monetary Policy Committee.

In Germany, the government purchased distressed assets of 80 billion euros through the *Financial Stabilization Fund*. A large-scale asset repurchase program (up to 400 billion euros) was adopted in Ireland. In Switzerland, the central bank bought illiquid assets worth $46 billion from the bank *BBS*.

Pursuant to the law of October 13, 2008, in Italy, a temporary exchange of government securities for bank portfolio assets or counter obligations of Italian banks was carried out. At the end of November 2008, a law was passed that authorized the Ministry of Economy and Finance to purchase before the end of 2009, financial instruments issued by Italian banks or bank holdings. The Bank of Italy will assess the state of the bank's capital and the characteristics of financial instruments. This measure is addressed to sustainable banks and is aimed at maintaining their ability to meet the demand for loans.

In Canada, the government purchased insured mortgages of local banks and mortgage-backed securities worth C$75 billion. In South Korea, the state fund *Korea Asset Management Corporation* redeemed depreciated construction loans from savings banks amounting to $900 billion. The Bank of Japan supported the financial sector with the unlimited purchase of shares, bills of exchange and corporate bonds from bank portfolios, and also accepted these securities as collateral for its loans for a period of three months at a preferential rate of 0.1%.

In general, the practice of buying distressed assets, despite some positive effect on mitigating the effects of the crisis, caused considerable criticism both from specialists and in public circles, since "the Federal Reserve received additional powers, including the right to exchange safe government bonds for toxic assets and even a more radical right to buy such assets and keep them on their balance sheet. Such measures, although effective, undermine the order established under the law"[100].

Another direction of maintaining liquidity and stimulating economic growth was an unprecedented decline in interest rates on loans from central banks. However, having lowered them to practically zero level, central banks failed to achieve sustainable economic growth, as the economies of developed countries fell into the "liquidity trap". The massive supply of practically free money from central banks did not lead to an increase in the lending activity of commercial banks, as credit risks remained at a high level. Lending to banks was preferred to operations in financial markets or the storage of cash on deposits at a central bank.

In addition to individual measures to maintain liquidity, the so-called Quantitative Easing (QE) programs were launched in the leading countries

---

[100] Roubini N., "Crisis Economics: A Crash Course in the Future of Finance", M., EKSMO, 2011 (in Russian language); p.159.

of the world, primarily in the US, UK, Japan and the EU. If initially anti-crisis measures were largely carried out at the expense of budget funds, the quantitative easing was linked to the large-scale use of the funds of central banks (e.g. the Federal Reserve funds for the purchase of assets). The American program QE-1 with volume up to USD 1.7 trillion was carried out until March 2010 and represented the purchase of mortgage securities of state agencies *Fannie Mae* and *Freddie Mac* from commercial and investment banks. In 2010 signs of economic growth appeared, which, however, proved to be unstable. It became obvious that without a constant flow of funds into the financial sector, growth could quickly turn into a recession.

Under these conditions, the Fed launched the QE-2 program, which lasted until mid-2011 and represented the purchase of US Treasury bonds. Within the QE-2 framework, a total of $600 billion worth of assets was purchased, but, as in the case of QE-1, the effect was short-term.

In August 2012, the QE-3 program was launched, designed to support liquidity in the financial sector, economic growth and employment decline. Within the framework of this program, 85 billion dollars were sent monthly to purchase securities, while the duration of the program was not established.

The quantitative easing program has caused a lot of criticism and pessimistic forecasts. So, according to experts of the credit rating agency Egan Jones, "QE-3 will inflate prices for stocks and resources, but, in our opinion, it will damage the American economy and, as a result, credit quality. Issuance of additional currency and suppression of interest rates through purchases of mortgage bonds is of little help to increase real US GDP, but it reduces the value of the dollar (due to the growth of money supply) and, in turn, increases the price of resources (recall the recent rise in prices for energy, food, gold and other resources). The increase in the cost of resources will put pressure on the profitability of enterprises, as well as increase the costs of consumers, reducing their purchasing power. Therefore, in our opinion, QE-3 will have detrimental consequences for credit quality for the US "[101].

---

[101] Michael Aneiro. «Egan-Jones Welcomes QE3 By Cutting U. S. Credit Rating» - Barron's, September 14, 2012

An even sharper assessment of this program was given by the famous US congressman R. Paul: "We are weakening the dollar ... trying to eliminate debts due to inflation. The consequences of the Fed's actions are much more serious than the simple growth of the consumer price index. The point here is in erroneous investments, and that people are doing wrong things at the wrong time ... We lost control, and the only thing that remains for us is an uninterrupted creation of new money from the air, which did not work before, will not work this time either "[102].

Fed Chairman Bernanke said: "Although I think that we can make a big and meaningful contribution to the solution of this problem, I do not think that we will be able to do anything about the results of the QE-3 program, in particular, solve it completely. We do not have sufficiently strong tools that can solve the problem of unemployment"[103].

In general, the policy of quantitative easing had a significant impact on a number of macroeconomic indicators, in particular, on the growth of money supply in the US (Figure 3).

The measures used to maintain liquidity, both in the form of loans and guarantees, and in the form of the purchase of distressed assets, have, on the whole, restored the activity of the financial sector, which had allowed to avoid dramatic consequences similar to those of the Great Depression. However, economists, politicians and society as a whole had a lot of questions about the consequences of the anti-crisis measures applied, because "many of them could be considered as contributing to increasing moral abuse. The Fed, in its desire to support the financial system, was saving financial institutions both that were simply experiencing liquidity problems and that were insolvent. This precedent may be difficult to get rid of, and in the long run it can lead to the collapse of market discipline which, in turn, can create preconditions for huge speculative "bubbles" and even more destructive crises"[104].

---

[102] Ron Paul: "Country Should PanicOver Fed's Decision" - Inforwars.com, Sept 14, 2012.

[103] Michael Snyder. «10 Shocking Quotes About What QE3 Is Going To Do To America». - Activist Post, September 15, 2012.

[104] Roubini N., "Crisis Economics: A Crash Course in the Future of Finance", M., EKSMO, 2011 (in Russian language); p.158.

Figure 3

Dynamics of money supply aggregates M1 and M2 in the USA, billion Dollars

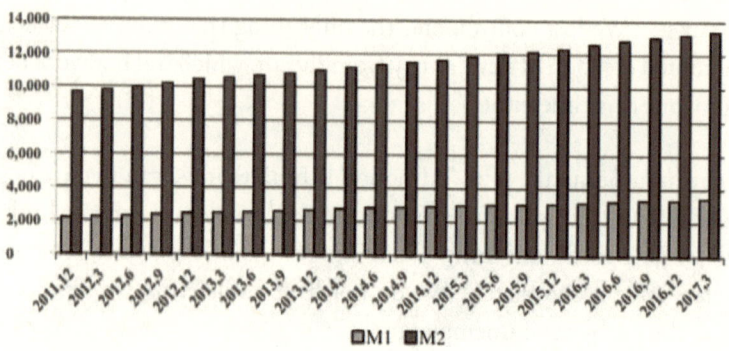

☐M1 ■M2

Source: Board of Governors of the Federal Reserve System. Economic Research and Data. Money Stock Measures, <u>www.federalreserve.gov</u>

In October 2014, the Federal Reserve decided to close the quantitative easing program and maintain the refinancing rate at 0% - 0.25% for a long time. At the same time, given the uncertainty of economic development, the Fed obviously envisaged opportunities for a flexible response to the changing macroeconomic situation in its decision in October 2014. In particular, the Fed statement said: "If the incoming data on the economy will indicate a faster advance towards the target values for employment and inflation, than the committee believes at the moment, in this case, the increase in interest rates is likely to occur earlier than expected. Conversely, if the rate of improvement in performance is slower, then interest rate increases are more likely to happen later than currently expected."

2.2. Restructuring of credit and financial institutions: does the end justify the means?

An important direction of the anti-recessionary measures was the restructuring of financial institutions, designed to restore and, if necessary, improve or even bring to a new qualitative level their liquidity, capital, asset quality, profitability, volume and quality of services provided. Restructuring, as a complex of measures to restore and improve the structure and activities of financial institutions, has long been used as an anti-crisis tool by owners, creditors and supervisors. However, many of the largest financial institutions of developed and developing countries, including banks, insurance companies, brokerage and dealer organizations, were subjected to restructuring to some extent.

Restructuring tools used were extremely diverse: the elimination and revocation of licenses were applied as a last resort, nationalization was effected and legal status was changed in some cases, but more often it was possible to see the provision of loans and financial assistance by the state, as well as purchase of distressed assets, participation of state institutions in the capital of banks, exchange of credit institution shares for government securities. Bank mergers, search of strategic investors, various forms of reorganization of financial institutions were also applied.

In the US, where the mortgage market became one of the epicenters of the crisis, the monetary authorities restructured the largest players in this market - mortgage companies *Fannie Mae* (Federal National Mortgage Association, founded as a state company in 1938 to support the secondary market of mortgage securities) and *Freddie Mac* (Federal Home Loan Mortgage Corporation, a private mortgage agency established in 1968 to demonopolize the secondary mortgage market). By the time of the *Fannie Mae* and *Freddie Mac* crisis, half of the US mortgage market was estimated at 12 trillion dollars. The mortgage portfolio of *Freddie Mac* as of March 31, 2008 constituted $709.8 billion, while the volume of guaranteed securities USD 1.44 trillion. By the end of March 2008, *Fanny May's* and *Freddie Mac's* total debt amounted to about 5.3 trillion dollars, which was then comparable to the size of the US public debt. In addition, the two companies supported their colossal operations with a rather limited equity capital of just 81 billion dollars.

In principle, these private companies had a special status, their reliability was always valued highly enough, since "investors proceeded from the implicit assumption that if these state-supported companies are in a dangerous situation, then, as quasi-state agencies established by the US government, they will be saved from bankruptcy "[105].

In times of crisis, *Fannie Mae* and *Freddie Mac* began to experience problems with liquidity, and the value of their shares began to decline rapidly. In 2008, the market capitalization of Fannie Mae declined from $40 billion to $7.6 billion, while of Freddie Mac - from $22 billion to $3.3 billion.

The rescue of these companies was one of the priorities for the US government, as, according to US Treasury Secretary Paulson, "Fannie Mae and Freddie Mac are so large and intertwined with the entire financial system of the country that their collapse will lead to tremendous upheavals in the national and international markets".

On September 7, 2008, it was decided to nationalize these mortgage companies. It should be noted that the nationalization of such large private companies is quite a revolutionary step for developed countries, who reluctantly applied extreme measures during the rule of the liberal doctrine. However, after the nationalization of *Fannie Mae* and *Freddie Mac*, this tool of anti-crisis management became quite widespread in many countries. US Treasury Secretary Paulson noted that "the step taken is" the best way to protect our markets and taxpayers from systemic risks in the current financial environment. " Ben Bernanke, the Federal Reserve Chairman said that he fully supported the government's decision and noted that "these forced measures will help to strengthen the US housing market and stabilize our financial markets."

The adopted program of restructuring *Fannie Mae* and *Freddie Mac* (one of the elements of which was the initial nationalization), according to the monetary authorities of the United States, was to operate for an indefinite period of time. After the recovery of the mortgage market, the decision on these companies was to be made by the US Congress.

As the owner of the companies the state carried out a whole complex of measures to restore the mortgage market and the activities of *Fannie Mae*

[105] Friedman J., Kraus V., "Man-made financial crisis. Systemic risks and failure ofregulation" (translated from English), M., Publishing House., «YRISEN» и «Mysl», 2012 (in Russian language);, p., 27.

and *Freddie Mac*. Management of these mortgage companies was entrusted to the *Federal Housing Finance Agency* (FHFA). During the restructuring of these companies, variety of instruments were used. Thus, the management of companies was changed, and the US government assumed more than $5 trillion of potential debt guaranteed by *Fannie Mae* and *Freddie Mac*. Significant funds ($148 billion) were spent on the purchase of preferred shares of companies.

In February 2009, the US Treasury Department decided to double the financial assistance to these companies and allocated $200 billion for each. However, only *Freddie Mac's* losses in 2009 reached $50.1 billion. In 2010, against the backdrop of the growing losses of *Fannie Mae* and *Freddie Mac*, the US Treasury announced that their fundamental restructuring was postponed until the final stabilization of the housing market and that in the future, these companies would not be supported by the government.

In June 2010, the Federal Housing Finance Agency announced the suspension of trading in the shares of these companies on the New York Stock Exchange, since the price of the stock fell unprecedentedly, for example, the price of *Fannie Mae* shares from $70 to 90 cents. In 2010, the companies also continued to suffer losses. At the same time, it should be noted that such losses were associated with loans and guarantees granted prior to 2007. During the restructuring, *Fannie Mae* and *Freddie Mac* succeeded in significantly changing the practice of granting loans, and starting from 2009, the loans issued corresponded to the established standards and as a whole were not loss-bearing.

In the course of restructuring, the *Federal Housing Finance Agency* conducted stress tests on *Fannie Mae* and *Freddie Mac*, depending on the changes in property prices and proposed three possible scenarios for the US housing market before the end of 2013: the rapid recovery of the market, freezing current prices and deep repeated recession. Under the first scenario, additionally $73 billion were required to finance the activities of mortgage agencies, while in accordance with the second scenario, $90 billion, and based on the third scenario, $215 billion.

According to analysts of the *Federal Housing Finance Agency* and the *Moody's* rating agency, the second scenario (slow market recovery) was most likely.

In all three scenarios, the cost of restructuring for *Fannie Mae* significantly would exceed the cost of supporting *Freddie Mac*, which was due to different levels of debt burden. Overall, the cost of restructuring for *Fannie Mae* was estimated at 102-192 billion dollars, and for *Freddie Mac*, 40-67 billion dollars.

One of the most common restructuring tools is attracting private investors, but at that time it was difficult to attract investment from mortgage agencies because of minimal dividends and huge debt burden. Moreover, some analysts, for example, Sean Egan, the president of *Egan Jones Ratings Agency*, forecasted new losses of agencies for guaranteed mortgage loans, which might require additional financial assistance of up to $1 trillion.

In the process of restructuring, mortgage agencies began to require banks to buy back previously refinanced loans that did not meet the established disbursement criteria. Thus, in 2007-2010 such claims amounted to more than $30 billion on 167,000 problem loans. Banks fulfilled their obligations to buy out troubled loans worth $21 billion.

During the restructuring of mortgage agencies, the facts of implementing unprofitable operations with banks were identified, which were based on incomplete or incorrect information provided by the latter. Under these transactions, banks were to pay significant fines. In particular, in 2013, the Department of Justice brought charges against the largest US banks (the charges were related to misleading consumers about the quality of the proposed assets, in particular, mortgage securities). Apparently, most of the charges could be settled in a pre-trial order, though the amount of payments could have been very large. For example, *JPMorgan Chase & Co.* concluded an agreement with the authorities according to which it would pay the US government 13 billion dollars for the fact that one of the units of the bank was providing buyers (including *Fannie Mae* and *Freddie Mac*) incorrect data on the quality of loans in these financial instruments. Similar charges were brought against *Bank of America*. At the same time, mortgage agencies suffered huge losses as a result of such actions.

Currently, the US is considering various options for further restructuring of mortgage agencies, the main owner of which continues to be the state. One of the proposals is liquidation with the transfer of their functions to private mortgage companies. The current US President at the time, President Obama, in his speech on the housing market in Arizona's capital of Phoenix noted: "so the bottom line is we don't think there's anything wrong with pursuing a profit, but we want to make clear the days of making bad bets on the backs of taxpayer money and then getting bailed out afterwards — we're not going back to that"[106]. Under the new scheme for refinancing mortgage loans, the government would act as the guarantor of last resort for mortgage loans, only when the possibilities of private mortgage agencies were exhausted.

In general, the US monetary authorities did not approve the proposal of several hedge funds and the *Fairholme Capital Management* to sell part of the shares of *Freddie Mac* and *Fannie Mae* (approximately $52 billion), based on the consideration that two large companies could be formed that would be too big to fail.

Thus, despite significant financial investments and a long period of restructuring, the fate of the largest mortgage companies in the US remained uncertain. Their operations were not fully recovered and they were facing the possibility of liquidation; at the same time, an alternative scheme for refinancing in the mortgage market, based on private investment companies, was not created.

Another example of a large-scale restructuring was the recovery of one of the largest US insurance companies - *American International Group* (AIG), which before the crisis was engaged in operations with credit-default swaps by mortgage transactions (the total value of such AIG obligations was estimated at $500 billion). As a result, "AIG had no way to cover damages for these tranches, and therefore its bankruptcy would ruin companies whose assets it insured. It was only emergency intervention by the American government that managed to avoid the catastrophe"[107].

The initial form of restructuring of this company in 2008 was its nationalization (like in case of mortgage agencies). The US government made a decision to allocate financial assistance in the amount of $182.5 billion for AIG, and 79.9% of the company's shares became state property.

---

[106] "Give the mortgage to the private person",07.08.2013., www.gazeta.ru

[107] Roubini N., "Crisis Economics: A Crash Course in the Future of Finance", M., EKSMO, 2011 (in Russian language); p.230.

In 2009, AIG's business was divided between various organizational structures. So the units involved in all types of insurance, with the exception of life insurance, were separated from AIG into a separate holding company *AIU Holdings*. Subsequently, this organizational structure was transformed into a special legal entity under the *Chartis* brand. Under its jurisdiction came the insurance of legal entities in the United States, Canada, personal insurance units outside the United States and Canada, services for private VIP customers. AIG invested funds in exchange for receiving shareholdings in the established structure. *Chartis* acquired the majority stake in the Japanese insurance company *Fuki Fire and Marine Insurance Company, Ltd.* This transaction allowed *Chartis* to become the fourth insurance company in Japan.

In 2008-2012, the group was engaged in the processes of improving finances, improving management, aligning the ratio of the share of private and corporate clients in the volume of collected premiums. Within four years after the crisis, AIG managed to fully pay off the debt to the US government. As of January 2013, the total profit of the Federal Reserve System and the US Treasury Department for investments in the company amounted to about $22.7 billion. In the same year, the Board of Directors decided to return the AIG brand to the personal and property insurance market, which meant the successful completion of the restructuring process.

Other major financial institutions were also restructured in various forms in the United States. Thus, in exchange for guarantees on mortgage securities, the US government received a package of preferred shares of *Citigroup* (7.8% of the capital). There were also further discussions on increasing the state share to 25% and even to 40%[108].

In January 2009, the US monetary authorities provided guarantees for USD 118 billion in exchange for preferred shares of *Bank of America* worth USD 4 billion. Later, the government acquired more shares of this bank for USD 20 billion and received warrants for further redemption[109].

---

[108] "Experts do not expect massive nationalization of banks in the US", RBC. "Finansy", 26 February 2009., www.rbc.ru

[109] Institute of State and Law of the Russian Academy of Sciences, Improving Legislation - a Way to Overcome the Global Financial Crisis, 2010.

In 2009 stress tests were performed for a number of American banks, measures for their restructuring and recapitalization were planned in accordance with the *Financial Stability Plan*. The *Capital Assistance Program* also embraced measures for the recapitalization of banks. N. Roubini, the researcher of the global crisis, provided a rather figurative description of the program for restructuring financial institutions in the US: "The Treasury decided to use part of USD 700 billion allocated under the TARP program to purchase of ownership interest in banks, thus provide "injections" of capital. The largest portions of injections went to such giants as *Bank of America, Citigroup, JPMorgan Chase, Goldman Sachs* and *AIG*, each of which received tens of billions of dollars. Hundreds of smaller banks also lined up for receiving government aid. As a result, the government - and through it the American taxpayers - had become a co-owner of a huge number of institutions of the financial system. In other words, the financial system was partly nationalized"[110].

However, recapitalization and financial support from the state were not the only forms applied for restructuring the banking sector. A prime example of the use of another tool - liquidation – is *Lehman Brothers*, the major American investment bank (assets as of August 1, 2008 – USD 600 billion). Generally, excessive investment in risky mortgage securities and the reluctance of the monetary authorities to provide the bank with large-scale support are named as the reasons for the collapse of this bank.

Back in 2007, rumors began to circulate that the bank embellished its reports, hiding losses from mortgage securities.

On June 9, 2008, *Lehman Brothers* officially announced plans to additionally issue shares worth USD 5 billion in order to attract new shareholders. However, on the eve of the placement of shares, *Standard & Poor's*, the international rating agency, lowered the ratings of the bank. A few days later, the bank published its reports, which shocked many investors. Investors began to hastily sell *Lehman Brothers'* shares, which led to the collapse of the share prices on the stock exchange. From January to June 2008, the bank's share prices fell by 64%. On August 25, 2008, *Lehman Brothers* put up its assets

---

[110] Roubini N., "Crisis Economics: A Crash Course in the Future of Finance", M., EKSMO, 2011 (in Russian language); p.199.

for sale (including securities, real estate and *Neuberger Berman*, the asset management company) with a total value of USD 40 billion.

On September 15, *Lehman Brothers* filed a petition with the bankruptcy court. Experiencing financial problems, the bank management launched negotiations with the US authorities with a proposal to nationalize the bank in order to save it from the collapse. However, *Lehman Brothers* were denied the financial aid by the monetary authorities. Many agencies and newspapers cited the words of Henry Paulson, the US Treasury Secretary: "To form discipline in the market and effectively contain risks, we must allow financial companies to go bankrupt. Our tools are now limited".

The US experience of overcoming the crisis is an excellent demonstration of the application of various instruments for restructuring financial institutions. Similar tools have been used in other countries as well.

The UK nationalized the banks of *Northern Rock* and *Bradford & Bingley*. *Royal Bank of Scotland* became state-controlled - the state share in the bank reached 70%. The British authorities gained control over 65% stake in *Lloyds Banking Group*. A special agency was created to manage assets that had been transferred to state ownership - the *Financial Investments of Great Britain*. One of the tasks of the agency was to make sure that the banks that had passed into the state ownership were making profit and sell the bank's shares to the private sector again after the situation on the securities market would improve.

Greece implemented a bank recapitalization program worth EUR 5 billion, Denmark – USD 13.4 billion, Luxembourg – EUR 2.9 billion euros, Finland – EUR 4 billion. Iceland nationalized the major banks in the country.

The Irish government decided to invest USD 7.7 billion in three major banks of the country: EUR 2 billion in *Bank of Ireland* and *Allied Irish Banks* each through a mechanism of preferred shares that would give the government 25% of the vote. Moreover, through investing EUR 1.5 billion in *Anglo Irish Bank* the state became the owner of a 75% stake in the bank.

Italy set up a program to recapitalize banks in accordance with the law "Urgent measures to guarantee the stability of the credit system". As part of this program, the Ministry of Economy and Finances was granted the authority to approve or guarantee an increase in a bank capital provided that the Bank of Italy considered it inadequate. In the interest of taxpayers, banks would have to adopt a stabilization and reinforcement plan and continue the dividend payment policy (required the approval of the Bank of Italy).

Kazakhstan nationalized *BTA Bank* through the purchase of 78.14% of the bank's shares by the *National Welfare Fund*. Moreover, the government allocated USD 1.75 billion for additional capitalization of the bank. The government reached agreement with *Kazkommertsbank* and *Halyk Bank* on the purchase of a 25% share in their capital to support the banks.

Norway set up a financial fund to increase banks' fixed assets (NOK 50 billion). All banks operating in Norway, including *Swedish Nordea Bank AB*, which is the major Scandinavian creditor, are eligible to get support from the financial fund.

Portugal carried out a EUR 4-billion program for the recapitalization of banks through the provision of preferred shares. Moreover, the country nationalized the banks that were on the verge of bankruptcy.

France set up a state holding company to recapitalize banks. Promptly, 13 credit institutions of the country were granted EUR 23 billion in loans at a rate of 4%. Moreover, several banks received financial assistance in the form of guarantees to restore confidence and liquidity. Thus, in October 2008, EUR 10.5 billion was allocated to six of the country's largest banks, including EUR 3 billion to *Credit Agricole*, EUR 2.55 billion to *BNP Paribas* and EUR 1.7 billion to *Societe Generale*.

Switzerland recapitalized *UBS* by a total of EUR 5 billion, while Sweden nationalized investment banks and allocated EUR 2 billion for the recapitalization of the banking sector.

In November 2008, Japan passed a law on the preventive injection of state funds into a bank's capital. In this regard, in March 2009, the *Financial Services Agency* (the mega-regulator of the financial sector) provided JPY 121 billion (about USD 1.27 billion) to three regional banks - *Sapporo Hokuyo Holdings*, *Minami-Nippon Bank* and *Fukuoka Bank*.

Generally, measures applied for restructuring financial institutions have played a significant role in overcoming the crisis. At the same time, massive financial assistance significantly increased public debt of many countries, had a negative impact on the volume and structure of the money supply, in some cases led to moral abuse and helped preserve in the financial sector the behavioral stereotypes generating speculative bubbles and causing inevitable crises.

2.3. Measures of Economic and Social Support

Along with the financial sector, the real sector and the social sphere were also supported during the crisis. The toolkit of anti-crisis measures was quite diverse. It included direct financial support from the budget in the form of subsidies, subventions, subsidies, equity participation and asset purchases. Credit support measures, tax credits, preferential taxation were also applied. To a certain extent, measures of customs support for the national economy were also applied, however, taking into account the negative experience of the Great Depression, customs barriers did not become one of the main tools for backing national markets. Furthermore, in an effort to overcome the crisis, various institutions were actively set up to support, for example, capitalization, investment and structural reforms.

Before the crisis, the construction was the most dynamically developing sector that experienced dramatic changes in many countries. Not surprisingly, the housing sector support measures had become one of the key areas of anti-crisis policy.

The state of the housing sector is very important not only for the US economy but also for the development of the global economy. Therefore, significant efforts were made in the United States to restore it. On July 30, 2008, the *Housing and Economic Recovery Act* was enacted. It provided new opportunities for refinancing mortgage debts and called for more stringent regulation of quasi-public companies and government agencies operating in the mortgage market. In October 2008, the *Hope for Homeowners* program was adopted, which provided assistance to borrowers in refinancing mortgage loans. In accordance with the *Financial Stabilization Plan* (February 2009), *Public-Private Investment Fund* (PPIF) of around USD 1 trillion was set up to support the real estate market.

The *American Recovery and Reinvestment Act* (ARRA) adopted in 2009 also aimed to overcome the crisis in general, including in the sphere of real estate. The *Homeowner Affordability and Stability Plan* (HASP) adopted in February 2009, called for mortgage refinancing provided that the collateral value fell below 20% of the loan, USD 75 billion support to borrowers in a difficult financial condition (loan modification) and additional capital injections of USD 200 billion in *Fannie Mae* and *Freddie Mac*.

In May 2009, the *Helping Families Save Their Homes Act* was passed. The act aimed to improve lending and better protect consumer rights in the housing market.

The housing market and the construction industry was supported in other countries as well. For example, Australia adopted an economic stimulus package of USD 26 billion, which provided for the construction of houses, new schools, infrastructure projects and the introduction of new technologies. In accordance with this program, it was proposed to save about 90 thousand jobs and increase the growth rate of the economy from 0.5 to 1%.

Argentina implemented a USD 21.5 billion employment program to create new jobs in the construction industry of the country.

In 2009, the UK announced a plan to build 20 thousand new affordable houses in the next two years (a GBP 1.5 billion worth program). At the same time, the borrowers were granted a three-month grace period for the payment of the principal amount of mortgage loans; the grace period for mortgage payments was increased to six months; interest was deferred to up to two years for mortgage loans of unemployed people or those whose income had sharply decreased; interest payment for other citizens was deferred for up to six months.

Kazakhstan allocated USD 5 billion to increase the affordability of houses. In order to stimulate the development of the housing market the marginal rates on bank mortgage loans were set at 12.5%, while the rate for a special mortgage program was set at 10.5%. Moreover, the mortgage lending rate as part of the anti-crisis program of Kazakhstan was defined at 9% for socially vulnerable groups of the population, while for other borrowers - up to 11%, the credit period increased to 20 years. USD 1 billion was allocated from the *National Fund* for the implementation of innovative, industrial and infrastructure projects. More than USD 3 billion was directed for a program designed to stimulate the real estate and mortgage market.

To support the dynamics of the housing market a set of measures were applied in China, including measures for the state support of the construction business and the reduction of various types of payments while making property transactions. A system of actions was developed to encourage regional authorities to allocate cheaper and longer-term loans for the purchase of houses by the middle class.

In Slovakia, the state provided financial support for those banks that decided to reduce interest rates on mortgage loans issued to financially distressed borrowers.

Along with supporting the driving force of the modern economy - the construction industry - many countries adopted programs to back the economy as a whole, develop infrastructure, stimulate consumer demand and protect the population socially.

For example, the US implemented a large-scale assistance program for the automotive industry, in particular, it restructured *General Motors*, which declared bankruptcy in 2009. Under the bankruptcy conditions, the US government provided around USD 30 billion in financial support for the company and received 60% of the company's shares. The Government of Canada, another large co-owner of the company (a 12% stake), provided financial support in the amount of USD 9.5 billion. 17.5% of shares appeared in hands of the *International Union, United Automobile, Aerospace and Agricultural Implement Workers of America*. Remaining 10.5% of shares were divided among the largest creditors of the concern. On July 10, 2009, a new independent company, *General Motors Company*, was founded. The old GM (General Motors Corporation) was renamed into *Motors Liquidation Company*. At the end of 2010, GM held an initial public offering of shares, which became one of the largest in history. During the placement, the US and Canadian governments, which became the main shareholders during bankruptcy in 2009, sold USD 23.1 billion worth of shares. At the end of 2010, GM held a public offering of shares, which became one of the largest in history. Moreover, in March 2009, the *New Path to Viability for GM &*

Chrysler, the Auto Supplier Support Plan was approved, which called for the provision of USD 5 billion to improve lending to suppliers of the automotive industry.

In 2009, the US Department of the Treasury announced the terms of the *Targeted Investment Program*, according to which, it makes decisions individually whether to provide financial assistance to companies, the bankruptcy of which may significantly damage the financial system.

In accordance with the *Recovery Act*, in 2009 the US implemented Obama's USD 790 billion economic stimulus program.

The UK government provided guarantees of GBP 10 billion for loans issued to SME. A program was implemented to encourage the replacement of old cars with new ones (allocation of GBP 2,000 to the owners of the cars with a service life of more than 10 years for the purchase of new vehicles).

In 2008-2009, GBP 3 billion was allocated for the maintenance of the employment level and creation of new workplaces as well as training and development of personnel. Special attention was paid to the employment of young people in the most promising sectors of the youth economy, including graduates of secondary schools and universities.

The amount of unemployment benefits was increased in the social sphere, especially for those who had been unemployed for a long time (more than a year), child allowances were also increased, a special savings plans were introduced for the poor, a maximum state pension rose, employer contributions under the national insurance program also went up by 0.5 percentage points on April 2011.

Moreover, the UK made important institutional changes aimed at improving the efficiency of the management of economy. In particular, the *UK Department of Trade and Industry* was transformed into the *Department for Business, Enterprise and Regulatory Reform*. This body was charged with the task of reducing the burden of administrative regulation on business and improving its quality. In October 2008, at the Cabinet the *National Economic Council* was set up. The council led by the Prime Minister has major business representatives as well among its members. The operational management of the economy was the task assigned to the council. In June 2009, the *UK Infrastructure Committee* was set up to improve the efficiency of infrastructure projects, primarily in the energy and transport sectors. In the framework of anti-crisis measures, the *Finance and Investment Committee* was set up, which is responsible, inter alia, for investments in the banking sector.

Germany approved a comprehensive program to support the real sector of the economy and the social sphere (Table 9).

Table 9

Anti-crisis measures to support the real sector of the economy and social sphere in Germany

	Amount of funding bln. EUR	
	2009	2010
Financing of entrepreneurial programs to maintain the employment rate	2,6	5,7
Liberalization of the temporary work sector, retraining	0,2	0,5
Investment in the development of transport infrastructure	1,0	1,0
Additional expenses on the structural regional policy, increase in the KfW capital	0,3	0,4
Reduction of income tax, increase in children's allowances	4,9	5,6
Reduction of rates of charges for medical insurance	3,0	6,0
Additional federal investments, including construction of schools and kindergartens	3,0	12,0
Federal support for research and innovation	0,7	0,7
Increase in child allowances for the unemployed with children aged 6-13 years	0,2	0,3
Subsidies for the creation of temporary jobs, retraining of staff, creation of 5 thousand new jobs in employment agencies	2,6	2,7
Other tax related incentives	5,9	2,4
Fighting unemployment	0,9	0,1

Changes in the payment of student benefits, housing subsidies, etc.	4,5	3,6
Amendments to the laws on medical and compulsory insurance	4,5	4,7

The anti-crisis program worth 200 billion rupees adopted in India (USD 4 billion) included additional budget expenses, stimulation of bank financing and reduction of excise duties. Moreover, a government plan to stimulate the national economy was adopted. The plan called for issuance of government bonds worth a total of USD 6 billion to implement infrastructure projects and facilitate foreign investment in the Indian economy.

In February 2009, Italy adopted an anti-crisis decree, according to which, additional EUR 1.1 billion, EUR 0.3 billion and EUR 0.4 billion obtained from budget cuts were directed to fight crisis in 2009, 2010 and 2011 consequently. These funds were used to stimulate the consumption of durable goods and to reduce the tax burden on enterprises. The law also allowed enterprises of the same industrial district to choose a formula of the collective tax regime. In this case, for at least three years, taxes would be calculated on the basis of an agreement with the local authorities and shared between participating enterprises. The law also provided for tax cuts in 2009 for enterprises involved in the financial group.

Kazakhstan allocated more than USD 4 billion from the budget to support the agro-industrial complex. The support program called for the creation of new farms, elevators, vegetable storehouses, mini-plants and factories for the processing of agricultural products, construction of new housing, hospitals and schools. Monetary authorities also provided USD 1 billion in loans to SME (for no more than 14% per annum).

Canada approved an economic stimulus package of USD 32 billion. Allocations for infrastructure development doubled (up to USD 6 billion). A significant number of funds were spent on home construction, maintenance of the aerospace, mining and forestry industries, professional retraining of the unemployed and as part of the employment insurance program.

In particular, USD 5.6 billion was allocated for the development of infrastructure projects, USD 3.2 billion was transferred to a special fund to develop the infrastructure of the provinces, territories and municipalities of the country; USD 1.6 billion was spent on the repair and construction of colleges and universities; USD 813 million - for the implementation of environmentally friendly infrastructure projects.

China implemented a set of measures in the real sector of the economy and social sphere in an effort to overcome negative consequences of the global financial crisis and ensure sustainable economic growth.

In order to support the stock market, the *Committee for Control and Management of State Property* carried out measures to stimulate centrally administered state-owned enterprises to repurchase shares of listed companies. Listed companies, the controlling interest of which was owned by the state, were encouraged to buy back their shares. The companies were also encouraged to repurchase shares through state financial injections into these companies. Moreover, measures were taken to motivate Chinese firms with foreign capital to make IPOs on Chinese stock exchanges.

A considerable attention was paid to fostering domestic demand in China, which was especially important in the context of a possible decline in exports to developed countries.

China adopted a large-scale program for the development of infrastructure and energy-saving technologies. The country took measures to increase employment, including through providing state support for SME and individual enterprises. The government refused to pursue the policy of restraining the issuance of bank loans in the conditions of "investment overheating". At the same time, measures were taken to redistribute credit resources in favor of SME. In particular, control over large investments in infrastructure was tightened, while control over lending to SME was reduced.

Tax regulatory instruments were actively involved, in particular, tax incentives were introduced for exporters, while taxes on interests of citizens' deposits in banks were abolished.

Moreover, internal demand and stable economic growth were fostered through the accelerated construction of social housing, rural infrastructure facilities, important transportation facilities (railways, highways and airports), the intensive development of health care, culture and education and the expansion of the construction of environmentally friendly facilities.

The pace of industry restructuring, introducing scientific and technical innovations, restoring the areas affected by the destructing earthquake was accelerated. Income of the urban and rural population increased.

Norway adopted USD 3 billion package of anti-crisis measures. Of the amount USD 500 million went to provide tax benefits to business as well as USD 1.5 billion to infrastructure and regional development, the rest was directed to road construction and the development and introduction of energy saving technologies.

To support demand for new cars, the Polish government decided to return the value-added tax (22%) to buyers of new cars.

Taiwan implemented infrastructure projects worth USD 2 billion and reduced taxes by USD 4 billion.

The Finnish government adopted a package of measures worth more than EUR 400 million to revitalize the country's economy. In particular, a number of projects related to the construction and repair of roads were carried out ahead of schedule. Airports in Helsinki and Oulu were repaired. Moreover, the government invested in construction, education, innovation and the development of new products. According to the estimates of the government of Finland, as a result of measures taken to revive the economy, 25,000 new jobs were to be created.

France introduced a comprehensive program of anti-crisis measures. Along with the already mentioned measures taken to support the financial sector, the country adopted large-scale programs in the real sector. In particular, the country set up a EUR 20 billion strategic investment fund (state intervention fund) subordinated to the national fund (Caissedes Depotset Consignations), Parliament and the National Assembly. The fund was tasked to participate in the capital of strategically important enterprises and protect these enterprises from being taken over by foreign companies.

France addressed the problem of ultra-high bonuses at enterprises having financial problems. The bonuses and premiums of the senior management of enterprises, employees of which faced partial unemployment or dismissal because of the crisis, were cancelled.

Other significant institutional changes were made, in particular, a special agency was set up to assist enterprises in getting loans and monitoring the credit market environment.

The tax sphere was also subjected to the reforms, in particular, the so-called local-level professional tax on company's fixed assets, which to some extent restrained their investments, was abolished. At the same time, losses of local budgets were compensated by the central government.

To overcome the crisis, public investments were actively made in promising sectors of the economy, which in the future would become the basis for the country's development: education, research and development complex, environment protection, digital and clean technologies.

Moreover, in December 2008, an additional comprehensive EUR 26.5 billion anti-crisis plan was approved. It called for different activities in the economy and social sphere (Table 10).

Table 10

Activities as per comprehensive anti-crisis plan to stimulate the economy of France (adopted in December 2008)

	Volume of financing, bln. euro
Support in providing liquidity of companies in the form of granting tax holidays and tax credits, three-year deferral of payment of debts to the budget, a rapid return of corporate income tax in the event of its overpayment, as well as additional funds for investment to companies, including through a special tax credit for investment in fixed assets and R&D for the financial years 2005-2008	11,4

Provision of funding for state investment programs, provision of social and housing programs, as well as an annual advance payment to the VAT Compensation Fund, doubling the number of non-interest-bearing housing loans	11,1
Provision of funds for the largest state companies (Electricite de France, Gaz de France, etc.) to upgrade and develop railway, energy infrastructure and postal service	4,0

As for additional actions taken in the social sphere, we can note an increase in the payment for partial unemployment from 60 to 70% of the existing wage, the payment of a one-time bonus (EUR 500) to the unemployed registered in the employment service after April 1, 2009, the creation of a separate social investment fund of EUR 2.5-3.0 billion for 2009-2010 at the suggestion of the trade unions, the partial abolition of the income tax on low incomes (covered about 6 million French families), the payment of one-time allowance (EUR 150) to families - recipients of the so-called "school benefits" (covered about 3 million French families).

The Czech Republic adopted a EUR 2.44 billion plan to stimulate the national economy and fight economic recession. As part of the plan, investment was made in infrastructure and ecology, loans were issued to automakers and small enterprises and taxes were reduced.

Switzerland implemented energy saving projects worth USD 290 million as well as highway and railroad construction projects worth USD 840 million. Tax relief was granted to 650 companies for the implementation of job creation programs (USD 460-million program).

Swedish monetary authorities granted EUR 2.9 billion in financial aid to car companies *Volvo Group* and *Saab AB*.

The Japanese government introduced four packages of budget incentives to support domestic demand. As part of these programs, SME were provided guarantees for their bank loans, cash assistance was provided for the population, tax incentives were introduced and funds were allocated for infrastructure construction.

2.4. Tightening the regulation of rating agencies

The development of markets, primarily credit and financial, in the late 19th - early 20th century required the formation of a respective infrastructure, including institutions designed to solve the problem of information asymmetry for investors and creditors. It was at this time when credit bureaus, audit and consulting companies and rating agencies started appearing in the developed countries. The rating agencies first appeared in the United States, where the famous 'Big Three' companies (*Moody's, Standard & Poor's,* and *Fitch Ratings*) were founded.

Prior to the Great Depression, the activities of rating agencies were not regulated in any way, which was in line with the prevailing concept of non-interference of the state in the Laisezz-Faire Market. However, a number of economic crises, first of all the Great Depression, forced the state to radically reconsider its views in the sphere of economic regulation, which affected activities of rating agencies as well.

In the face of sharply increased risks in the economy, the role of institutions designed to solve the problem of information asymmetry increased. It was then, in the 1930s, that US rating agencies were included in the system of state regulation. In 1936, in accordance with a government act, the *US Securities and Exchange Commission* received the right not to allow the securities rated by national rating agencies below the investment level to take part in stock trading sessions.

Thus, the state recognized the ratings of national rating agencies as a part of the system of economic regulation. In the 1970s the *Securities and Exchange Commission* adopted Rule 15c3-1 (*"Universal Net Capital Rule"*), according to which the ratings of specially recognized rating agencies were used to calculate the net capital of brokers and dealers. In practice, this role was assigned to the so-called big three rating agencies (later the special role of these agencies was also secured by other governing documents of the United States' monetary authorities).

Subsequently, the special status of the 'Big Three' was virtually spread to all developed and most developing countries and was recorded in international regulatory documents. At the same time, no regulatory system was set up for the rating agencies in those years.

Affected by a number of factors, the situation began to change in the past years.

Firstly, the 'Big Three' failed to give an objective assessment of the financial condition of some large companies, which suddenly became bankrupt despite their high ratings (*Enron, WorldCom, Parmalat*). The lack of adequate ratings of issuers of securities and structured financial products caused even more destructive consequences on the eve of the global economic crisis of 2007-2009.

Secondly, the monopolization of the rating services market began to gradually deteriorate, national rating agencies started appearing both in the developed and developing countries, they competed with the 'Big Three'.

In the early 2000s in the wake of scandals related to the bankruptcy of high-rated companies, two models of regulation of the activities of rating agencies were introduced into the *European Union* (EU). The models were considered by the *European Parliament,* the *European Commission* and the *Committee of European Securities Regulators* (CESR).The first model provided for a fairly detailed regulation of the activities of rating agencies at the legislative level. The second focused on the self-regulation of the activities of rating agencies on the basis of internal codes of conduct, which were consistent with the CRA Code of the *International Organization of Securities Commissions* (IOSCO).

In general, following the discussions, there was a prevailing view that a soft option of the self-regulation based on the IOSCO CRA Code would be enough. A number of other countries also followed the path of self-regulation in those years. The rating agencies there joined the national professional codes of conduct of rating agencies.

However, the world economic crisis of 2007-2009 exposed many problems in the activities of rating agencies: insufficient disclosure of information, in particular, on the methods used for assigning a rating, difficulties associated with the comparability of ratings assigned by different rating agencies; conflict of interests between the main activity of an agency and support services, such as counseling; lack of responsibility for improper assigned ratings or for other shortcomings in activities; absence of a global regulation system.

Under these circumstances, on June 20, 2008, the *EU Parliament* decided to create a legislative framework for the regulation and supervision of credit rating agencies at the EU level. Consulting documents were prepared. The documents called for the adoption of a directive or the introduction of rules on the authorization of activities and external supervision of credit rating agencies operating in the territory of the EU.

In 2009, the EU adopted and enacted Regulation No. 1060/2009 on credit rating agencies establishing a unified procedure for their registration in the EU; for the purposes of regulation, ratings assigned by only registered agencies could be used. A rating agency registered in one of the EU countries had the right to assign ratings throughout the EU territory. If a credit rating was assigned in a third country, in order to be recognized in the EU, it had to be confirmed by the agency registered on its territory. At the same time, the confirming rating agency had to be ready to prove on an ongoing basis that the rating agency from the third country complied with the requirements established by the EU regulation on the independence and transparency of the rating agencies. In this case, the credit rating of companies (and securities) created (issued) outside the EU, could also be used for regulatory purposes. The use of a rating without confirmation is also possible if it does not have a systemic importance for the financial stability or integrity of the financial market of one or more EU countries.

In the regulations much attention is paid to the independence of a rating agency and the prevention of conflicts of interest. Thus, a rating agency is obliged to have in its structure a supervisory unit that ensures that the rating process is not related to the political or economic conjuncture and the conflict of interests has been accurately identified, controlled and publicly disclosed. Rating agencies cannot provide advisory services but they are allowed to engage in additional activities, for example, market analysis. When assigning ratings to structured financial products, analysts of rating agencies are not allowed to give recommendations on their schemes.

The document contains quite detailed requirements for the independence of analysts' estimates. They cannot assign ratings to the enterprises, financial instruments of which they own. They cannot receive money, gifts, and privileges from contractors of the rating agency.

The regulations also contain requirements for transparency in the activities of the rating agency, including the disclosure of methodologies, models and key assumptions. Techniques and ratings should be updated and revised. If the rating agency changes the methodology, it must inform which ratings have been affected by the changes. Agencies are required to publish all ratings, as well as decisions to refuse to assign a rating, including justification. Information on the existing or potential conflict of interests, the list of support services, methodologies and models, changes in resources, systems and procedures should be disclosed. Also, information on the top 20 clients of the rating agency should be disclosed annually, indicating the income received from them.

The document determines the procedure for registering rating agencies. It is carried out by a board of supervisors that is made up of representatives of the competent authorities of the EU country where the rating agency is located, in close coordination with CESR.

Competent authorities of the EU countries are responsible to oversee and monitor whether a rating agency complies with its obligations, have great powers to access to any information related to the activities of the rating agency. The regulations stipulate that sanctions against offenders will be developed later.

In the US, the Treasury Department proposed to increase the transparency of the activities of rating agencies and prevent conflicts of interest. Regulations were tightened both due to harsh criticism of rating agencies for providing inaccurate information on investment and credit risks on the eve of the crisis and the impact of stricter requirements introduced in this sphere in the EU. Thus, it was proposed to prohibit rating agencies from advising the companies that were subject to their rating assessment. The reports of the rating agencies will contain information on payments of issuers made for rating services for the last two years.

The SEC was entitled to verify the rules, procedures and methodologies for determining ratings. According to the statement of the US Treasury

Department, "the proposed measures will lead to the strengthening of the regulatory system of all rating firms".

The following trends and prospects can be pointed out in the sphere of regulation.

In recent years, most countries in the world have begun to intensively develop a system for regulating rating agencies. It has become clear, especially in the context of the global economic crisis, that a mild regulation model - taking commitments by rating agencies voluntarily, creating self-regulating associations, joining the codes of conduct - is not very effective.

In order to regulate the activities of rating agencies, most of the developed countries have embarked on the development of a legislative base. This trend is most fully manifested in the EU - the adoption of the Regulation No. 1060/2009 on credit rating agencies has radically changed the situation in this sphere.

At the national level, relevant initiatives are also being taken, both at the legislative level and in the form of departmental regulations. Due to the importance of the problem, in the short term we can expect further development of the legal framework for the regulation of rating agencies in both developed and developing countries.

Along with the legislation, the institutional framework of regulation is being formed through granting supervisory and regulatory powers to certain state institutions. The emergence of new regulatory agency is quite possible.

The methods for regulating the activities of rating agencies have not been developed fully yet. However, exclusively remote and discrete methods proposed in a number of countries may not correspond to the level of risks in this segment of the economy.

The emerging regulatory system is aimed at increasing the transparency of the activities of rating agencies, including such important information as data on owners, the management, revenues, procedures, applied techniques, assigned, revised and withdrawn ratings. It is important that this information be public, accessible not only to regulators, but also to a wide range of users.

It is important to regulate the optimal ratio of formalized procedures and methodological approaches in assigning ratings with subjective judgments of experts, which in any case should be motivated and documented.

Taking into account serious regulatory requirements for the independence of rating agencies and prevention of conflict of interests, it will be difficult to resolve the problems with providing unbiased and adequate ratings without creating an environment for the development of competition in the rating services market and improvement of the transparency and responsibility (financial and legal) of the agencies for the results of their activities. The formation of the regulatory system must be supplemented with measures to promote competition and even encourage the development of national rating agencies.

The situation objectively requires a rapid increase in the effectiveness of the regulation of rating agencies; recent regulatory initiatives in many countries point to significant steps that have been made in this direction.

CHAPTER 3
Institutional and Regulatory Reforms Implemented in Response to the Crisis

The global crisis which was the deepest one since the Great Depression, required not only implementation of urgent and medium-term anti-crisis measures (such as support for liquidity of financial institutions and industrial companies, their restructuring and recapitalization, stimulation of economic growth, social support for the population and fiscal consolidation), but also deep institutional reforms in vital social and economic spheres, especially in the field of regulation and supervision. In the past few years, both during the acute phase of the crisis and the post-crisis period, regulatory and supervisory reforms have begun to be actively pursued at the national, regional and international levels. At the national level, thorough regulatory reforms were carried out in both developed and developing countries, but especially in the world's leading economies, especially in the United States, where the adoption of the *Dodd-Frank Law* and other regulatory innovations lay the foundation for the formation of a new economic model of development. Serious regulatory and supervisory reforms were also implemented at the regional level, for example in the European Union and the euro area. At the international level, significant changes were initiated at the G8 and G20 forums, and institutions such as the *International Monetary Fund, World Bank, Financial Stability Board* and *Basel Committee on Banking Regulation and Supervision* became the vehicles of these changes. This chapter discusses the most important regulatory and supervisory reforms implemented at the international, regional and national levels.

3.1. Measures Taken by the Financial Stability Board for Creating Conditions for a New Economic Growth

During the global crisis it became apparent that efforts taken only at the national or even regional levels were not enough to overcome its consequences. A coordinated policy of developed and developing countries at the international level was required. In the most important areas of anti-crisis policies and measures such coordination was carried out primarily at the forums of leaders and ministers of G8 and G20 countries. It became necessary to create relevant institutions which would actually implement the decisions taken at these forums. As a result, in June 2009, the *Financial Stability Board* was established to implement regulatory and supervisory reforms at the international level. This institute was established on the basis of the *Financial Stability Forum*, which was founded in 1999 on the initiative of the finance ministers and central bank governors of the G7 countries.

At present, the *Financial Stability Board* (FSB) includes the G20 countries, as well as international organizations such as the *International Monetary Fund, World Bank, Organization for Economic Cooperation and Development, Bank for International Settlements, European Central Bank, European Commission, Basel Committee on Banking Supervision, Committee on the Global Financial System* (CGFS), *Committee on Payment and Settlement Systems* (CPSS), *International Association of Insurance Supervisors* (IAIS), *International Accounting Standards Board* (IASB) and *International Organization of Securities Commissions* (IOSCO).

The plenary sessions of the *Financial Stability Board* are attended by the directors or deputy directors of central banks, heads or first deputies of the main regulatory bodies, deputy finance ministers, and representatives of leading international organizations.

At the G20 summit in Cannes on November 4, 2011, the strengthening of the FSB's institutional framework was approved by changing its charter and transforming the FSB into a legal entity – an association under the Swiss law (with the possible subsequent transformation into a full-fledged international organization with appropriate immunity and privileges).

The *Financial Stability Board* was tasked to improve functioning of financial markets, identify the vulnerabilities of the financial system, strengthen financial stability in all regions of the world and reduce systemic risks through information exchange and international cooperation between national and international supervisory authorities.

The FSB authorities are the plenary meeting (meets at least 2 times a year, if necessary, conferences calls are organized), *Coordination Committee, Sectoral Standing Committees* (and their working groups) and the *FSB Secretariat*. The Chairman of the FSB is appointed by a plenary session for a term of three years, convenes and leads the work of plenary sessions and the *Coordination Committee*, and oversees the activities of the *Secretariat*. The plenary session takes decisions on changing the charter and membership in the FSB, approves the FSB programs, reports, principles, standards, recommendations and guidelines developed by the FSB. During the year, the results of the work of all FSB committees and working bodies are submitted for discussion at plenary sessions.

In order to ensure implementation of the FSB's tasks, the plenary session may establish standing committees and working groups and grant them the necessary authority. Currently, there are five standing committees: the *Steering Committee* (manages operation and implementation of the instructions between plenary sessions and prepares plenary sessions); The *Standing Committee for Assessment of Vulnerabilities in the Financial System* (identifies, assesses, and monitors vulnerabilities in the financial system and develops recommendations for addressing them; provides input for the Early Warning Exercise conducted in collaboration with the IMF), the *Standing Committee on Standards Implementation* (monitors implementation of the recommendations adopted by G20 members and FSB; implements thematic reviews and the promotes adherence to international standards), the *Standing Committee of Supervisory and Regulatory Cooperation* (develops recommendations on strengthening regulation and supervision in various areas of the financial system and measures conducive to the effective implementation of these recommendations), the *Standing Committee on Budget and Resources* (provides the plenary with assessments of the resource needs of the *Secretariat* taking into account the current mandate and reviews the budget).

In addition, the FSB has an *Analytical Group of the Standing Committee for Vulnerabilities Assessment*, six regional advisory groups (for countries in the Americas, Asia, CIS, Europe, the Middle East, North Africa, and sub-Saharan Africa) and a number of working groups.

The *Financial Stability Board* is entrusted with a number of fundamental tasks to reform the regulatory and supervisory system.

Thus, the *Financial Stability Board* continued the work on development of the *Compendium of Standards*, which was previously implemented by the *Financial Stability Forum*. The compendium includes internationally accepted economic and financial standards. At the moment – it consists of more than 150 documents, ranging from broad principles to detailed instructions. Nevertheless, the experts mark out 12 key standards, which are defined by the council members as the highest priority for implementation. In particular, three of the standards touch upon macroeconomic policies and data transparency: transparency of monetary, financial and fiscal policies and dissemination of data. In the field of institutional and market infrastructure there are six standards: bankruptcy procedure, corporate governance, financial reporting, audit, payments and settlements, and market integrity. Finally, financial regulation and supervision includes three standards: banking supervision, regulation of the securities market, and supervision of the insurance.

Under the auspices of the FSB, measures are also being implemented to motivate countries to comply with key regulatory standards in the financial sector. For this purpose, implementation of international standards by countries is regularly monitored. In its work the FSB uses the results of the *Financial Sector Assessment Program*, conducted by the *IMF* and *The World Bank*.

One of the most important and for many reasons difficult tasks of the FSB is regulation of the activities of systemically important financial institutions. This sphere of the FSB activities is based on the decisions of several G20 summits, in particular, the Seoul summit in 2010, which set the goal of reducing the risk of unfair behavior of all systemically important financial institutions, including banks.

Within the framework of the task, in November 2011 the *Financial Stability Board* developed the basic principles of an effective regime for resolution of insolvency of financial institutions. The key principle was creation of conditions for resolution of the insolvency of any financial institution without serious consequences and the risk of losing taxpayers' funds. In addition, effective resolution of insolvency should provide options for both financial recovery and liquidation of financial institutions. At the same time, a continuity of systemically important banking functions should be ensured, and the mechanism for protecting their depositors and insured persons must be quickly implemented. Principles of effective bankruptcy regulation also include cooperation with authorities of other countries, and exclusion of unsustainable financial institutions from the market. In accordance with the FSB approaches, the authorized bodies of states should have a wide arsenal of powers and instruments, including the possibility to dismiss the management of a financial institution, demand return of a certain part of the remuneration paid to the bank executives, take actions stipulated by law in respect of bank owners, transfer assets and liabilities to another company, create a special institution for ensuring continuity of systemically important functions, write of debts to a number of creditors and introduce a temporary moratorium on the right to demand the early execution of contractual obligations.

The problem of shadow banking is also in the area of the *Financial Stability Board's* monitoring. Shadow banking institutions are involved in credit intermediation, but their activities are poorly or insufficiently regulated, which creates significant risks and leads to large losses for many market participants in times of crisis. It is now well known that it was these institutions that made a significant contribution to the global crisis. The study carried out by FSB in 2012 on the extent of shadow banking indicates that the total assets of shadow banking institutions in FSB member countries make up about 25% of the assets of the entire financial system. The scale of shadow banking is the highest in the Netherlands, where the assets of shadow institutions reach 45% of all assets of the financial system (mainly at the expense of Special Financial Institutions, which are subsidiaries of transnational corporations). After the Netherlands, the biggest scale of shadow banking is characteristic to the United States and Hong Kong (where these institutions account for 35%

of all assets). In the UK, Switzerland, Singapore, and South Korea, the ratio of shadow banks' assets to all assets of the financial sector reaches 25%. In the FSB's study it was noted that in the pre-crisis years there was a rapid growth of assets of such institutions in the FSB member countries. In particular, assets of such institutions grew from 26.3 trillion dollars in 2002 to 61.5 trillion dollars in 2007, or almost 2.5 times. During the crisis, they slightly decreased (to 58.9 trillion dollars), but after the acute phase of the crisis, their further growth was observed (up to 66.1 trillion dollars by the end of 2011). Such data convincingly testify to the scale and topicality of the problem of shadow banking assets. The FSB also analyzed the structure of the assets of shadow banking institutions by types of companies working with such assets and concluded that the bulk of such assets (34%) was concentrated in investment funds (excluding money market funds), and 14% of assets (the second largest concentration) was accounted for brokerage and dealer structures.

Since 2011, the *Financial Stability Board* has begun to explore opportunities to identify shadow banking structures in order to strengthen their regulation and supervision. The report prepared by the FSB "The Shadow Banking System: Strengthening Supervision and Regulation" provides for two stages of regulating such structures. At the first stage, all credit mediation cases outside the regulated banking system are investigated, while at the second stage, institutions that have asset maturity and liquidity transformation risks, incomplete risk transfer, high leverage and regulatory arbitrage are identified. After identifying of such institutions at the second stage, the FSB will develop measures to build effective systems for regulating the shadow banking business.

In 2012, FSB, together with the *Basel Committee and the International Organization of Securities Commissions* (IOSCO), established 5 working groups on various aspects of shadow banking structures. The first group deals with the issues of banks' cohesiveness with shadow structures, develops additional recommendations on the bank consolidation order for risk management and reporting purposes, as well as on risk management related to large investments of banks, and the rules for calculating the risk of banks' investments in the funds capital.

Money market investment funds fall within the competence of the second group, which includes requirements for management of these funds, methods for assessing assets, managing liquidity, using a model with a constant or variable value of assets, using credit ratings and disclosure of information.

The third group within the FSB is engaged in other shadow banking structures. This is a fairly wide range of financial institutions, including, for example, institutions that manage customers' cash (when there is a risk of massive withdrawal of funds). This group also includes organizations that provide loans using funds attracted for short-term; brokerage companies that provide services that depend on short-term funding or funding against customer assets; Firms specializing in the issuance of guarantees, sureties and securitization. In accordance with the FSB's recommendations regulation of such institutions should be based on the following principles: regulators must have all necessary powers in their field; at their disposal there should be all the information necessary for assessing the risk degree of the shadow banking institutions' activities, in particular, the level of leverage, maturity of assets and other liquidity parameters; standards of information disclosure must constantly increase so that the market participants properly assess the risks of operations with such institutions; appropriate regulatory tools should be applied taking into account the operations of shadow banking structures.

Securitization issues are the responsibility of the fourth group, which has developed recommendations on the requirements for retaining part of the credit risk by the originator of asset-backed securities, as well as measures to improve transparency and standardization of securitization products.

The fifth group deals with an aspect of the shadow banking business, such as repo transactions and securities lending. It elaborated recommendations on increasing the transparency of such transactions, regulation of secured financing, structural aspects of securities lending and repo markets.

Another important direction of the FSB's activities was reformation of the OTC derivatives market. The FSB's activities are based on the implementation of the tasks of reforming the OTC derivatives market, formulated at the G20 summit in Pittsburgh (USA) in 2009: clearing of all standardized OTC derivatives should be carried out through a central counterparty; information about transactions should be sent to trading repositories; higher capital and margin requirements and higher risk ratios must be applied to transactions with OTC derivatives which are not cleared through a central counterparty;

all standardized transactions with OTC derivatives should be carried out through organized trades and electronic trading platforms.

Currently, national and international regulators have managed to implement some of the set tasks, in particular, international principles and standards have been developed in this area. Work is underway to establish a global system of centralized clearing. All countries made statements about their approaches to centralized clearing. In a number of countries (in particular, those that have the largest OTC derivatives markets), the necessary legislation has been largely prepared and entered into force, and the financial markets' infrastructure for centralized clearing and reporting on transactions carried out in developed markets was created for all classes of OTC derivatives.

The *Financial Stability Board* pays much attention to reducing the automatic dependence of banks and other financial market participants on external credit ratings, since this situation contributed to the accumulation of credit and market risks by banks on the eve of the global crisis. In 2010, the FSB published the principles of reducing the dependence on ratings. In accordance with these principles, national authorities and international standards-setting organizations should work to reduce dependence on ratings by making appropriate changes to standards, legislative and regulatory acts, and to stimulate measures aimed at increasing transparency and competition in the credit ratings market.

In November 2012, the heads of central banks and finance ministers of the G20 countries approved a roadmap for national regulators and supervisors, as well as international standards setting organizations, to reduce dependence on rating agencies' ratings. In compliance with this roadmap, all member countries pledged to publish draft regulatory changes minimizing the use of references to external rating agencies' estimates by July 1 2014, and to ensure implementation of these changes by market participants by the end of 2015.

Creation of the *Global Legal Entity Identifier* (LEI) system, which is necessary for solving many problems of financial stability, is also one of the FSB's current tasks. It is expected that this tool will be used, in particular, to improve the risk management quality in companies, improve assessment of macro prudential risks, reduce the amount of fraud and machinations in the financial markets, and generally improve the quality and accuracy of financial data. The *Global Legal Entity Identifier* system will consist of three elements: *Regulatory Oversight Committee* (ROC), *Central Operating Unit* (COU), *Local Operating Units* (LOU).

In addition, the FSB regularly publishes various thematic reviews, such as reviews on employee incentive compensation practices of financial institutions, the practice of initiating and underwriting mortgage loans, disclosure of risk information, deposit insurance systems, and risk management practices, as well as reviews on different countries. For example, the review on financial incentives for employees of financial institutions analyzes the discrepancies between international recommendations and the practices spread in different countries and assesses the progress achieved in this direction. The review of the deposit insurance system examines the functioning of such systems in member countries and effective reforms implemented in this area. An overview of risk disclosure is devoted to structured finance transactions and disclosure of all information about the risks associated with them.

Under the auspices of the FSB, measures are also being taken to reform the regulation of insurance companies, in particular, global systemically important insurers (G-SIIs). Taking into account the FSB's recommendations, the *International Association of Insurance Supervisors* has developed a document proposing measures to regulate the G-SIIs, which include strengthening their supervision, building an effective insolvency regime, and additional capital requirements.

The *Financial Stability Board* pays special attention to the problem of regulating financial indices. After discussing this issue at the plenary session of the FSB in 2013, regulators both at the international and national levels have taken certain steps to eliminate deficiencies in this area. In particular, after the publication of the report by the Head of the Office of Financial Regulation and Supervision M. Whitley about the drawbacks in calculating the LIBOR rate, the UK government put forward proposals for amending the legislation in order to implement a number of recommendations specified in the report. The *International Organization of Securities Commissions* also published an advisory report on this issue in 2013. The *European Securities and Markets Authority* and *European Banking Supervision Authority* have prepared and published a consultative document on the principles for regulating the process of calculating indices.

3.2. Basel Accords in the Light of the Global Crisis

The changes made in the regulation and supervision played an important role in overcoming the consequences of the global crisis, as well as in increasing the stability of the global economy. Over the past 25 years, the risks in the banking sector have been largely governed by the recommendations of the *Basel Committee on Banking Supervision* (the Basel I, Basel II and Basel III Accords).

On the eve of the crisis, banking regulations of most countries were based on a set of recommendations of the Basel Committee known as the *Basel II Agreement*. In particular, the regulatory authorities were guided by the document "International Convergence of Capital Measurement and Capital Standards: New Approaches". Basel II was based on three components: minimum capital requirements, supervisory process and market discipline.

The main modification made in Basel II in comparison with Basel I was the choice between three ways of calculating credit risk: a standardized approach (SA) based on data from external rating agencies; approaches based on internal ratings (IRBA), in which banks were allowed to use their own internal rating system, coordinated with the supervisory authority; improved approach (A-IRBA). Basel II encouraged the use of IRB approaches as more sensitive to risk assessment, but at the same time required certification of the bank's credit rating system and alignment of its methodology with supervisors.

Even before the crisis, shortcomings of this regulatory approach were revealed during implementation of Basel II requirements. In particular, the researchers noted that banks and supervisors excessively concentrated their efforts on the first component of the agreement (minimum capital requirements) and paid insufficient attention to the other two components (supervisory process and market discipline). Often banks focused on compliance with the rules established by this agreement, but did not try to build a highly efficient management process which would be based on adequate risk assessment, business planning and pricing strategies.

Another drawback of the current regulatory practice was that, due to the possibility of using internal models, large banks actually received a competitive advantage and reduced requirements for their own capital, while medium and small banks using a simplified approach could not use this opportunity.

In addition, when moving to the Basel II standards, it was difficult to accurately assess the effects of capital recalculation for different countries. Innovative approaches were hampered by a lack of information, especially in emerging economies. Not all regulators required banks to create an effective internal system to ensure sufficient capital and cover a full range of banking risks, including those that were not covered by the first component (in particular, liquidity and concentration risks).

It is necessary to note dual approach of Basel II to stress testing of capital. On the one hand, Basel II provides for stress testing within the first and second components, within which capital must also correspond to stressful conditions. On the other hand, the Basel II approach allows to estimate one-year capital requirement, which essentially leads to procyclicality. The capital regulation model underlying Basel II had to simultaneously meet development needs and create conditions for the sustainability of the economy and the banking sector, which was impossible in case of the procyclical regulation.

The global economic crisis clearly showed all existing shortcomings of the *Basel II Agreement*, starting from the asset quality assessment criteria and ambiguity of including a number of financial instruments in the calculation of capital, before the negative effect of the mechanism of procyclical regulation. In accordance with the decision of the heads of government of the G20 countries, the *Basel Committee*, with participation of the *Financial Stability Board*, took a number of steps to change the active regulation rules.

Capital Requirement Directive 3 (CRD 3) initiated the process of reforming the regulatory framework at the international level. It contained an adjustment of the market risk measurement. In accordance with the new requirements, it was necessary to use not only the VaR risk assessment methodology, but also the risk of changing instrument ratings without an active market, using an incremental risk charge (IRC).

Later on, *Capital Requirement Directive 3*, formulated additional regulatory requirements that had to be implemented over a number of years. The new *Basel III Accord* largely preserved the approaches used earlier, in particular, the three-component structure of regulatory rules, asset and capital valuation approaches and the possibility given to banks to use their own risk assessment models for calculation of capital ratios.

At the same time, Basel III introduced many cardinal innovations, in particular, leverage. This innovation is of particular importance, given the recent experience of banks, when due to many reasons the degree of asset risk was not adequately assessed and sometimes deliberately understated. The debt ratio had to be introduced in 2013-2017.[111]Rather heated discussion unfolded around introduction of this indicator, given the fact that in calculating this ratio, high-risk assets (usually those that generate higher income) and low-risk assets (with a lower yield) are treated identically, which limits the potential profit of banks.

Most regulators support the introduction of this indicator as mandatory. In the United States, for example, it is proposed to include the new standard into the mandatory list. Besides, the level of minimum sufficient capital is defined as the larger of two capital adequacy indicators (calculated with or without a risk factor). At the same time, a number of European countries are very cautious about this coefficient, suggesting that it can remain mandatory at the discretion of national regulators.

The new *Basel III Accord* also proposed that companies should not include into the capital a number of financial instruments, in particular subordinated loans, banks' shares of in insurance companies and minority stakes of third parties to banks and banking groups (they will be withdrawn from capital gradually during 2013-2022). In addition, it was decided to highlight the main (consisting of ordinary shares) and additional capital (also having a very high degree of reliability) within the framework of tier 1 capital. In contrast, division into subcategories was abolished for the second-tier capital. The requirements contained in the accord for the magnitude of capital adequacy ratios (by levels and taking into account the capital buffer) are presented in Table No. 11.

---

[111]   Basel Committee on Banking Supervision. Basel III phase – in arrangements, www.bis.org

Table N 11

The Minimum Capital Adequacy Coefficients Provided for in Basel III (%)

	2013	2014	2015	2016	2017	2018	2019
Debt Ratio	Calculated in parallel from 01.01.2013-01.01.2017, disclosed from 01.01.2015					Included into Section 1 of the Accord	
Sufficiency of the fixed capital of the 1st tier	3,5	4,0	4,5	4,5	4,5	4,5	4,5
Capital conservation buffer				0,625	1,250	1,875	2,500
Sufficiency of the fixed capital of the 1st tier plus the capital conservation buffer	3,5	4,0	4,5	5,1	5,8	6,4	7,0
Subtraction from the fixed capital of the 1st tier of financial instruments previously accounted for in equity		20	40	60	80	100	100
Sufficiency of the 1st tier capital	4,5	5,5	6,0	6,0	6,0	6,0	6,0
Sufficiency of the capital	8,0	8,0	8,0	8,0	8,0	8,0	8,0
Sufficiency of the capital plus the capital conservation buffer	8,0	8,0	8,0	8,6	9,1	9,9	10,5

Source: Basel Committee on Banking Supervision. Basel III phase – in arrangements, www.bis.org

Another innovation of Basel III was introduction of a countercyclical capital buffer designed to cover possible capital losses in the event of an increased systemic risk caused by banks' credit expansion. Its value fluctuated in the range from 0 to 2.5% of the sum of assets weighted by the risk degree. It is assumed that the value of the buffer for a particular bank will be determined as a weighted average for the countries in which it conducts its lending operations. At the national level, the value of the buffer will be determined depending on the ratio of the current volume of loans given to the private and non-financial sector to the gross domestic product (GDP) and taking into account a long-term trend in this indicator. The buffer is proposed to be set at 0%, if the increase of the credit-to-GDP ratio is less than 2% compared to the long-term average and at 2.5%, if this increase is more than 10%. For other values of the gain, the buffer size should be determined based on linear interpolation.

In Basel III, in addition to changes in the regulation of capital adequacy, there have also been significant innovations in the area of liquidity risk management, which had not previously received significant attention. In particular, it provides for stress testing of banks by simulating a situation when there is no possibility to raise funds in financial markets.

Basel III also provides for introduction of a liquidity cover ratio (LCR), calculated as the ratio of highly liquid assets to net obligations that have up to 30-day maturity period. In 2015, the value of this coefficient was established at the level of minimum 60%, starting from 2016 - at the level of minimum 70%, from 2017 – minimum 80%, in 2018 - minimum 90%, and in 2019 – minimum 100%.[112]

One more important tool for regulating liquidity was the *net stable funding ratio* (NSFR), calculated as the ratio of available stable funding to the required stable funding. Basel III established that the value of this coefficient should be more than 100%. At the same time, available stable financing is defined as part of the sources, represented by own capital and borrowed funds which are weighted with a certain coefficient. For example, fixed capital is included into calculation of the net stable financing indicator with a coefficient of 100%, stable small business deposits with up to one-year maturity - with a coefficient of 90%, liabilities to non-financial companies with less than one-year maturity - with a coefficient of 50%.

The required stable financing is calculated as the aggregate value of assets also weighted with a certain coefficient, for example, cash, securities under one year, and securities transferred under reverse repurchase agreements have a weighting factor of 0%; secured bonds and bonds of non-financial companies

---

[112] Basel Committee on Banking Supervision. Basel III phase – in arrangements, www.bis.org

with AA and higher rating and the term exceeding one year have a weighting factor of 50%; retail loans and loans to small businesses with up to one-year maturity period - 85%. From 2018, the value of the net stable financing indicator is set at a level of at least 100%.

The situation with the transition to Basel III standards varies significantly across countries. The EU countries have consistently adopted all the changes in the Basel Agreements, so they smoothly move from Basel II to Basel III standards. The United States will begin to implement the new standards based on the Basel I. Japan, Hong Kong, Singapore and Australia have made significant progress in this direction, but the situation in Eastern Europe, the Middle East, Africa, and the Asia-Pacific region remains unclear. There are other problems related to the transition to Basel III standards, which many experts pay attention to. Thus, according to P.-E. Shabanel - senior director of Moody's Analytics we have a situation "when some countries may also have another operating system of regulation, which in some cases may mean replacement of a part of internal standards with the requirements of Basel III. However, parallel the implementation of domestic and international standards may be necessary. Global differences complicate the situation even further, because banks may have to comply with different norms in different jurisdictions. Some banks will have to report according to the requirements of Basel II in one country and according to the requirements of Basel III in another, depending on their location".[113]

In recent years, the *Basel Committee on Banking Supervision* has also been actively involved in the issue of compiling a list of the world's systemically important (system-forming) financial institutions (SIFIs), which will have to be under particularly strict supervision by regulators.

The principles and criteria for selecting systemically important banks have provoked heated discussions between banks, national governments and international supervisory bodies. As a result, banks tend to present themselves in the most modest light, to be in the last places in the SIFIs list or, even better, do not get into it at all. "Regulators around the world agree that financial institutions influencing the global system should be subject to more intensive

---

[113] Shabanel P., "Implementation of Basel III standards: complexity, options and opportunities", Analytical Banking Journal, 2011, № 10 (in Russian language); № 10.

banking supervision," said Andreas Dombret, Executive Board Member of Bundesbank (Germany), in an interview with Handelsblatt.

During the discussion of this problem, experts proposed various criteria for backbone institutions, for example, the number of branches and subsidiary banks, the amount of exchange capitalization, the ratio of the volume of loans and own assets. Inclusion of financial institutions in the list of international backbone institutions is often not admired by banks and at the national level. Economist H. Beninka of the University of Tilburg in the Netherlands notes, that lobbyists will do their best to convince regulators that a bank "Perhaps, is a backbone for the financial system, but not at the global level". And, indeed, for example, the government of Japan pointed out that the magnitude of the risks for the world financial system depends not only on the size of the bank, but on how extensive its international activities are, therefore the global system-forming institutions are not Japanese, but American and European banks. In Japan, they made their own list of global backbone banks from 60 institutions, giving the first places to *Deutsche Bank, Goldman Sachs* and *JP Morgan Chase*.

Despite the ambiguous attitude to the future list of global backbone banks in France, they still agree that objectively *BNP Paribas* and *Societe Generale* can be recognized as such institutions.

In Italy, the real candidates are *UniCredit* and *IntesaSanpaolo*. "They are preparing in advance for the increased requirements related to the size of their own capital, in order to avoid problems in case if they get into the SIFIs List", - said one of the Italian analysts in an interview with Handelsblatt. At the same time, the expert noted that these banks prudently pre-sell some of their "daughters".

In Spain they are also engaged in this problem. According to the representative of the *Spanish Central Bank, Banco Santander* and *BBVA* are obvious candidates for getting into the SIFIs list. German experts named one candidate for the world system-forming institutions - *Deutsche Bank*.

Given the active discussion in the banking community, the *Financial Stability Board* and *the Basel Committee on Banking Supervision* have developed a system of indicators that allows the bank to be classified as a global systemically important institution. In accordance with this methodology, the following

5 criteria (groups of indicators), which have the same weighting factor (20%) in calculation, are used to determine a bank's global importance: the size of the bank, its interconnectedness with other institutions, the lack of readily available substitutes for the services they provide, their global (cross-jurisdictional) activity and their complexity. With the exception of the size criterion (which has only one indicator), the Basel Committee provides for several indicators in the remaining four groups with an equal weighting factor. For example, if there are two indicators in the group of indicators, then each has a weighting factor of 10%, if there are three indicators in the group, then the weighting coefficient of each will be 6.67% etc.

Global systemically important banks are selected by regulators from the list of candidate banks. This list, in turn, is also formed by the regulatory bodies, based on the following three criteria: such credit institutions should either be among the 75 largest banks in the world in terms of the debt to equity ratio calculated at the end of the fiscal year; or they should be systemically significant on the basis of past calculations of regulatory bodies; or they should be proposed by national supervisory authorities.

Since 2011, the *Financial Stability Board* and the *Basel Committee on Banking Supervision* have been publish a list of global systemically important banks annually, on a regular basis (Table 12).

Table 12

The List of Global Systemically Important Banks (Classified into 5 Groups)

The Group of Banks (According to the Additional Capital Buffer Coefficient)	The Bank's Name
Group 5 (3.5%)	(empty)
Group 4 (2.5%)	Citigroup JP Morgan Chase
Group 3 (2%)	Bank of America BNP Paribas Deutsche Bank HSBC

Group 2 (1.5%)	Barclays Credit Suisse Goldman Sachs Industrial and Commercial Bank of China Limited Mitsubishi UFJ FG Wells Fargo
Group 1 (1%)	Agricultural Bank of China Bank of China Bank of New York Mellon China Construction Bank Groupe BPCE GroupeCréditAgricole ING Bank Mizuho FG Morgan Stanley Nordea Royal Bank of Scotland Santander Société Générale Standard Chartered State Street Sumitomo Mitsui FG UBS Unicredit Group

Source: Financial Stability Board. 2016 list of global systemically important banks (G-SIBs). – www.fsb.org.

As a result of applying the methodology and cluster analysis, five groups of global systemically important banks were formed in order to establish their additional capital requirement values. Each group of such banks will have its own additional requirements to the general requirements for a step-by-step increase in the value of capital adequacy. For the first group of banks, such additional requirements will be minimal and amount to 1%; for the second group additional requirements will be 1.5%, for the third group - 2%, for the fourth group - 2.5%, for the fifth group - 3.5%. Additional capital requirements can be met only by means of the fixed capital (which includes only ordinary shares and retained earnings) and act as the capital conservation buffer.

Additional capital requirements for global systemically important banks were applied from 2014, with a phased introduction until 2019. In addition, these institutions also had to comply with increased requirements for risk management systems, data aggregation and internal control.

The methodology for determining the list of global systemically important banks became the basis for recommendations to identify national systemically important banks and to draft a methodology for identifying global systemically important insurance companies.

In addition, in 2012, the *Banking Supervision Committee* developed guidelines for a mechanism regulating the activities of national systemically important banks. In accordance with these guidelines, national regulators and supervisors had to develop their own methodologies for assessing the systemic importance of banks, taking into account the consequences of their possible bankruptcy and characteristics of the national economy.

3.3. Institutional and Regulatory Changes in the EU

The global crisis has led to serious institutional changes at the national and regional levels, especially in such areas as regulation and supervision, maintaining financial stability, and guaranteeing deposits. Important institutional changes have occurred in the EU.

In 2010, the *European Financial Stability Facility* (EFSF) and the *European Financial Stability Facility* (EMFS) were created, which have a significant role to play in overcoming the effects of the crisis and strengthening financial sustainability. Since the need to combat the crisis was urgent, these institutions were established in a short time frame. Their activities were supposed to end in 2013. EMPS was under the management of the European Commission and had 60 billion euros allocated from the EU budget.

The EFSF was established as a separate organization with the task of providing financial support to problematic Eurozone countries, under the guarantees of all EU countries. Having a high credit rating due to these guarantees, this institution was also able to borrow funds in open markets on favorable terms. One of the activities of the EMFS was provision of loans to those countries that experienced difficulties in servicing their debts. Thus, the EFMS, together with the IMF, opened credit lines for Ireland (a credit line with a limit of 85 billion euros), Portugal (78 billion euros) and Greece (164 billion euros). These funds were allocated in separate tranches as needed, taking into account fulfillment of agreed budgetary savings programs by the borrowing countries.

Initially, the EU countries provided IMFS with guarantees for 440 billion euros. Later, this amount was increased to 780 billion euros. Specific numbers on contributions of European countries in the EMFS is presented in Table 13.

Table 13

Contributions of European Countries in the EMFS
(In absolute and relative terms)

	Guarantee Deposits (Increased)	
	In Bln. Euros	Share (%)
Austria	21,6	2,78
Belgium	27,0	3,47
Germany	211,1	27,10
Greece	21,9	2,80
Ireland	12,4	1,59
Spain	92,6	11,87
Italy	139,3	17,86
Cyprus	1,5	0,20
Luxemburg	2,0	0,25
Malta	0,7	0,09
Netherlands	44,5	5,70
Portugal	19,5	2,50
Slovakia	7,7	0,99
Slovenia	3,7	0,47
Finland	14,0	1,79
France	158,5	20,33
Estonia	2,0	0,26
Eurozone (17 countries)	780,0	100,00

Source: *www.ecb.europa.eu*

Recently one more European institution - the *European Stability Mechanism* (ESM), has also been established. It will replace EFSF and EMFS and provide financial assistance to the Eurozone countries. The capital of this institution is formed from contributions from the Eurozone countries (80 billion euros) and their financial guarantees (620 billion euros). The contribution to the fund's capital is defined according to the country's GDP. The largest share is provided by Germany (27.1%), France (20.4%) and Italy (17.9%).

In order to form its own resource base, the ESM also actively attracts funds in the financial markets and has achieved significant results in this area. The head of the European Stability Mechanism K. Regling described the situation in the following way: "The European Fund for Financial Stability, and now the European Stability Mechanism, have operated quite successfully in the market. Over the past two and a half years we have managed to raise 140 billion euros, and we started from scratch. So, now both funds have a reserve of 700 billion euros. At the same time, 90% of them are not yet allocated and can be used if necessary. It seems to me that this fact is quite convincing for the market, we have many resources".[114]

The new institute - ESM has some differences from the previously established EFSF and EMFS. Only the Eurozone countries take part in its financing, and the ESM itself is integrated into the structure of the EU institutions, which means that its loan allocation process is guided by the requirements of the founding treaties and Euro-group's decisions. In addition, only those Eurozone countries that will ratify the *Treaty on Stability, Coordination and Governance* of the *Economic and Monetary Union* (EMU) signed in March 2012 will be able to receive assistance. This treaty sets mandatory norms for reducing the national debt of those countries where it exceeds 60% of GDP, establishes a procedure for monitoring the budget deficit, provides for monitoring over the budgetary policies of troubled countries by the EU authorities and severe sanctions for violating commitments.

Starting from March 1, 2013, one more precondition for receiving the ESM assistance is the existence of a fully ratified European fiscal agreement. After receiving an application for the EU support, the so-called Troika (European

---

[114] Regling K., "The eurozone crisis: Half or even two-third of the case is done", Interview to the news channel Euronews 01.08.2013 r, www.euronews.com (in Russian language);

Commission, ECB and IMF) must analyze and assess the country in terms of financial stability parameters in order to decide which of the five assistance programs can be proposed:

1. Stabilization credit within the framework of the macroeconomic adaptation program (sovereign loan);
2. The bank recapitalization program;
3. Preventive financial assistance;
4. Primary market assistance.
5. Secondary market assistance.

Along with the organization of financial assistance to troubled countries in recent years, the EU has been paying considerable attention to the normative framework and institutions in charge of regulation and supervision. In particular, the EU is in the process of forming a banking union that provides for a single bank supervision mechanism (Single Supervisory Mechanism, SSM) and a single mechanism for working with problem banks (SRM). Both mechanisms will apply to all Eurozone countries and the EU member states that wish to join them. It is also planned to unify the deposit guarantee. Assessing these changes, the EU Commissioner for Financial Markets M. Barnier noted that "we are introducing revolutionary changes to the Europe's financial system, so that taxpayers no longer foot the bill when banks make mistakes".[115]

To a large extent based on Germany's initiative, a clause on the so-called "cascade of liability" was introduced into the banking union. Shareholders of banks, bondholders and depositors whose assets in a troubled bank exceed EUR 100,000, will be obliged to finance the bank's liquidation before aid comes from the outside. At the same time, within ten years, banks will have to create an emergency fund of 55 billion euros from their own funds. Before it is fully formed, it is possible to use the resources of the *European Stability Mechanism* (ESM) and the stabilization funds of the Eurozone members.

Despite the importance of creating a banking alliance to maintain financial stability in the EU, the new institution in its present form, according to

---

[115] Lenta.ru.,"Ekonomika", 15 January 2014., EU finance ministers agreed to establish a banking union, www. Lenta.ru

experts, has shortcomings and weaknesses. So, if any European bank falls into a difficult financial situation, the issue of its liquidation will be decided by an ad hoc committee created from representatives of national regulators and the European Commission. At the same time, the European Commission has the right of veto. If the veto is applied, the fate of the troubled bank will have to be decided by the ministers of finance. According to analysts of the *Financial Times*, an agreement of nine commissions and committees and about 140 votes at various levels will be needed for liquidation of a troubled bank.

The press service of the European Commission reported that on January 1, 2016, the *Single Resolution Mechanism* (SRM) has become fully operational in the territory of the European Union. "The banking union already possesses the necessary tools for regulating the Eurozone banks. And on January 1, the single mechanism of financial curing of banks began to work. This means that now we have a system for solving banking problems that will protect taxpayers from the need to help banks in case of bankruptcy. Errors of banks will no longer rest on the shoulders of others",[116] — said European Commissioner for Financial Stability and Financial Services Jonathan Hill.

There are also quite skeptical assessments regarding creation of the new institutions in terms of the possibility of preventing future crises. Thus, German expert T. Knedlik (Institute for Economic Research in Halle) notes the following: *"Can an emergence of a new financial crises in the Eurozone be prevented even by a single banking supervision? The question remains open. After all, in many countries the reason for the recent crisis is not the banks' risks, but the government expenses beyond the budget. Yes, a single banking supervision will partially help some crises, but exclude them completely – hardly".*[117]

At the present time, a Pan-European financial regulator has been established with a staff strength of 1,000, which since January 1, 2014 was headed by D. Nui. Initially, it was planned that the supervision at the Pan-European level, which would be carried out by the ECB, would be extended to all 6,000 European banks. However, later, at the initiative of Germany, where more than a third of the euro area banks are operating, an approach has

---

[116] In the EU, a single mechanism for the rehabilitation of bankswas launched. – www.banki.ru

[117] Seninsky S., Banking Union of Europe, Radio Liberty, 20.12.2013, www. svoboda.org (in Russian language); www.svoboda.org

been developed according to which the ECB would control only those banks that meet the following criteria: the bank's assets exceed either EUR 30 billion or 20% of its GDP of its country; the bank conducts business in at least two countries. Also, the three largest banks of each Eurozone country would be included into this group. According to the preliminary calculations of the European Commission, these criteria is met by about 130 banks in which about 70% of the Eurozone's assets are concentrated. The remaining banks will remain under the control of national regulators. Such a system, according to the president of the Bavarian Center of Finance (Munich), Professor W. Gerke, "will limit the ability of so-called "System" banks that have a significant influence on the economy to conduct high-risk financial transactions. *While the national supervision bodies will be better able to cope with the control of small banks - provided that all the bank criteria of the EU are complied with.*"[118]

The third component of the European banking union - deposit insurance - is still under development. It is possible that the idea of creating a single European Deposit Insurance Fund has not received sufficient support. On the eve of the EU summit in December 2013, the finance ministers agreed only to standardize the national rules for formation of private deposit insurance funds in the Eurozone countries – using up to EUR 100,000. It is assumed that in most cases it will be sufficient to accumulate in these Funds 0.8% of the total amount of private deposits held in banks of a particular country so that in the event of bankruptcy of an individual bank is able to pay off the depositors within the deposit insurance limits, no later than in a seven-day period. In addition, experts note that deposit insurance of up to 100 thousand euros has almost been introduced in the Eurozone countries at the national level, which makes creation of a single fund unnecessary.

3.4. Reforms of the Regulatory and Supervisory System in the USA

In the world's largest economy - the US - in recent years there have been significant changes in the institutional and regulatory environment aimed at changing the economic model that led to the biggest crisis in the last 70 years.

---

[118] Seninsky S., Banking Union of Europe, Radio Liberty, 20.12.2013, 20.12.2013., www. svoboda.org

To a large extent, the implemented and planned changes are contained in the well-known *Dodd-Frank Wall Street Reform* and *Consumer Protection Act*. The authors of the bill are the Chairman of the Financial Services Committee of the House of Representatives B. Frank and the Chairman of the Banking Committee of the Senate K. Dodd. The Dodd-Frank law was adopted by the US Congress and signed by President Barack Obama in 2010.

The *Dodd-Frank Act* provides for several major institutional changes. One of the most important is the regulatory reform. In accordance with the law, a special institution - the *Financial Stability Oversight Council* (FSOC) was created, which is headed by the US Minister of Finance. This new body will monitor macro-prudential risks and the stability of the entire financial system in the United States. The *Council for the Supervision of Financial Stability* began its work on October 1, 2010. During regular meetings, its participants consider recommendations for the implementation of the *Dodd-Frank Act* and develop their own rules and instructions on matters within the competence of the Council (FSOC). Such issues, in particular, include the implementation of the so-called *Volcker rule*, the limit set for the concentration of obligations in the financial system, and the criteria for determining the non-bank backbone financial companies that must be subject to more stringent supervision by the Fed.

In recent years the role of backbone companies in the US economy and financial sector has undoubtedly increased significantly, as evidenced by statistics. Thus, the ratio of the assets of the six largest US banking holding companies to the gross domestic product increased from 18% in 1995 to 68% in 2009.[119] The significant role of several large financial institutions in the US economy has been recognized by regulators for a long time, but it was particularly significant during the crises. This special role became especially noticeable during the last crisis, when the decision to bankrupt one of the largest investment banks - *Lehman Brothers*, dramatically increased negative trends in the US and world economy. At the same time, taking into account the consequences of *Lehman Brothers* bankruptcy, many countries, including the US, had to provide unprecedented financial assistance to financial institutions, especially those that were "too big to fail". Therefore,

---

[119] Grover E., Dodd-Frank ushers in a corporatist era in banking, American Banker, 2012, 14 November.

the oversight bodies of almost all countries faced the task of identifying such backbone companies and financial institutions and establishing a special regulatory and supervision regime.

The *American Financial Stability Oversight Council* (FSOC) was also tasked with developing a system of criteria by which the *Financial Stability Board* would identify system-forming organizations. In January 2011, the *Financial Stability Oversight Council* published a draft document containing a system of criteria for classifying backbone financial institutions. In particular, the proposed criteria included the company's size, lack of alternative financial products, and interdependence with other financial institutions, the level of leverage, liquidity risks, and the existing level of regulatory oversight.

The banking community of the United States actively discussed the criteria proposed by the FSOC. Based on the results of the heated discussion, it was decided that the largest and interdependent bank holding companies (with assets in excess of $50 billion) would be among the systemically important companies in the financial sector. Non-bank holding companies can be recognized as systemically important if one of the five additional thresholds associated with the volume of transactions with derivatives and the level of using borrowed funds is increased. In case of such an approach it is very likely that organizations such as hedge funds, asset management companies, utility companies of the financial market, and insurance organizations will fall into the system-forming ones.

A special procedure for supervision and regulation is being developed for the backbone organizations, in particular, it provides for stricter requirements for liquidity, leverage, capital adequacy, credit risk per borrower, risk management and stress testing. They are subject to the "rapid problem-solving system", which envisages four levels of supervisory measures up to the resolution of the situation in the case of insolvency.

The *Dodd-Frank Law* provides that in order to minimize the risks of losses from deteriorating financial positions of systemically important institutions, all US bank holding companies (BHCs) must develop and submit to the regulator plans for the effective resolution of crisis situations at the corporate level. Submission of such anti-crisis plans was carried out by the BHC in stages (depending on the size of these companies). By July 1, 2012, the first group of BHC, whose assets exceeded $250 billion, presented them. BHC with assets ranging from $50 billion to $150 billion submitted such plans to regulators by July 1, 2013, and the rest by December 31, 2013. When analyzing the submitted documentation, regulators had to make sure that systemically important credit institutions that had complex organizational structures, management system and operating model and were geographically diversified would be ready for negative external influences and could be divided into separate organizational structures if necessary, without negative consequences for the markets.

The plans presented by the bank holding companies contained a wide range of measures to overcome the crisis. For example, in its anti-crisis plan, *Bank of America* provided for the regrouping resources, return to traditional banking activities, strengthening the role of risk management, increasing equity and liquidity while reducing the long-term debt burden and increasing the market capitalization of the bank. The plan envisages launch of the "Make a new Bank of America" program, cutting the bank's spending by $5 billion by the end of 2014, based on closer integration of customers' current needs and corporate strategy. The plan envisaged putting into practice a system for estimating the economic capital necessary for the proper operation of the bank in case of sudden credit, market and operational risks and losses, with the distribution of risk shares by structural units, depending on the degree of riskiness of their activities. It was also planned to shift priorities towards risk management on an ongoing basis and add to the management reports an indicator on additional liquidity (in the whole global excess liquidity) which had to be preserved for minimum 21 months.

In its anti-crisis plan, *ContiGroup* intends to bring the volume of highly liquid assets to 22% of their total value, in order to achieve early compliance with the requirements of Basel III in terms of the Liquidity Coverage Ratio, and to create a unit for the banking regulation reform.[120]

It is planned to establish a special body - the *Orderly Liquidation Authority -* under the *Federal Deposit Insurance Corporation* to control banks in crisis conditions (including during bank liquidation). It is assumed that this

---

[120] Banking information and regulation. Resolution plans Board of Governors of the Federal Reserve System (2012).

institution can re-register in its own name and manage assets and liabilities of a bankrupt institution, participate in the restructuring of creditors' debts, in particular, in its conversion into shares, and carry out recapitalization of the troubled credit organization at the expense of public funds. It is assumed that the bankruptcy prevention costs of the FDIC will be reimbursed at the expense of other systemically important banks.[121]

Of the recent initiatives of the US supervisory authorities regarding the backbone organizations, we can note introduction of a standardized minimum liquidity requirement, which was generally developed in accordance with the recommendations of the *Basel III Accord* for regulation of short-term liquidity of banks. Speaking about the need to introduce such liquidity requirements, a member of the FRS Board of Governors D. Tarullo, in particular, noted that "since a financial crisis usually begins with a liquidity deficit that further weakens the position of the vulnerable firms' capital, it is important to adopt liquidity rules that would complement enhanced capital adequacy requirements, stress-testing, and other regulatory changes that we have been implementing for the past few years."[122]

In accordance with the regulatory reform, systemically important American organizations should have a certain amount of high quality liquid assets, for example, reserves in the central bank, government and corporate debt securities, which can be easily and quickly converted into cash. This liquidity amount should be equal to the projected liquidity outflow minus the forecasted receipt of liquidity for some short stress period. The ratio of the organization's liquid assets to the projected net outflow of cash is its liquidity coverage ratio (LCR). In proposing the introduction of this liquidity ratio, the Chairman of the FRS Board, Bernanke noted, that "liquidity plays a key role in the bank's viability and smooth functioning of the financial system. For the first time in the US, the proposed rule will establish a quantitative liquidity standard, which, combined with other reforms, will make the financial system more stable and secure."[123]

---

[121] Wallison P. J., Dodd-Frank Liquidation plan is worse than bankruptcy, Bloomberg, 2012, 12 June.

[122] Quoted after: Federal Reserve press release. 24.10.2013., www.fedspeak.ru

[123] Quoted after: Federal Reserve Press Release. 24.10.2013., www.fedspeak.ru

The LCR indicator will be applied to backbone non-banking financial institutions and to all banking organizations actively engaged in international transactions (whose total consolidated assets exceed $250 billion, or whose net position for foreign assets exceeds $10 billion). A less stringent LCR approach will be applied to bank holdings and credit and savings holdings that do not conduct international transactions, but have assets worth more than $50 billion. It should be noted that this regulatory rule does not apply to bank holdings and credit and savings holdings with large insurance subsidiaries and backbone non-banking financial institutions with significant insurance operations.

The proposals of the *Council for the Supervision of Financial Stability* (CSFS) and the *Federal Reserve System* (FRS) contain a procedure for classifying assets by category in terms of their liquidity, as well as a mechanism for calculating an organization's projected net cash outflow during a stressful period, using common standard assumptions on liquidity outflows and inflows associated with specific liabilities, assets and off-balance sheet liabilities.

The proposed regulatory rule that sets a number of parameters, in particular, the list of liquid assets and the rate of outflow for some types of funding, is more stringent than that provided for in Basel III. The initiative of the US oversight bodies also establishes a shorter transitional period than envisaged in the Basel Accords. The reason for this is the desire to promote better liquidity of the US financial institutions achieved after the crisis, in part as a result of the supervisory efforts implemented by the FRS and other banking regulators. According to the proposal, the transition period to a new LCR for US organizations will begin on January 1, 2015 and will be fully completed by January 1, 2017. While making comments on the supervisor's decision, a member of the FRS Board of Governors D. Tarullo noted, that "this regulation will help to ensure that liquidity positions in our banks do not deteriorate as the crisis is forgotten."[124]

Supervisory bodies also established new requirements for the capital adequacy of backbone organizations, which are generally based on the regulatory rules of Basel III, but at the same time are more stringent on a number of parameters. The fundamental approaches of the supervisory bodies in this matter were

---

[124] Quoted after: Federal Reserve Press Release. 24.10.2013., www.fedspeak.ru

set forth in the speech of the member of the Board of Governors of the FRS, D. Tarullo, at the Peter G. Peterson Institute for International Economics in Washington on June 3, 2011. The Federal Reserve also received the authority to strictly supervise and regulate the payment, clearing and settlement systems of systemic importance. In particular, these institutions will have to follow tougher risk management standards (based on international standards) to warn regulators ahead of time about the intention to make changes in the rules of their operation. At the same time, systemically important payment institutions have the right to open accounts with FRS banks and use various payment services of the Federal Reserve System, as well as apply for loans, including emergency loans for liquidity problems.

Another important component of the *Dodd-Frank law* was the introduction of changes in the regulation of the derivatives market. The requirements of the law relate to those derivative financial instruments that have a source and are implemented and regulated in the US, or those which are settled in the US or through a US-based financial institution. In particular, the *Dodd-Frank Act* contains requirements for separation of large buyers and sellers operating in the US derivatives market into *Major Swaps Participants* (MSPs) and *Swaps Dealers* (SD). Such persons must be registered with the regulatory authorities, in particular the US Futures Trading Commission and/or the US Securities and Exchange Commission, and also comply with a number of new regulatory rules.

In addition, the law provides that clearing settlements for swaps that meet the regulatory requirements of regulators are carried out through a central counterparty. Admissible trading operations are carried out in the specialized market of derivatives (*Designated Contract Market*, DCM) or a site for swap transactions (*Swaps Execution Facility*, SEF). Additional requirements were established for the capital of transaction participants, ensuring trade operations, both with and without the participation of clearing organizations. Strict rules for protection of clients' assets are provided. In particular, rapid reporting to the *Swaps Data Repository* (SDR) on all derivative transactions in should be followed. Quantitative restrictions are set on certain primary commodities.

It should be noted that under the new legislation, the requirements for derivative financial instruments are determined by the *US Futures Trading*

Commission or the *Securities Exchange Commission* (and sometimes both) depending on the nature of the swap or its underlying asset.

Another of the main directions of the American financial system reform was adoption of so-called "Volcker Rule", named after the author of the legislation amendments P. Volcker, who was an economic adviser to the President Barack Obama, and previously served as a Chairman of the Board of Governors of the Federal Reserve System. The *Dodd-Frank Act* prohibits those banks that attract deposits from the public, to use their own funds for making investments in hedge funds and direct investment funds and for implementing trade operations with securities. At the same time, the law does not prohibit banks from carrying out such operations at the expense of clients' funds or use market makings, hedging of risks, and underwriting, as well as many other operations that are often similar to those that implementation of which is prohibited at the bank's own expense.

In the *Dodd-Frank Law*, the "Volcker Rule" is also supplemented with the derivatives *Push-out Rule*, which prohibits banks from dealing with the following types of derivatives: commodity swaps (except for gold and silver swaps), stock swaps, credit default swaps, that do not have an investment class. Banks will have to create separate branches with their own capital in order to trade such derivatives.

These provisions of the *Dodd-Frank Act* sparked heated discussions in the banking community, because many experts believe that such regulatory innovations should have a negative impact on the incomes of the largest financial institutions. Bankers also pointed to the vagueness of the criteria for certain operations contained in the regulatory innovation. In particular, the head of *JP Morgan Chase*, J. Dimon noted that adoption of such innovations would lead to the fact that each trader would need assistance of a psychologist and a lawyer to figure out whether the "Volcker Rule" is violated or not. Opponents of the law also argued that trade at the bank's own expense had nothing to do with the crisis, and restrictions on the bank activities could make financial markets more volatile.

In 2010-2012 the regulatory bodies received about 17 thousand comments and suggestions from representatives of the banking community on the norms contained in the "Volcker Rule." There were opinions that the "Volcker Rule" would not be implemented in practice. The initiative of American regulators was criticized in other countries. So, in the opinion of a Deputy Governor of the Bank of Japan, K. Nishimura, "this rule could have significant implications for important market-making activities, as well as for market liquidity."

In 2013, the situation was as follows: according to Bloomberg, trading in securities provided 14% of *Bank of America's* income and 44% of *Goldman Sachs'* income. At the same time, by 2014 most of the largest banks, including GS, have already disbanded their trading departments using their own funds.

In 2012, *JP Morgan Chase* received losses of $6 billion as a result of risky operations implemented at the company's own expense by its dealer in London, B. Iksel. This example became a weighty argument for the supporters of the "Volcker Rule". Responding to the critics of this initiative, Secretary of the US Treasury T. Geithner noted that "banks cannot own hedge funds, since this can put us in an awkward position. If hedge funds go bankrupt, too many innocent people will suffer. Despite the fears of some governments and central banks, I do not believe that the "Volcker Rule" poses significant liquidity risks in these countries.

In December 2013, despite the financial sector's criticism and lobbying, the "Volcker Rule" was approved by five regulatory organizations (*Securities and Exchange Commission, Federal Reserve, Federal Deposit Insurance Corporation, Office of the Comptroller of the Currency, Commodity Futures Trading Commission*). It was assumed from April 2014, banks would have to ensure full compliance with the "Volcker Rule", while in 2015 the supervisory authorities would start strict monitoring over the compliance. However, according to the RNS news agency referring to Reuters, a number of large American banks applied to the FRS with a request to give them additional five years (to 2022) to fulfill the Volcker Rule.[125]

Thus, since 2014 banks cannot trade at their own expense. They will be able to continue trading operations on behalf of clients or work in the markets provided that regulators have clear and convincing evidence that these transactions are not trade at their own expense.

---

[125] RNS. 12.08.2016. Large American banks are asking the Fed for a delay in fulfilling Volcker's rule for five years. – www.rns.online

In addition, the "Volcker rule" establishes that banks can invest in the capital of hedge funds or private equity funds no more than 3% of Tier 1 capital. In this case, the share of banks in the capital of these institutions also cannot exceed 3%.

The *Dodd-Frank Law* also established a special liquidation regime for those large financial institutions (Orderly Liquidation) whose bankruptcy could threaten the financial stability of the United States. In accordance with the norms of the Law, the US government must finance the entire liquidation procedure and take actions to prevent possible panic in the market and sell the bankrupt assets at the maximum cost. After the completion of the procedure, the owners of the liquidated company will be obligated to fully reimburse the costs incurred by the state.

Another rule of the Law provides for the possibility of a forced return of bankrupt assets if they were transferred to third parties shortly before the bankruptcy. It also imposes personal responsibility on the top managers, under whose leadership the company has gone to bankruptcy: suspension from management of the company, compensation of the company's damages by the top managers and prohibition of further administrative activities in other financial companies.

One of the directions of changes in the regulatory framework was the establishment of a limit on concentration in the financial system. This measure, also contained in the *Dodd-Frank Act*, prohibits the acquisition of one bank by another bank if, as a result of this purchase, the incorporated company will own more than 10% of all liabilities of the financial system. Thus, this provision limits mergers and take-over. According to regulators, this rule limits the possible mergers of the four largest financial institutions of the United States (*Bank of America, JP Morgan Chase, Citigroup, Wells Fargo*), each of which has over 5% of the total liabilities of the financial system on its balance sheet.

The *Dodd-Frank Act* also contains legal norms aimed at protecting consumers' rights and tightening the rules of business conduct of companies. In particular, a new institution was created - the *Consumer Financial Protection Bureau* (CFPB), which both establishes rules in this sphere, controls their implementation and even has the right to charge with a criminal offence.

Currently, this institution mainly regulates retail lending, but in the long term the scope of its activities can be expanded. The law provides for setting a limit on the amount of commissions charged on transactions with bank cards. A requirement is introduced that securitization organizations are required to bear 5% of the credit risk associated with securitization of assets. The possibility of introducing a single standard for fiduciary obligations of investment consulting firms and brokers/dealers is being discussed.

The law provides for the registration of consulting firms and the provision of reporting on private funds (Form PF). Registration is carried out at the *US Securities and Exchange Commission* or the *US Commodity Futures Trading Commission*, depending on the type of assets for which the consultation services are provided. There is a rigid system of internal certification and the volume of benefits for foreign private consulting firms is decreasing.

The *Dodd-Frank Act* also contains requirements for improving the quality of corporate governance, including the disclosure of remuneration information and the possibility of taking away previously paid remuneration.

In the US, there are also some other regulatory instruments that are also actively used in addition to the regulatory norms contained in the *Dodd-Frank Act*, in particular - stress testing of banks first conducted by the FRS in 2009 (the second round was held in 2011). Application of this tool allows to assess the adequacy of the capital base of credit institutions and the impact of possible negative external changes on their financial situation. An important change in the regulation and supervision practice will be implementation of stress tests of financial institutions on a regular annual basis.

In general, despite the adopted system of measures to reform regulation and supervision in the United States, heated discussions on the effectiveness of these measures in practice are still going on. The success of the innovations contained in the *Dodd-Frank Act* will to a large extent be determined by the consistency and persistence of the regulators in the implementation of these innovations, and, when necessary, by their timely adjustment. Moreover, coordinated actions of regulators of different countries in reforming regulatory and supervisory systems will also be of great importance in the modern global economy.

3.5. Regulatory Reform in the UK

On the eve of the global crisis, almost all segments of the financial market of Great Britain were under the jurisdiction of the *Financial Services Authority* (FSA). This state regulatory agency was established in 1997 on the basis of the *Institute for Securities and Investments*. Since 2000, this institution has been operating under the *Financial Services and Markets Act*. By 2005 the area of its supervision included banks, insurance companies, financial consultants, housing and consumer cooperatives, asset management, mortgage business and intermediary operations in insurance. The *Financial Services Authority* has thus become a mega-regulator accountable to the Ministry of Finance.

The global crisis demonstrated that the financial sector had accumulated a lot of excessively high risks at both the macro and micro levels and that the existing regulatory system could not prevent such a situation. On December 7, 2011, speaking at the event of the *Geneva Insurance Association*, the Financial Secretary of the UK Treasury M. Hoban described the current state of affairs in the field of regulation in the following way: "The UK simply cannot afford to repeat the past crisis ... It is vital that regulatory changes keep pace with changing markets, products and services. Regulatory reform is of a paramount importance - it is designed to ensure that what is happening in the financial sector will not undermine the stability in the rest of the economy."[126]

In 2010, the UK published a regulatory reform plan that divided the FCA into two parts: The *Prudential Regulation Authority* (PRA) and the *Financial Conduct Authority* (FCA). In compliance with the reform plan, prudential supervision of financial institutions' condition was to go to PRA, while the task of FCA would be to monitor the behavior of companies in the markets. In fact, the reorganization of the FCA began from 2010.

The *Financial Services Act*, adopted in 2012, has become the legal basis for the regulatory reform in the UK. The Law established an independent *Financial Policy Committee* within the Bank of England. The Committee's functions included monitoring and countering systemic risks, issuing PRA and FCA guidelines and participation in the implementation of the government's economic policy.

---

[126] Quoted after: www.expert-rating.com

The guiding principles based on which the Financial Policy Committee had to implement its activities were: proportionality (the restrictions placed on individuals or their activities should be commensurate with the expected positive result), transparency (namely the obligation to publish information on the systemic risks and the Committee's measures in this area), compliance with international obligations of the UK, especially regarding the functions of the Committee in relation to the FCA and PRA.

The *Law on Financial Services* provides for the introduction of a new Appendix 1 to the *Bank of England Act* (1998) with provisions related to the *Financial Policy Committee*. In particular, it defines the rules of forming the committee from representatives of regulatory bodies, their terms of office, and the procedure for appointment and removal from office. It also contains the procedure for holding the committee meetings and determining the quorum as well as the rules for the implementation of the committee's functions.

In accordance with the *Financial Services Law*, the *Prudential Regulation Authority* (PRA) was also established. Its main purpose was to ensure safe and reliable operation of the organizations under its jurisdiction (including banks, building societies, insurance companies and some types of investment firms), without negative consequences for the financial system.

In the event of failure of any of these financial institutions, the *Prudential Regulation Department* should take control over the bankruptcy process or apply the financial recovery regime in accordance with the *Banking Act* (2009). The recovery regime can be carried out in various forms: sale of the organization on market conditions, transfer to another financial organization for management, and temporary transfer into the state ownership.

In order to achieve its goals, the *Prudential Regulation Authority* elaborates a strategy and revises it minimum once a year. While working on the draft strategy and its new versions, the PRA consults with the board of directors of the Bank of England. The approved version of the strategy must be published. In addition, the *Prudential Regulation Authority* must develop and implement a procedure for consultations with its subordinate institutions and persons representing their interests (for example, associations of industries). To this end, it must establish a special body - the *PRA Practitioner Panel*, under the *Prudential Regulation Authority*.

In exercising the supervisory functions, the *Prudential Regulation Authority* works closely with the departments of the Bank of England, including the *Financial Policy Committee* and *Special Resolution Unit*.

In addition to the *Prudential Regulation Authority*, the *Financial Services Authority* was also established in accordance with the *Financial Services Act*. The FSA was entrusted with the following tasks: ensuring proper functioning of financial markets, the market for regulated financial services, consumer protection and competition protection.

In addition, the *Financial Services Act of 2012* provides for additional regulation of the clearing and settlement chambers of the UK, in particular, when they face financial difficulties. In such cases, the financial recovery regime provided for in Part 1 of the *Banking Act* (2009) is applied. The law requires that the Bank of England must be notified about initiation of bankruptcy proceedings against the settlement and clearing house of the UK and allows the Bank of England to participate in the proceedings.

CHAPTER 4
Post-crisis development of the world economy: trends and prospects

4.1. The real sector of the economy: structural disproportions restrain economic growth

The world economy, in recent years, according to most experts, has been at the stage of recovery after a devastating crisis. However, this process is unsustainable, because it is largely a consequence of the constant large-scale stimulation of the economy, the volume of which reached USD 3.9 trillion in the US, USD 1.4 trillion in Japan and GBP 375 billion in Great Britain. Persisting structural imbalances that led to the crisis do not contribute to long-term sustainable growth. Overall, the growth rates of the world economy and individual groups of countries vary greatly.

In 2016, the world economy grew by 3.1%, which was less than in 2015 (3.4%). However, the IMF forecasted acceleration of economic growth up to 3.5% in 2017. Experts agree that such growth rates are not sufficient to ensure sustainable development of the economy and social sphere of most states, especially given the continuing uneven economic development of regions and countries. In general, the macroeconomic situation in most developed countries looks quite good, while in a number of developing countries and countries with economies in transition (including the largest), there are negative development trends.

Economic growth in developed countries amounted to 1.7% in 2016, which is below the indicator of 2015 (2.2%). In 2017, the IMF predicts the acceleration of economic development in this group of countries to 2% (Table 14).

In 2016, the US GDP growth rate (1.6%) was significantly lower than in 2015 (2.6%). The IMF predicted an increase in US economic growth to 2.3% in 2017.

In the UK, GDP in 2016 grew by 1.8%, which was less than in 2015 (2.2%). In 2017, the growth of the British economy is projected at the level of 2.1%.

In Japan, despite the active policy of quantitative easing, in 2016 the economy showed a small increase (1%), though in 2017, it is forecasted that the rate of economic growth will accelerate to 1.3%.

Leaders by economic growth among developed countries in 2016 were Iceland (7.2%), Ireland (5.2%), Israel (4%), Luxembourg (4%), Malta (5%) and New Zealand (4%). In the euro zone, in 2016, slowdown in economic growth was identified: 1.7% compared with 2.1% in 2015. However, in 2017 the IMF expects a slight acceleration to 2%. Germany's economy in 2016 grew by 1.8%. In 2017, it is expected to grow by 1.6%. In France, in 2016, GDP growth rate was 1.2% and in 2017, it will increase to 1.4%. In Italy, there was a weak economic growth observed: in 2015 by 0.8%, in 2016 by 0.9%. In 2017, GDP is expected to increase by 0.8%.

Table 14

GDP Dynamics in developed countries (%) by years

	2015	2016	2017
All developed countries	2,2	1,7	2,0
Euro zone countries	2,1	1,7	1,7
Australia	2,4	2,5	3,1
Austria	1,0	1,5	1,4

Belgium	1,5	1,3	1,6
Canada	0,9	1,4	1,9
Cyprus	1,7	2,8	2,6
Czech Republic	4,5	2,4	2,8
Denmark	1,6	1,1	1,5
Estonia	1,4	1,6	2,5
Finland	0,3	1,4	1,4
France	1,3	1,2	1,4
Germany	1,5	1,8	1,6
Greece	-0,2	0,0	2,2
Hong Kong	2,4	2,0	2,4
Iceland	4,1	7,2	5,7
Ireland	26,3	5,2	3,5
Israel	2,5	4,0	2,9
Italy	0,8	0,9	0,8
Japan	1,2	1,0	1,3
Korea	2,8	2,8	2,7
Luxembourg	3,5	4,0	3,7
Malta	7,4	50	4,1
Netherlands	2,0	2,1	2,1
New Zealand	3,1	4,0	3,1
Norway	1,6	1,0	1,2
Portugal	1,6	1,4	1,7
San Marino	0,5	1,0	1,2
Singapore	1,9	2,0	2,3
Slovakia	3,8	3,3	3,3
Slovenia	2,3	2,5	2,5
Spain	3,2	3,2	2,6
Sweden	4,1	3,3	2,7
Switzerland	0,8	1,3	1,4
Taiwan	0,7	1,4	1,7
Great Britain	2,2	1,8	2,1
USA	2,6	1,6	2,3

Source: *IMF. World Economic Outlook Database, April 2017, www.imf.org*

Economic growth is largely related to the level of savings and investment.

In 2016, in the global economy, savings reached a record level of 26% of GDP. In 2017, their slight decrease to 25.8% of GDP is forecasted. The main contribution to the high level of global savings is made by developing Asian countries.

In developing and transition economies, the level of savings in 2016 was 32% of GDP, while in 2017 it is estimated at 31.7% of GDP. The highest values of this indicator in 2016 were recorded in developing Asian economies (41.1% of GDP).

The level of savings in developed countries in 2016 amounted to 22.3% of GDP. In 2017, savings will drop to 21.8% of GDP.

In the Post-Soviet countries, the savings rate in 2016 was 26.2% of GDP, and in 2017 it is expected to decline to 24.9% of GDP. At the same time, the value of this indicator is highly differentiated by countries of the region. In 2016, it was 14.6% of GDP in Tajikistan, 17.9% of GDP in Ukraine, 20.8% of GDP in Kyrgyzstan, 18.3% of GDP in Armenia, 19.4% of GDP in Georgia, 27,4% of GDP in Russia, 21.4% of GDP in Azerbaijan, 22.1% of GDP in Kazakhstan and 25% of GDP in Belarus.

In countries of Latin America, savings in 2016 amounted to 17.3% of GDP, while in 2017 they will decline to 17.2%. In Eastern European countries with transitional economies, this indicator in 2016 amounted to 22.7% of GDP, and in 2017 it is projected at 22.1%. In the countries of the Middle East and North Africa, savings reached 24.1% in 2016, and in 2017 they are expected to increase to 26.5%.

Despite unsustainable economic growth, investments in the world economy in 2016 reached a very high level of 25.2% of GDP, and in 2017 they will grow to 25.4% of GDP (mainly due to developing Asian economies).

In developing countries and countries with economies in transition, investments in 2016 reached 32.2% of GDP and in 2017 they are projected at 32% of GDP. At the same time, the leaders in terms of investment are still "Asian tigers": 39.8% of GDP in 2016 and 2017.

Investment activity in developed countries in 2016 slightly decreased and equaled 20.8% of GDP (in 2015 - 21.1% of GDP). In 2017, it is expected that it will rise slightly to 21.1%. In the euro zone, the investment level in 2016 was 19.9% of GDP, and in 2017 it is estimated at 20% of GDP.

In the Post-Soviet space, the level of investment in 2016 amounted to 25.9% of GDP, which is higher than in 2015 (23.3% of GDP). In 2017, investment is projected to decline to 23.1%. At the same time, the level of investment (as well as savings) varies greatly across countries. In 2016 this indicator was 19.7% of GDP in Tajikistan, 21.5% of GDP in Ukraine, 31.8% of GDP in Georgia, 21.2% of GDP in Armenia, 25.1% of GDP in Azerbaijan, 25.6% of GDP in Russia, 28.2% of GDP in Kazakhstan and 29.3% of GDP in Belarus.

Some improvement in recent years in the economic situation of most developed countries has led to a decrease in the unemployment level (Tab.15). In 2016, this indicator in developed countries equaled 6.2% (for comparison: in 2012 it was at 8%, and in 2013 - 7.9%). In 2017, according to the IMF forecasts, unemployment in this group of countries will drop to 6%.

At the same time, high unemployment remains in the euro zone: in 2015 it was 10.9%, while in 2016, 10%. In 2017, its reduction to 9.4% is projected. This group of countries still urgently needs systemic measures on the part of the state to revitalize the labor market. The growth of public and private investments, for example, in infrastructure and programs for professional retraining can have a certain positive effect.

The employment situation in the group of developed states is highly differentiated by country. In the USA, unemployment has been steadily declining in recent years: in 2014 it was 6.2%, in 2015 - 5.3%, while in 2016 - 4.9%. In 2017, it is expected to be 4.7%. This figure in Great Britain in 2016 was 4.9 %, in Japan - 3.1%, in Canada - 7%, in Germany - 4.2%, in France - 10%, in Italy - 11.7%, in Spain - 19.6%, in Portugal - 11.1% and in Greece - 23.8%.

Despite the economic recovery that has begun, the unemployment rate, the most important indicator of the economic state, is forecasted by international financial organizations to be still at a high level in a number of developed countries in the coming years. Consequently, the growth potential is insufficient for a radical change in the socio-economic situation for the better, which once again speaks of the need for deep structural and institutional reforms designed to provide a new qualitative level of economic growth.

Table 15

Unemployment rate in developed countries, in%

	2015	2016	2017
All developed countries	6,7	6,2	6,0
Euro zone countries	10,9	10,0	9,4
Australia	6,1	5,7	5,2
Austria	5,8	6,1	5,9
Belgium	8,5	8,0	7,8
Canada	6,9	7,0	6,9
Cyprus	14,9	12,9	11,3
Czech Republic	5,1	4,0	3,8
Denmark	6,2	6,2	5,8
Estonia	6,1	6,9	8,3
Finland	9,4	8,8	8,5
France	10,4	10,0	9,6
Germany	4,6	4,2	4,2
Greece	24,9	23,8	21,9
Hong Kong	3,3	3,3	3,2
Iceland	4,0	3,0	3,0
Ireland	9,4	7,9	6,5
Israel	5,3	4,8	4,8
Italy	11,9	11,7	11,4
Japan	3,4	3,1	3,1
Korea	3,6	3,7	3,8
Luxembourg	6,8	6,4	5,9
Malta	5,4	4,8	4,7
Netherlands	6,9	5,8	5,4
New Zealand	5,4	5,1	5,0
Norway	4,4	4,8	4,5

Portugal	12,4	11,1	10,6
San Marino	9,2	8,6	8,0
Singapore	1,9	2,1	2,1
Slovakia	11,5	9,7	7,9
Slovenia	9,0	7,9	7,0
Spain	22,1	19,6	17,8
Sweden	7,4	7,0	6,7
Switzerland	3,2	3,3	3,0
Taiwan	3,8	3,9	4,0
Great Britain	5,4	4,9	4,9
USA	5,3	4,9	4,7

Source: *IMF. World Economic Outlook Database, April 2017. – www.imf.org*

Economic growth in developing countries and countries with economies in transition also varies (Tab.16).

In developing countries and countries with economies in transition, in 2016 economic growth was 4.1%, which was significantly lower than in the pre-crisis decade (5.4%). In 2017 the IMF predicts a slight acceleration of economic development of this group of countries (up to 4.5%). At the same time, we must note a sharp differentiation in the rates of economic growth in this group of countries.

Thus, in developing Asian economies, GDP growth in 2016 was 6.4%, which is lower than in 2015 (6.7%). The IMF predicts that in 2017 the GDP growth rates of these countries will be the same as in 2016. In China, GDP in 2014 grew by 7.3%, while in 2015, its growth slowed down to 6.8%. In India, in 2014, GDP growth rate reached 7.3% and remained at that level in 2016. For this group of countries, the task of stimulating domestic demand while preserving macroeconomic stability is still important.

In Latin America in 2016, there was a decline in production (negative 1%). However, in 2017, the IMF expects a 1.1-fold growth in production in this region. The fastest GDP growth is expected in Bolivia (4.1%), Panama (6%), and the Dominican Republic (5.5%). The economic decline is projected in Venezuela (negative 10%), Brazil (negative 3%), and Ecuador (negative 0.6%).

GDP growth will equal 0.4% in Argentina, while in Mexico and Chile will equal 2.3%.

Economic growth in countries of the Post-Soviet space in 2016 was only 0.4% (after a decline in production by 2.2% in 2015). In 2017, the IMF forecasts growth in the economy of this group of countries by 1.7%. In Russia in 2015, the decline in production totaled 2.8%, while in 2016 - 0.3%. In 2017, the IMF forecasts growth of the Russian economy by 1.4%. The economic decline in 2016 was also recorded in Azerbaijan (negative 3.8%) and Belarus (negative 3%).The leaders of economic growth among the Post-Soviet states in 2016 were Turkmenistan (6.2%), Uzbekistan (7.8%), Tajikistan (6.9%), and Moldova (4%).

In the Eastern European countries with economies in transition, the GDP growth in 2016 was 3%. And the growth is projected at the same level for 2017. In the countries of Middle East and North Africa, economic growth in 2016 was 3.9%, and in 2017 it is expected to slow down to 2.6%. The rate of economic growth in Sub-Saharan Africa in 2016 was small (1.4%). In 2017, their acceleration is predicted to reach 2.6%.

Table 16

**GDP dynamics of a number of developing countries
and countries with economies in transition (%)**

	2015	2016	2017
Countries of Central and Eastern Europe	**4,7**	**3,0**	**3,0**
Bulgaria	3,6	3,4	2,9
Hungary	3,1	2,0	2,9
Poland	3,9	2,8	3,4
Romania	3,9	4,8	4,2
Turkey	6,1	2,9	2,5
Post-Soviet Countries	**-2,2**	**0,4**	**1,7**
Azerbaijan	1,1	-3,8	-1,0
Armenia	3,0	0,2	2,9

Belarus	-3,8	-3,0	-0,8
Georgia	2,9	2,7	3,5
Kazakhstan	1,2	1,1	2,6
Kyrgyzstan	3,5	3,8	3,5
Moldova	-0,4	4,0	4,5
Russia	-2,8	-0,3	1,4
Tajikistan	6,0	6,9	4,5
Turkmenistan	6,5	6,2	6,5
Uzbekistan	8,0	7,8	6,0
Ukraine	-9,8	2,3	2,0
Developing Countries of Asia	**6,7**	**6,4**	**6,4**
India	7,9	6,8	7,2
Indonesia	4,9	5,0	5,1
China	6,9	6,7	6,6
Malaysia	5,0	4,2	4,5
Thailand	2,9	3,2	3,0
Countries of Latin America	**0,1**	**-1,0**	**1,1**
Argentina	2,7	-2,3	2,2
Brazil	-3,8	-3,6	0,2
Mexico	2,6	2,3	1,7
Chile	2,3	1,6	1,7
Countries of Middle East and North Africa	**2,7**	**3,9**	**2,6**
Egypt	4,4	4,3	3,5
Iran	-1,6	6,5	3,3
Pakistan	4,0	4,7	5,0
Saudi Arabia	4,1	1,4	0,4
African Countries	**3,4**	**1,4**	**2,6**
Republic of South Africa	1,3	0,3	0,8

Source: *IMF. World Economic Outlook Database, April 2017, www.imf.org*

In developing countries and countries with economies in transition, the employment situation is also very different.

In developing countries in Asia, the unemployment rate remains relatively low. So, in China it has for some years been about 4%. In 2016, this figure was 5.6% in Indonesia, 3.5% in Malaysia and 0.8% in Thailand.

In the Post-Soviet space, the employment situation varies widely by country. In 2016, a high level of unemployment was recorded in Armenia (18.8%) and Ukraine (8.8%). Traditionally, this indicator is very low in Belarus (1%). In Russia in 2016, unemployment was 5.5%. In Latin America, there is also a marked differentiation of this indicator. So in 2016 this figure was 8.5% in Argentina, 11.3% in Brazil, 4.3% in Mexico and 6.5% in Chile.

Table 17

The unemployment rate in developing countries and countries with economies in transition,%

	2015	2016	2017
Countries of Central and Eastern Europe			
Bulgaria	9,2	7,7	7,1
Hungary	6,9	4,9	4,4
Poland	7,5	6,1	5,6
Romania	6,8	6,0	5,4
Turkey	10,3	10,8	11,5
Post-Soviet Countries			
Azerbaijan	6,1	6,1	6,1
Armenia	18,5	18,8	18,9
Belarus	0,9	1,0	1,0
Georgia	12	n/a	n/a
Kazakhstan	5,0	5,0	5,0
Kyrgyzstan	7,6	7,5	7,4
Moldova	4,9	4,2	4,3
Russia	5,6	5,5	5,5
Tajikistan	n/a	n/a	n/a
Turkmenistan	n/a	n/a	n/a
Uzbekistan	n/a	n/a	n/a

Ukraine	9,1	8,8	9,1
Developing Countries of Asia			
India	n/a	n/a	n/a
Indonesia	6,2	5,6	5,4
China	4,1	4,0	4,0
Malaysia	3,1	3,5	3,4
Thailand	0,9	0,8	0,7
Countries of Latin America			
Argentina	n/a	8,5	7,4
Brazil	8,3	11,3	12,2
Mexico	4,4	4,3	4,4
Chile	6,2	6,5	7,0
Countries of Middle East and North Africa			
Egypt	12,9	12,7	12,6
Iran	11,0	12,5	12,5
Pakistan	5,9	6,0	6,0
Saudi Arabia	5,6	5,7	n/a
African Countries			
Republic of South Africa	25,4	26,7	27,4

Source: *IMF. World Economic Outlook Database, April 2017, www.imf.or*

4.2. Monetary Factors of Development and Balance of Payments

Monetary and price factors play a significant role in the economy and their stability is very important for sustainable growth. This postulate is reflected in many economic studies, and, most importantly, this is convincingly confirmed by practice. In recent years, as a result of anti-crisis measures and actions to support the economy, for example, quantitative easing programs, the money supply has significantly increased. Such measures could not but affect the growth of the money supply. For example, in the United States in 2013, the aggregate of the M1 money supply increased by 8.9%, and in 2014 - by 9.7%, in 2015 - by 6%, in 2016 - by 7.9%. The M2 aggregate increased by 5.5% in 2013, and by 5.9% in 2014, by 5.9% in 2015 and by 7.1% in 2016[127].

Noticeable growth in the money supply was also observed in developing countries. In 2011, the broad aggregate of money supply in developing countries increased by 16.4%, in 2012 - by 14.3%, in 2013 - by 14.1%, in 2014 - by 12.2%, in 2015 - by 12.6% and in 2016 - by 11.6%[128].

Despite the relatively high growth rates of the money supply, prices in most countries (primarily in developed ones) have not yet reacted with a noticeable increase. Apparently, the liquidity that enters the economy through credit institutions is largely channeled to the financial markets and thus influences the growth of prices of exchange-traded assets. In particular, liquidity does not flow to the real sector of the economy and to consumers, so its impact on consumer prices is not significant. At the same time, many economists note that the influence of the quantitative easing policy on macroeconomic stability is not fully understood, therefore uncertainty remains in this issue.

Table 18

Dynamics of prices in developed countries, as a percentage of annual growth

	2015	2016	2017
All developed countries	**0,3**	**0,8**	**2,0**
Euro zone countries	**0,0**	**0,2**	**1,7**
Australia	1,5	1,3	2,0
Austria	0,8	1,0	2,1
Belgium	0,6	1,8	2,0
Canada	1,1	1,4	2,0
Cyprus	-1,5	-1,2	1,5
Czech Republic	0,3	0,7	2,3
Denmark	0,5	0,3	0,6

---

[127] Board of Governors of the Federal Reserve System. Economic Research and Data. Money Stock Measures, www.federalreserve.gov
[128] IMF, World Economic Outlook Database, April 2017, www.imf.org

Estonia	0,1	0,8	3,2
Finland	-0,2	0,4	1,4
France	0,1	0,3	1,4
Germany	0,1	0,4	2,0
Greece	-1,1	0,0	1,3
Hong Kong	3,0	2,6	2,6
Iceland	1,6	1,7	2,2
Ireland	0,0	-0,2	0,9
Israel	-0,6	-0,5	0,7
Italy	0,1	-0,1	1,3
Japan	0,8	-0,1	1,0
Korea	0,7	1,0	1,8
Luxembourg	0,1	0,1	1,4
Malta	1,2	0,9	1,5
Netherlands	0,2	0,1	0,9
New Zealand	0,3	0,6	1,5
Norway	2,2	3,6	2,6
Portugal	0,5	0,6	1,2
San Marino	0,1	0,6	0,7
Singapore	-0,5	-0,5	1,1
Slovakia	-0,3	-0,5	1,2
Slovenia	-0,5	-0,1	1,5
Spain	-0,5	-0,2	2,4
Sweden	0,7	1,1	1,4
Switzerland	-1,1	-0,4	0,4
Taiwan	-0,3	1,4	1,4
Great Britain	0,1	0,6	2,5
USA	0,1	1,3	2,7

Source: *IMF. World Economic Outlook Database, April 2017, www.imf.org*

In developed countries in 2015-2016, there was a clear slowdown in inflation. In 1999-2008, it was at average 2.2%, in 2013-2014 - 1.4%, while in 2015 and 2016 only 0.3% and 0.8% respectively. Even more pronounced was the inflation slowdown in the euro zone countries: in 2015-2016 the prices practically did not grow. Such a sharp slowdown in the rate of price growth could have a deterrent effect on the pace of economic growth. At the same time, in 2017, the IMF predicts an acceleration in the rate of price growth in developed countries to 2%, including in the euro area - up to 1.7%. In developing countries in recent years, inflation processes have also slowed, but not as much as in developed countries. So, if in 1999-2008 years, in developing countries, prices grew by an average of 7.5% per year, in 2013 they increased by 5.5%, in 2014-2015 only by 4.7%, and in 2016 by 4.4%. In 2017, they are expected to grow by 4.7%. In the US in 2016, inflation was 1.3% (in 2015 -0.1%). In 2017, its acceleration is predicted to reach 2.7%. In the UK in 2016, prices rose by 0.6% (after almost zero growth in 2015). However, in 2017, they are expected to increase by 2.5%.

In Japan, in 2016, there was a slight deflation (minus 0.1%). In 2017, according to the IMF forecast, the price increase in Japan will be 1%. In 2016, the price increase in Germany was 0.4%, while in France - 0.3%. In Italy, deflation was noticed (minus 0.1%). Thus, despite a large-scale policy of quantitative easing, in many developed countries (Japan, Italy, Spain, Ireland, Slovakia, Slovenia, Cyprus, Switzerland, Singapore and Israel) deflation was observed in 2016, which had a negative impact on the economic development. In developing Asian countries, inflation in 2016 slowed to 2.9%, and in 2017 it is expected to be slightly accelerated to 3.3%. Price growth in 2016 reached 2% in China, 4.9% in India, and 3.5% in Indonesia.

In Latin America in 2016, overall inflation was at a relatively low level (with the exception of Venezuela, where it reached 255%). In 2016, in Brazil, it was 8.7%, in Mexico 2.8% and in Chile 3.8%. In countries of the Post-Soviet space in 2016, inflation slowed to 8.3% (in 2015 it was 15.5%). In 2017, the price increase in this region will see a further slowdown in price growth to 5.7%. In 2016, the greatest increase in prices in this group of countries was recorded in Ukraine (13.9%), Kazakhstan (14.6%), Belarus (11.8%) and Azerbaijan (12.4%).

In the Eastern European countries with transition economies in 2016, inflation was 3.2%, and in 2017 it is expected to accelerate to 5.7%.

In the countries of the Middle East and North Africa, inflation in 2016 was 5.1%, and in 2017 it will accelerate to 7.6%. In Sub-Saharan Africa, this indicator in 2016 was at the level of 11.4%, and in 2017 it will reach 10.7%.

Table 19

Price dynamics in developing countries and countries with economies in transition, in% of annual growth

	2015	2016	2017
Countries of Central and Eastern Europe	**3,2**	**3,2**	**5,7**
Bulgaria	-1,1	-1,3	1,0
Hungary	-0,1	0,4	2,5
Poland	-0,9	-0,6	2,3
Romania	-0,6	-1,6	1,3
Turkey	7,7	7,8	10,1
Post-Soviet Countries	**15,5**	**8,3**	**5,7**
Azerbaijan	4,0	12,4	10
Armenia	3,7	-1,4	2,0
Belarus	13,5	11,8	9,3
Georgia	4,0	2,1	5,7
Kazakhstan	6,7	14,6	8,0
Kyrgyzstan	6,5	0,4	3,6
Moldova	9,6	6,4	5,5
Russia	15,5	7,0	4,5
Tajikistan	5,8	5,9	5,8
Turkmenistan	7,4	3,5	6,0
Uzbekistan	8,5	8,0	8,6
Ukraine	48,7	13,9	11,5
Developing Countries of Asia	**2,7**	**2,9**	**3,3**
India	4,9	4,9	4,8
Indonesia	6,4	3,5	4,5
China	1,4	2,0	2,4
Malaysia	2,1	2,1	2,7
Thailand	-0,9	0,2	1,4
Countries of Latin America	**5,5**	**5,6**	**4,2**
Argentina	n/a	n/a	25,6
Brazil	9,0	8,7	4,4

Mexico	2,7	2,8	4,8
Chile	4,3	3,8	2,8
Countries of Middle East and North Africa	**5,7**	**5,1**	**7,6**
Egypt	11,0	10,2	22,0
Iran	11,9	8,9	11,2
Pakistan	4,5	2,9	4,3
Saudi Arabia	2,2	3,5	3,8
African Countries	**7,0**	**11,4**	**10,7**
Republic of South Africa	4,6	6,3	6,2

Source: *IMF. World Economic Outlook Database, April 2017. –*

www.imf.or

The world trade growth rate in 2016 amounted to 2.2%, which has been one of the lowest indicators in recent decades. In 2017, according to the IMF forecast, the volume of world trade will grow by 3.8%. In 2017, world prices in US dollars are expected to increase for most commodity groups, in particular, for manufacturing products - by 2.8%, oil - 28.9%, food - 3%, metals - 23.2%, agricultural raw materials - 7%. Imports to developed countries will grow by 4% in 2017 (in 2016 it increased by 2.4%), in developing countries - by 4.5% (in 2016 it increased by 1.9%). Exports from developed countries will increase by 3.5% in 2017 (an increase by 2.1% in 2016), from developing countries - by 3.6% (in 2016, by 2.5%). In general, the growth rates of exports and imports both from developed countries and from developing countries still lag far behind those in the pre-crisis decade.

In 2017, as in the previous 5 years, a small surplus of the current account balance of developed countries (0.7% of GDP) is predicted, which indicates that this group of states managed to get rid of the chronic balance of payments deficit. In general, the structure of the global trade and payment balance is experiencing positive changes related to the equalization of trade imbalances. At the same time, the euro zone countries in 2017 will have a balance of payments surplus at 3% of GDP. At the same time, the US will maintain the traditional chronic current account deficit, which in 2017 will be 2.7% of GDP. Germany will have a significant positive balance in 2017 (8.2%

of GDP), as well as Switzerland (10.8% of GDP), the Netherlands (9.2% of GDP), Slovenia (5.5% of GDP), the Republic of Korea (6, 2% of GDP), Luxembourg (5.1% of GDP), Norway (5.7% of GDP), Denmark (7.5% of GDP), Sweden (4.6% of GDP), Taiwan (14.8% of GDP) and Singapore (20.1% of GDP). At the same time, the chronic deficit of the current account balance is preserved in such countries as the USA, Great Britain, Australia, New Zealand, Canada, Latvia and Lithuania.

In emerging Asian economies, the traditional surplus of the current account balance in 2017 will be at the level of 0.8% of GDP (in 2016 - 1.3% of GDP). China in 2017 will have a surplus of 1.3% of GDP and Malaysia - 1.8% of GDP. At the same time, India will still have a current account deficit, which is estimated at 1.5% of GDP.

Countries in the Post-Soviet space, overall, in 2017 will have a surplus of the current account balance (1.6%). In Russia, the surplus will be 3.3% of GDP (in 2016 - 1.7% of GDP). However, most Post-Soviet states in 2017 will have a negative current account balance, in particular, Armenia - 3.2% of GDP, Belarus - 4.7% of GDP, Georgia - 12.9% of GDP, Kyrgyzstan - 12% of GDP, 3.8% of GDP, Ukraine - 3.6% of GDP, Tajikistan - 5.5% of GDP and Turkmenistan - 12.8% of GDP.

Eastern European countries with economies in transition in 2017 will traditionally have a current account deficit in the balance of payments (2.8% of GDP). The countries of Latin America will not be able to overcome the current account deficit in 2017 (as in other years after the global crisis), which will reach 2.1% of GDP. In the Middle East and North Africa, the current account deficit of 1.1% of GDP is also projected. After the global crisis, the countries of Sub-Saharan Africa also had a negative current account balance (in 2017 it will reach 3.8% of GDP).

4.3. State of Public Finances

The global crisis had an extremely negative impact on the public finances virtually of all countries: decrease in government revenues and other payments to the budget, an avalanche-like growth of spending and budget deficits at all levels, primarily in the state budget (largely as a result of anti-crisis measures) and a rapid increase in public debt. Such a sharp deterioration in the state of public finances has led investors to view the purchase of government securities as a risky investment, which in turn caused an increase in yield (in some cases, a critical one) on these government obligations. Governments had to undertake fiscal consolidation measures, which had a noticeable effect. However, the need for state support of the economy is still on the agenda, and therefore there is a fairly sharp conflict between the forced reduction in public spending and the need for further support for the economy. In part, this problem is being addressed through large-scale quantitative easing programs implemented through central banks, but there are certainly economic limitations of using these resources.

In developed countries, public expenditure increased from 37.7% of GDP in 2005 to 43.5% of GDP in 2009. The fiscal consolidation policy allowed to reduce the public spending to 38.8% of GDP in 2015. In 2016, they amounted to 38.7% of GDP. According to the IMF forecasts, in 2017 they will drop to 38.3% of GDP[129].

Government revenues of developed countries during the crisis declined from 36.5% of GDP in 2007 to 34.7% of GDP in 2010, however in post-crisis years they increased slightly and amounted to 36.2% of GDP in 2015. At the same time, in 2016, budget revenues fell again to 35.8% of GDP. It is expected that in 2017 revenues will amount to 35.6% of GDP.

Developed countries traditionally have a deficit of the state budget, but prior to the 2007 crisis it was at a low level. During the crisis, the deficit sharply increased and reached 8.7% of GDP in 2009. By 2015, it was reduced to 2.6% of GDP. In 2016, this indicator again rose to 2.9% of GDP. According to the IMF forecast, in 2017 the deficit of the state budget of developed countries will be at the level of 2.7% of GDP.

Despite a slight reduction in the state budget deficit, developed countries have not succeeded in reducing public debt in recent years, which has grown significantly during the global crisis.

In 2016, the public debt of developed countries reached 106.5% of GDP. According to the IMF, in 2017 this figure will be 105.9% of GDP. This size

---

[129]   IMF, World Economic Outlook Database, April 2017, www.imf.org

is a serious problem for developed countries, as it distracts from the budget significant funds for debt servicing, constrains the ability to support the economy and social sphere, undermines investor confidence in the government securities market.

At the same time, the situation with the state of public finances in developed countries differs greatly (Table 20).

Table 20

Dynamics of the state budget and public debt balance of developed countries,% of GDP

	Balance of state budget			Public debt		
	2015	2016	2017	2015	2016	2017
All developed countries	**-2,6**	**-2,9**	**-2,7**	**104,4**	**106,5**	**105,9**
Euro zone countries	**-2,1**	**-1,7**	**-1,5**	**92,6**	**91,4**	**90,1**
Australia	-2,7	-2,7	-2,2	37,6	41,1	42,9
Austria	-1,0	-1,4	-1,1	85,5	83,9	81,2
Belgium	-2,5	-2,7	-2,1	105,8	105,5	104,3
Canada	-1,1	-2,0	-2,4	91,6	92,3	91,2
Cyprus	-1,5	-0,3	-0,3	107,5	108,0	109,3
Czech Republic	-0,6	0,2	-0,2	40,3	37,7	36,0
Denmark	-1,3	-1,0	-1,2	39,6	39,9	39,8
Estonia	0,1	0,3	0,3	10,1	9,5	9,0
Finland	-2,7	-1,9	-2,1	63,7	63,6	64,4
France	-3,5	-3,3	-3,2	96,2	96,7	97,4
Germany	0,7	0,8	0,6	71,2	67,7	64,7
Greece	-3,4	0,0	-1,5	179,4	181,3	180,7
Hong Kong	0,6	4,8	1,6	0,1	0,1	0,1
Iceland	-0,8	11,3	0,6	68,1	53,2	45,9
Ireland	-1,9	-0,9	-0,5	78,7	76,4	74,8
Israel	-2,7	-2,5	-3,3	64,1	62,2	62,5
Italy	-2,7	-2,4	-2,4	132,0	132,6	132,8
Japan	-3,5	-4,2	-4,0	238,0	239,2	239,2
Korea	0,3	0,3	0,8	37,8	38,6	38,6

Luxembourg	1,6	1,7	0,3	22,1	22,6	23,2
Malta	-1,4	-0,7	-0,6	60,6	59,4	58,0
Netherlands	-2,0	-0,5	0,0	65,1	62,6	59,7
New Zealand	0,6	0,6	0,6	29,6	29,5	27,5
Norway	5,7	2,9	3,6	33,2	33,2	33,2
Portugal	-4,4	-2,3	-1,9	129,0	130,3	128,6
San Marino	-0,3	-0,6	-1,1	19,7	21,6	21,8
Singapore	3,7	3,3	1,7	103,2	112,0	112,0
Slovakia	-2,7	-2,0	-1,8	52,5	52,3	51,9
Slovenia	-3,3	-1,8	-1,5	83,2	78,9	77,7
Spain	-5,1	-4,6	-3,3	99,8	99,3	98,6
Sweden	0,2	-0,2	-0,3	42,9	41,7	40,4
Switzerland	0,1	-0,1	-0,1	45,8	45,4	44,5
Taiwan	-1,8	-1,7	-1,3	36,3	35,4	33,7
Great Britain	-4,4	-3,1	-2,8	89,0	89,2	89,0
USA	-3,5	-4,4	-4,1	105,6	107,4	108,3

Source: *IMF. World Economic Outlook Database, April 2017, www.imf.org*

The budget deficit of the world's largest economy - the USA - in 2016 was 4.4% of GDP, and in 2017, according to the IMF forecasts, it will drop to 4.1% of GDP.

It was possible to achieve improvement in this indicator also in Great Britain in 2016 - up to 3.1% of GDP. The budget deficit of Japan in 2016 amounted to 4.2% of GDP. In Canada, there was an increase in the budget deficit (up to 2.4% of GDP in 2017). In many countries of the euro zone there is a certain improvement in the balance of the state budget. In 2016, the budget deficit in France amounted to 3.3% of GDP, in Italy to 2.4% of GDP, in Spain to - 4.6% of GDP, in Netherlands to 0.5% of GDP and in Portugal to 2.3% of GDP. Germany had a surplus of 0.8% of GDP. The positive balance of the state budget in 2016 was also observed in the Republic of Korea, Hong Kong, Estonia, Czech Republic, Iceland, Luxembourg, Norway and Singapore.

Despite some improvement in the state budget, in most developed countries in 2016 the public debt continued to grow. In the US in 2016, public debt reached 107.4% of GDP, in Britain - 89.2% of GDP, in Japan - 239.2% of

GDP, in France - 96.7% of GDP, in Italy - 132.6% of GDP and in Spain - 99.3% of GDP. At the same time, in a number of developed countries in 2016 there was a decrease in the size of the public debt: in Germany - to 67.7% of GDP, in the Czech Republic - to 37.7% of GDP, in Estonia - to 9.5% of GDP, in Iceland - to 53.2% of GD and in Slovenia - to 78.9% of GDP.

Table 21

Dynamics of the state budget and public debt balance of developing countries and states with economies in transition, as% of GDP

	Balance of state budget			Public debt		
	2013	2014	2015	2013	2014	2015
Countries of Central and Eastern Europe	**-2.5**	**-2,3**	**-1,9**	**46,5**	**44,9**	**44,6**
Bulgaria	-1,8	-3,7	-2,0	17,6	26,9	28,6
Hungary	-2,5	-2,6	-2,7	77,4	77,0	75,3
Poland	-4,0	-3,2	-2,8	55,7	50,1	51,1
Romania	-2,5	-1,9	-1,8	38,8	40,6	40,9
Turkey	-1,3	-1,0	-0,8	36,1	33,6	32,1
Post-Soviet Countries	**-0,8**	**-0,9**	**-4,9**	**16,6**	**21,1**	**24,8**
Azerbaijan	1,4	-0,4	--7,9	13,8	15,9	20,6
Armenia	-1,6	-1,9	-4,1	38,0	41,3	46,1
Belarus	-0,9	0,2	-2,4	38,1	40,5	40,4
Georgia	-1,2	-1,8	-1,4	32,2	34,8	45,4
Kazakhstan	5,1	1,8	-3,2	12,9	14,9	18,3
Kyrgyzstan	-3,7	0,1	-2,5	46,1	53,0	60,0
Moldova	-1,8	-1,7	-3,9	23,8	31,5	44,8
Russia	-1,3	-1,2	-5,7	14,0	17,8	20,4
Tajikistan	-0,8	0,0	-1,9	29,2	28,3	32,9
Turkmenistan	1,3	0,8	-0,9	21,1	16,8	18,7
Uzbekistan	2,4	2,2	0,1	8,3	8,5	11,6
Ukraine	-4,8	-4,5	-4,2	40,7	71,2	94,4
Developing Countries of Asia	**-2,2**	**-2,1**	**-2,8**	**42,7**	**44,1**	**45,6**

India	-7,6	-7,0	-7,2	65,8	66,1	65,3
Indonesia	-2,0	-2,1	-2,3	24,9	25,0	26,6
China	-1,1	-1,2	-1,9	39,4	41,1	43,2
Malaysia	-4,3	-3,6	-3,5	55,9	55,2	55,6
Thailand	0,4	-0,9	-1,2	42,2	43,5	43,5
Countries of Latin America	**-3,1**	**-4,9**	**-5,8**	**48,7**	**51,9**	**54,8**
Argentina	-2,0	-2,7	-4,9	40,2	45,3	52,1
Brazil	-3,1	-6,2	-7,7	62,2	65,2	69,9
Mexico	-3,7	-4,6	-4,0	46,4	49,8	52,0
Chile	-0,5	-1,5	-3,3	12,8	15,1	18,1
Countries of Middle East and North Africa	**2,6**	**-1,5**	**-10,5**	**29,2**	**30,6**	**377**
Egypt	-14,1	-13,6	-11,7	89,0	90,5	90,0
Iran	-0,9	-1,1	-2,9	15,4	15,8	16,4
Pakistan	-8,4	-4,9	-5,3	64.8	64.9	64,7
Saudi Arabia	5,8	-3,4	-21,6	2,2	1,6	6,8
African Countries	**-3,1**	**-3,5**	**-4,2**	**28,5**	**30,3**	**34,3**
Republic of South Africa	-4,1	-3,8	-4,1	43,3	46,0	48,4

Source: *IMF. World Economic Outlook Database, April 2017, www.imf.org*

Most developing countries in Asia in 2016 had a deficit of the state budget, including China (1.2% of GDP), India (7% of GDP), Indonesia (2.1% of GDP) and Malaysia (3.6% of GDP). In China, the public debt is growing: in 2015, it was 39.4% of GDP, in 2016 it grew to 41.1% of GDP, and in 2017 it will reach 43.2%.

In countries of the Post-Soviet space in recent years, deterioration in the state of public finances has been identified. In most states, the imbalance in the state budget was noted. In Russia, the budget deficit in 2016 amounted to 3.7% of GDP, while in 2015 it increased to 5.7% of GDP. However, next year it is expected to decline to 3.9% of GDP. The negative balance of the budget reached 3.7% of GDP in Russia in 2016, in Armenia - 5.6% of GDP, in Azerbaijan - 1.4% of GDP, in Belarus - 4.6% of GDP, in Georgia - 1.6% of GDP, in Kazakhstan - 4.4% of GDP, in Kyrgyzstan - 4.6% of GDP, in Moldova - 2.1% of GDP, in Tajikistan - 4.4% of GDP, in Turkmenistan - 1.3%

of GDP and in Ukraine - 2.2% of GDP. Growth in public debt was noted practically in all countries. So, in 2016, in Armenia this indicator amounted to 51.8% of GDP, in Belarus to 52.3% of GDP, in Kyrgyzstan to 58.5% of GDP and in Ukraine to 81.3% of GDP. Deterioration in public finances is observed in Latin America. Thus, the state budget deficit of Argentina in 2016 reached 2.7% of GDP, while the public debt - 45.3% of GDP. In Brazil these indicators accounted for 6.2% of GDP and 65.2% of GDP, while in Mexico - 4.6% of GDP and 49.8% of GDP, respectively.

The budget deficit is also observed in many countries of the Near and Middle East and North Africa, and in a number of countries it is quite large. The imbalance in public finances is also characteristic to most countries of Sub-Saharan Africa.

4.4. Banking sector of the world economy: success and problems

The banking sector, which received huge financial assistance from the state during the crisis, generally demonstrates good development indicators. Banks play a very important role in ensuring economic growth, primarily through the smooth execution of settlements and payments, accumulation of savings, continuous lending to all sectors of the economy and implementation of long-term investments. Therefore, the relatively good state of the banking sector in most developed and developing countries, creates certain prerequisites for the resumption of economic growth.

Indeed, most developed countries have sufficiently high capital adequacy ratios for the banking sector as a whole, especially Denmark, Estonia, Finland, Luxembourg, the Netherlands, Sweden, Switzerland and the UK (Tab.22). However, this figure was significantly lower in most developed countries. A good state of capital adequacy in these countries is associated with significant efforts of monetary authorities to increase the capitalization of banking systems during the crisis, as well as to reduce the magnitude of bank risks. In general, "active measures to strengthen the capital base of the banking sector were undertaken not only in developed countries, but also in developing countries with economies in transition. Important sources of growth of own funds were various forms of state participation in the capital of banks: subordinated loans granted by monetary authorities to credit institutions, direct state participation in capital, temporary nationalization of some banks"[130].

However, the situation with the indicator of "bad" loans (the share of non-performing loans) in the developed countries looks worse than with the capital adequacy. This indicator has grown significantly in a number of countries during the crisis years and does not tend to decline noticeably. Very high proportion of "bad" loans is observed in Cyprus, Greece and Italy, which reflects the poor macroeconomic situation in these countries.

Table 22

The most important indicators of the banking sector in developed countries, in%

	Capital Adequacy	Share of "bad" loans	ROA	ROE
Australia (2016 A1)	13,6	1,0	0,8	11,0
Austria (2016 A1)	18,0	2,7	0,5	7,0
Belgium (2016Q3)	18,5	3,5	0,7	10,2
Canada (2016 A1)	14,8	0,6	1,0	19,9
Cyprus (2016 Q1)	16,3	47,0	0,7	7,0
Czech Republic (2016 Q3)	16,0	4,8	1,3	17,4
Denmark (2016 Q3)	19,9	3,3	0,7	11,9
Estonia (2016 A1)	31,8	0,9	1,6	12,8
Finland (2016 Q3)	23,1	n/a	0,5	9,4
France (2016 Q3)	17,2	3,9	0,4	7,5
Germany (2016 A1)	18,8	2,0	0,4	7,5
Greece (2016 A1)	16,9	36,3	0,1	0,8
Hong Kong (2016 A1)	19,2	0,9	1,1	16,0
Israel (2016 A1)	14,7	1,6	1,0	13,9
Italy (2016Q2)	15,0	17,5	0,1	1,4

---

[130] Kovzanadze I., "Post-crisis development of the global banking sector: trends and prospects", «Dengy y credit», M., 2013, № 3 (in Russian language);

Japan (2016Q3)	16,2	1,4	0,3	8,3
Korea (2014 A1)	14,0	0,5	0,5	6,0
Luxembourg (2016 A1)	24,6	0,2	0,8	11,0
Malta (2016 A1)	16,0	5,4	1,2	15,9
Netherlands (2016A1)	22,4	2,5	0,6	10,1
Norway (2016Q1)	19,1	1,2	0,9	9,7
Portugal (2016Q3)	13,5	5,4	0,1	1,2
Singapore (2016 A1)	16,5	1,2	1,1	11,3
Slovakia (2016 A1)	18,0	4,4	1,4	13,0
Slovenia (2016 A1)	19,2	5,1	1,1	8,8
Spain (2016 A1)	14,8	5,6	0,4	5,5
Sweden (2016 A1)	26,8	1,0	1,2	16,0
Switzerland (2016 Q2)	22,4	0,8	0,4	5,5
Great Britain (2016Q3)	20,6	1,1	0,4	5,6
USA (2016 A1)	14,2	1,3	0,4	3,2

Source: *IMF. Data and Statistics. Financial Soundness Indicators, www.imf.org*

Notes to the table:

1. Data are presented at the last reporting date (indicated in parentheses for the country in question).
2. Capital adequacy is calculated as the ratio of regulatory capital to risk-weighted assets.
3. ROA - return on assets.
4. ROE - return on equity.

For development prospects of the world economy, the state of the economy and the banking sector in the US is of great importance, the development tendencies of which have recently instilled some optimism.

In the past three years, the resource base of American banks has been growing steadily. So in 2012, the volume of deposits attracted by US banks with insured deposits increased from USD 9,257 billion to USD 10,012 billion, or by 8.2%, while in 2013 - by 3.7% to USD 10,385 billion, in 2014 - by 5.3%

to USD 10,939 billion and in 2015 by 3.8% to USD 11,350 billion[131]. The loans provided by the US banking sector in 2012 increased from USD 6,719 billion to USD 7.042 billion, or by 4.9%. In 2013, the lending growth rate amounted to 2.9%, and the total amount of loan debt reached USD 7,243 billion. In 2014, loans increased to USD 7,633 billion, or by 5.4%. In 2015, the volume of loan debt reached USD 8,172 billion (an increase of 7%). Thus, in 2015, a record growth in lending in recent years was recorded.

Loans for real estate transactions in 2012 increased by 1.7% (from USD 3,547 billion to USD 3,607 billion). In 2013, such loans even slightly decreased (to USD 3,597 billion). In 2014, loans for real estate transactions increased by 2.8% to USD 3,700 billion. In 2015, there was a record growth in recent years of such lending by 6% to USD 3,921 billion.

Bank loans to industry and trade grew very rapidly, which undoubtedly played a positive role in accelerating economic growth in the United States. So in 2012, these loans increased from USD 1,276 billion to USD 1,438 billion, or by 12.7%. In 2013, this segment of lending grew by another 4.7% (to USD 1,506 billion). In 2014, commercial loans increased to USD 1,651 billion, or by 9.6%. In 2015, they grew to 1,779 billion dollars (an increase of 7.8%).

Crediting of individuals also grew, although at a more modest pace. So in 2012, loans to individuals grew from USD 1,213 billion to USD 1,231 billion, or by 1.5%, and in 2013 by 1.5% (to USD 1,249 billion). In 2014, this segment of lending grew by another 4% - to USD 1,299 billion. In 2015, such loans increased to USD 1,363 billion (an increase of 4.9%).

The capital of the banking sector also grew steadily. In 2012, it increased from USD 1,404 billion to USD 1,489 billion, or by 6.1%, while in 2013 by 2% (to USD 1,519 billion), in 2014 –by another 5.8% % (to USD 1,607 billion). In 2015, the capital rose to USD 1,676 billion dollars, or by 4.3%.

In developing countries, the performance of the banking sector varies considerably across countries and regions, although most countries have a relatively high level of capital adequacy (Table 23). The situation with the level of "bad" loans is much worse, especially in the countries of Eastern and Central

---

[131]   Federal Deposit Insurance Corporation. Bank Data and Statistics, www.fdic.gov.

Europe and the Post-Soviet space. This indicator reflects all macroeconomic and institutional problems inherent in this group of countries, in particular, frequent economic crises, instability of the legal situation, weakness of state and public institutions. At the same time, in most developing countries and countries with economies in transition there are quite high profitability indicators, which show a high profitability of banking operations (the reverse side of high risks).

Table 23

The most important indicators of the banking sector of developing countries and countries with economies in transition, %

	Capital adequacy	Share of "bad" loans"	ROA	ROE
Countries of Central and Eastern Europe				
Bulgaria (2016 A1)	22,2	13,2	1,4	10,4
Hungary (2016 A1)	16,4	7,4	1,7	17,4
Poland (2016A1)	17,2	4,0	0,8	9,0
Romania (2016Q3)	18,8	10,0	1,3	12,3
Turkey (2016 Q3)	16,0	3,2	2,0	17,5
Post-Soviet Countries				
Armenia (2016 A1)	20,0	6,7	1,1	7,0
Belarus (2016 A1)	18,6	12,8	1,6	12,6
Georgia (2017M3)	16,8	3,7	3,8	27,6
Kazakhstan (2016A1)	16,3	6,7	1,9	17,9
Moldova (2016A1)	30,1	16,3	2,1	11,9
Russia (2016A1)	13,1	9,4	1,2	9,8
Tajikistan (2015 Q3)	16,1	19,1	2,6	18,5
Uzbekistan (2016A1)	23,5	0,4	2,0	17,8
Ukraine (2017Q1)	13,7	55,1	0,8	7,8
Developing Countries of Asia				
India (2016 A1)	13,0	9,2	0,4	5,1
Indonesia (2016 A1)	20,6	2,9	3,0	20,7

China (2016 Q2)	13,1	1,7	0,6	7,6
Malaysia (2016 A1)	16,5	1,6	1,3	12,3
Countries of Latin America				
Argentina (2016 A1)	16,7	1,8	5,3	43,4
Brazil (2016 A1)	17,2	3,9	1,1	11,3
Mexico (2017M1)	15,1	2,1	2,6	25,8
Chile (2016 M3)	12,9	1,9	1,1	13,8
Countries of Middle East and North Africa				
Saudi Arabia (2016 A1)	19,5	1,4	1,8	12,6
African Countries				
Republic of South Africa (2017 M1)	15,9	2,9	1,7	22,0

Source: *IMF. Data and Statistics. Financial Soundness Indicators, www.imf.org*

Notes to the table:

1. Data are presented at the last reporting date (indicated in parentheses for the country in question).
2. Capital adequacy is calculated as the ratio of regulatory capital to risk-weighted assets.
3. ROA - return on assets.
4. ROE - return on equity.

4.5. Georgia's Economy and Banking Sector - Trends of Development

Georgia's economic growth rate in 2014 reached 4.6%, in 2015 it was 2.9%, in 2016 - 2.7%[132], while in the first half of 2017 - 4.5 %, which is much higher than the average pace of development in the entire Post-Soviet space in the same period and the IMF forecast (3.5%) for 2017 (1.7% increase is forecasted in the post-Soviet space on the whole).

The volume of industrial production in 2016 amounted to GEL 8,649.9 million, which represents a 1.7% growth for one year. The number of employed

---

[132] National Statistics Office of Georgia. MainStatistics. www.geostat.ge

in the industry by July 1, 2017 reached 117,599 people, which is higher by 4.6% compared to the previous year.

The volume of agricultural production in 2016 exceeded the 2015-year level by 7.5%. The growth in this sector of the economy has been noticed since 2013. At that time, it became possible to reverse the trend formed in the 1990s when agricultural production growth during one year used to be followed by decline the next year. In 2015, the growth rate of agricultural production reached 8.1%.

In 2016 direct foreign investments amounted to USD 1,565.9 million, which in fact repeated the level of the previous year (USD 1,564.5 million; average quarterly indicators of direct foreign investments for the first half of 2017 also almost repeated the average quarterly figures of the previous year (USD 380 million)).

In 2014 Georgia's foreign trade turnover reached its historical maximum of USD 11,463 million (a 4.9% increase over the 2013 indicator). However, in 2015 the trend of sustainable growth in Georgia's foreign trade turned into an opposite one. In 2015 this figure was USD 9,497 million (17% decrease). In 2016 the foreign trade turnover, according to preliminary data, amounted to USD 9,407 million.

If the processes taking place in January-August 2017 are maintained, the volume of Georgia's foreign trade in 2017 may increase by 5.5 percent as compared to 2016 (including exports growth by 19.5 percent and imports growth by 1.5 percent).

It should be noted that there is still an extremely high disproportion between the volume of exports and imports in favor of the latter. The export coverage ratio of imports in 2016 was only 29.0%, and for January-August 2017 - 34.1%. As a result, there is a chronic deficit in the country's trade balance, which reached USD 5,741 million in 2014, USD 5,096 million in 2015 and USD 5,181 million in 2016. For 2017 it is forecasted to decline to USD 4,880 million. In general, the continuing high trade balance deficit remains a serious macroeconomic problem requiring close attention on the part of institutional regulators.

Georgia has managed to keep relatively low inflation rate in recent years: in 2014 the inflation rate made up 3.1%, in 2015 - 4.0%, while in 2016 - 2.1% and for the January-August period of 2017, 4.0%. In 2015 the state budget deficit accounted for 1.1% of GDP, while in 2016 - 1.4% of GDP and according to forecasts it is expected to decline to 0.2% of GDP in 2017. The public debt of Georgia amounted to 41.4% of GDP in 2015 and 44.6% of GDP in 2016. More than ¾ of the national debt of Georgia - external bilateral and multilateral debts, and the interest of their servicing in recent years has 'stabilized' and is about USD 100 million a year. It should be noted that the problem of increasing public debt is typical for most developed and developing countries. In general, Georgia has managed to maintain the level of public debt at a relatively safe level from the point of view of macroeconomic stability and the possibility of repeating the so-called 'Greek scenario'.

The banking sector of Georgia has demonstrated quite good development indicators. Achievements in this area clearly point to the generally good level of development of the Georgian economy. The financial and banking sector, along with the population of Georgia, has learned a serious lesson from the hyperinflation and collapse of the economy of the first half of the 1990s and has accurately followed the strict recommendations of international financial institutions in its further development. Since economic stabilization in the mid-1990s, the introduction of Lari, the national currency (September 1995) and curbing the galloping inflation, the Georgian banking sector was actually rebuilt from scratch. In the subsequent period, it showed an enviable, dynamic growth, outpacing the nominal increase in GDP. In the pre-crisis period, in 2005-2007 bank assets grew at record double-digit rates (for example, in 2006, growth made up 67%, while in 2007 - 71%)[133].

Today, the banking system is well-organized economic sector, which has a developed branch network throughout Georgia, modern technical facilities and technologies and qualified personnel. The total assets of the banking sector in August 2017 amounted to GEL 31.518 billion, which is a 22.6 % higher over the August 2016 indicator. The income of Georgian banks

---

[133] Kovzanadze I., Systemic and Borderline Banking Crises. iUnivrce Inc., New York, 2010, p. 173.

amounted to GEL 3,370 million in 2016, which is slightly less than in 2015 (GEL 3,455 million). At the same time, for the first 4-8 months of 2017, the income of Georgian banks reached GEL 2,778.6 million, which is by 30.6% more than in the same period in 2016.The net profit of the banking sector reached GEL 679 million in 2016, which is up by 26.4% compared to the profit in 2015. In the first 4-8 months of 2017 it made up GEL 561 million, exceeding the similar indicator of 2016 by 39%. The return on assets (ROA) of the Georgian banking sector in June 2017 was 3.4%, while return on equity (ROE) was 24.9%. Indicators of financial activity of Georgia's banking system are among the best in the Post-Soviet area.

A well-organized banking system, adherence to the recommendations of the IMF, *World Bank*, other reputed international financial and economic institutions, and the legislative framework that meets the requirements of the time have contributed significantly to the stability of the Georgian national currency. Although the volume of Lari in circulation has increased 32.5 times for almost twenty two years since its introduction (with GDP growing 5.4 times for that period), the average annual rate of inflation was only 5.4%, including the inflation rate for the past 5 years (2013-2017), which was even less, 2.5%. The national currency has devalued against the US dollar for this twenty-year period by only 84.4%, which is not a large indicator for such a small, relatively easily vulnerable to exogenous negative factors economy.

The main long-term resource and loss buffer - the capital of the banking sector - has an impressive volume for the scale of the Georgian economy. It increased from GEL 270 million in 2001 to GEL 1.8 billion in 2010 and up to GEL 4.1 billion by August 2017. Moreover, Tier 1 capital of the banking sector rose from GEL 0.2 billion in 2001, to GEL 1.3 billion in 2010 and to GEL 3.6 billion in January 2017[134]. The capital adequacy ratio of the banking sector by August 2017 was 16.3%, which indicates that the Georgian banking system currently has a high level of capitalization, which allows it to withstand the possible negative external impacts, which have become so common in the context of globalization.

---

[134] National Bank of Georgia. Statistics, www.nbg.gov.ge

In general, the banking system of Georgia maintains a high level of capitalization. By august 2017 the primary capital ratio (Tier 1 capital) calculated in accordance with the *Basel Accords* recommendation was 10.4% (which is 2.4 percentage points up the minimum level required by the National Bank of Georgia), and the ratio of supervisory capital (regulatory capital) - 17.416.5% (4.5 points higher than the level required by the National Bank of Georgia).

Deposits of commercial banks are steadily growing, which largely contributes to the growth of loans to individuals and legal entities (Figure 4).

It should be noted that loans issued by banks are distributed rather unevenly among different industries considering the share of the industries in the country's GDP. They are more or less comparable only in the construction industry and real estate operations. In other industries their share in GDP exceed the sectoral share of issued loans (agriculture, transport and communications, education etc.), or vice versa - the share in loans exceeds the share of corresponding industries in GDP (industry, trade, hotel and restaurant business, etc.), which is clearly seen in Fig. 5

Figure. 4.

Ratio of some monetary aggregates to the GDP of Georgia (%)

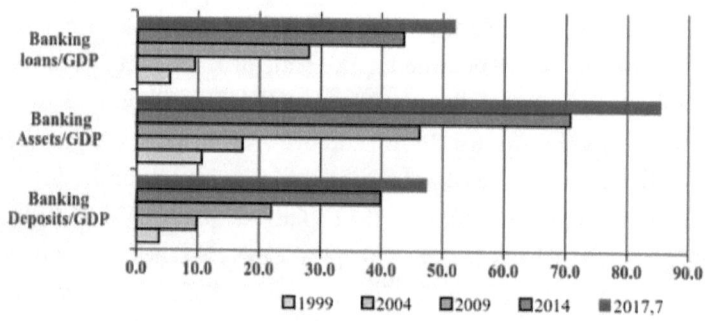

Source: National Bank of Georgia. Statistics. www.nbg.gov.ge

198

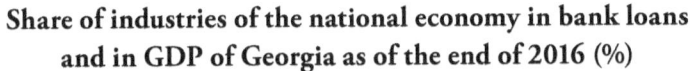

Fig. 5.

Share of industries of the national economy in bank loans and in GDP of Georgia as of the end of 2016 (%)

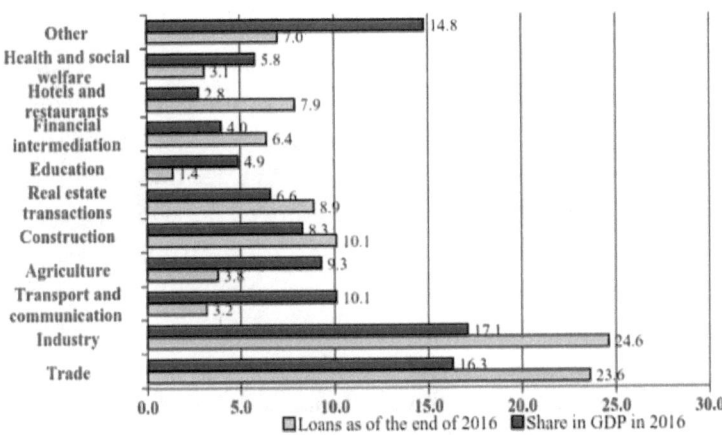

Source: National Statistics Office of Georgia. MainStatistics. www.geostat.ge

At the same time, with obviously successful development and sustainability of both the entire economy and the banking system of Georgia, it is still necessary to note some problems that make them vulnerable in the face of the growing negative processes in the world economy.

High dollarization rate of the economy may be called "a weak spot" of the money circulation[135]. Although the dollarization rate has declined for the past several years, it has stayed at a relatively high level in view of high degree of dependence on the import (power resources, food products, consumer goods etc.) and a solid negative trade balance (over 65%[136]). The level of dollarization in relation to the obligations of commercial banks is even higher, where it amounted to 65.5% in August 2017. This dates back to the 1990s, when, due to a relatively high share of the informal sector, with a weak

---

[135] Although foreign currency deposits and loans are denominated in other currencies as well, the process fully justifies its name. Almost ¾ of all deposits in foreign currency are denominated in the US dollars.

[136] In IVQ 2014r. – 60.3%, inIIQ 2015 – 63.0%.

institutionalization of the economy, the level of dollarization began to go off scale (by 2001 the level of dollarization reached 86%, while in 2002 - 85%).

Due to the implementation of economic reforms, improvement of fiscal discipline and administration, reduction of the shadow economy in a short period (literally in two or three years), it was possible to ensure a more than two-fold increase in the ratio of tax receipts to GDP; increase in foreign direct investment (in 2007 the foreign direct investment reached USD 2.1 billion – the indicator that has not been challenged so far) and large-scale privatization of state property. As a result, it was possible to significantly reduce the level of dollarization of the economy, strengthen the national currency and the reputation of the banking sector as the most accepting of innovation and a dynamically developing sphere of the economy.

Moreover, the global financial and economic crisis of 2008-2009 had a negative impact on the de-dollarization process. The period coincided with the August 2008 Georgian-Russian war, when the de-dollarization process was not only suspended but also reversed (the level of dollarization of deposits for the six months of 2008 increased by more than 16.4 points – from 56.12 points in July to 72.55 points in December).

The worsening trend of the ratio of banks' liquid assets both to their aggregate assets and to short-term liabilities, which carries an increased risk of financial instability, should be noted among other problems that require attention from the National Bank, the government of the country and the very credit institutions (Figure 6).

Fig. 6.

The ratio of liquid assets of Georgian commercial banks to total assets and short-term liabilities in 2001-2017 (%)

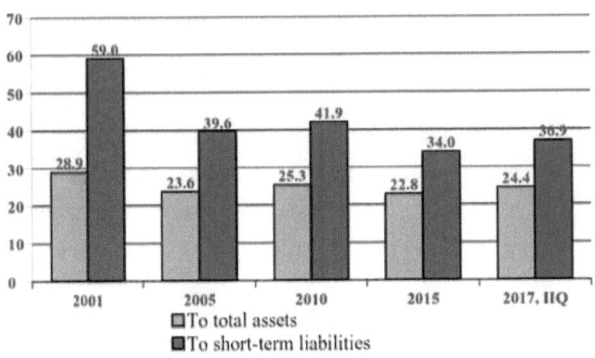

Source: National Bank of Georgia. Statistics. www.nbg.gov.ge

The rapid growth of household debt is another negative trend in the economy and the banking sector. As of September 1, 2017, more than GEL 10.1 billion was disbursed to the population in the form of loans. Compared to the end of 2010, the amount of debt increased about by 4.5 times, while the total cash income of the population for the same period rose only 1.8 times. As a result, household debt for IQ – 2017 accounted for 199.6% of their disposable income i.e. increased by more than two times during the last 5 years.

The financial and the banking system of Georgia would have had far better indicators if they had not been affected by the global crisis of 2007-2008 and the August 2008 war between Russia and Georgia. Provisions to cover probable losses, which remained at a relatively low level for a long time (5% of the value of the entire banking portfolio) began to increase rapidly after August 2008 reaching about 20% by the end of 2009.

The August developments had a quite serious impact: for only 3 months the bank assets decreased by 12 percent (by more than GEL 1 billion). It took almost two years from the banking system to regain the July 2008 level. Reduction in assets took place at the expense of 'working' assets. The banks reduced the issuance of new loans sharply. It took them 28 months to regain the 2008 July level. Naturally, these circumstances negatively affected the profitability of the banking system: the banking sector saw a loss of GEL 215.7 and GEL 65.3 million in 2008 and 2009 respectively.

These negative events also significantly impacted the profitability of the Georgian banking system: In 2004-2007, an average indicator of ROA amounted to 3.1%, ROE - 13.5%, while in the next 18 months (from the second half of 2008 to the end of 2009) these indicators had a negative value (setting a kind of 'anti-record' in Q4 2008 - minus 2.5% and minus 12.6% respectively).Under the influence of these events, the level of overdue loans quadrupled to almost GEL 500 million. Then this indicator fell to the pre-war level, and now it equals 2.2% of the total amount of credits.

Analyzing the general economic situation of 2007-2009, one can say that Georgia's banking system was definitely experiencing problems. The 2008 August events contributed to the exposure of all internal economic inconsistencies and imbalances, including in the banking sector. From September-November 2008, when the global crisis broke out, these imbalances got even worse and had a serious impact on the medium-term development of the economy and banking sector of Georgia.[137]

In this process, the assistance provided to Georgia by international financial institutions (IMF, *World Bank*, IBRD, EBRD, etc.) and individual developed states played an important positive role. In this context, it is difficult to overestimate the decision of the Brussels Donor's Conference (October 2008) to provide large-scale assistance to Georgia. Given the importance of the reforms undertaken by Georgia in recent years and the gravity of the problems that ensued the global economic crisis and the war with Russia, international financial institutions and donor countries decided to support Georgia through the allocation of USD 4.5 billion (of which USD 2.5 billion in a soft loan, and more than USD 2.0 billion as a free transfer). This aid was actually equivalent to more than 35% of GDP and almost 1.5 times more than the revenues of the Georgian budget in 2008.

---

[137] Kovzanadze I., Systemic and Borderline Banking Crises. iUnivrce Inc., New York, 2010, pp. 178-179.

This financial support turned out to be practically a 'safety cushion' for Georgia's economic stability and sustainability, preventing it from falling into a deep recession because of the accumulation of the above-mentioned negative circumstances. Georgia's GDP in 2009 decreased by only 3.7%. For comparison - for the same period in the most post-Soviet countries the economy shrank on a more impressive scale. For example, in 2009 GDP in Ukraine, Latvia and Estonia declined by 15% (in each of these countries), in Latvia and Armenia by 14%, in Russia - by 8%, Moldova - by 6%. Even the countries acted as Georgia's donors did not escape the economic recession. For example, the GDP of Germany (which contributed USD 360 million to the pool of donor funding) and Japan (contributed USD 315 million) declined in 2009 by 6%, while the GDP of US (contributed USD 1 billion) - by 3%.

In view of the above data, one can only try to guess the level at which the Georgian economy could have been reduced without the timely and large-scale aid of the above-mentioned donors.

Of the assistance provided, almost USD 1 billion was used to rehabilitate and ensure the stability of the Georgian banking sector; almost the same amount was used to support the state expenditure budget to cover sharply decreased tax revenue in the second half of 2008 - the first half of 2009.

Nevertheless, in general, the years 2008-2009 proved depressive for the Georgian banking sector – due to increased risks, only in the first half of 2009 the loan portfolio of banks decreased by more than 10%.

However, foreign aid was not the only one received by the banking sector of Georgia to overcome the difficulties and go ahead with its development. Internal factors undoubtedly played a positive role in this. For example, the measures taken by the Government and the National Bank of Georgia to reduce the financial burden of the banking sector proved in a way to be a turning point for reviving the banking sector.

The positive dynamics of key indicators of Georgia's banking sector are presented at Fig.7.

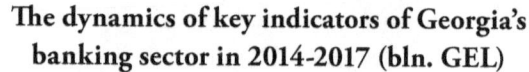

Fig. 7.

The dynamics of key indicators of Georgia's banking sector in 2014-2017 (bln. GEL)

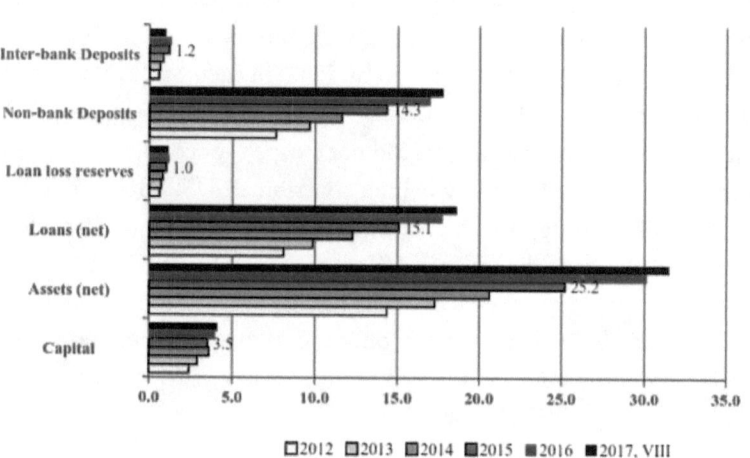

Source: *National Bank of Georgia. Statistics. www.nbg.gov.ge*

Thus, in recent years both the economy and the banking sector of Georgia have seen a fairly steady development. The dynamics of many macroeconomic parameters of Georgia is better than the average indicator in the post-Soviet area and in the Central and Eastern European states. At the same time, further efforts are needed to upgrade and diversify production, improve infrastructure and develop public, state and private institutions. The banking system of Georgia should also play an increasing role in the reform process.

CHAPTER 5
The Time-related Challenges and Possible Ways of Development

5.1. Towards a New Model of Economic Development: System Reforms Needed

In previous chapters, the reasons, the nature of development and consequences of the global crisis were discussed in detail. The analysis of all these components provide strong evidence of the disparities and problems existing both at the level of the national and global economy. Now many economists and politicians clearly say that the existing economic model shall undergo sweeping reforms at all levels: national, regional and global.

The clearest appeal for cardinal reforms came from scientists in the field of economy, some of whom predicted the occurrence of destructive global crisis. Thus, N. Roubini, a world-famous economist and Professor of Economics at New York University, stated quite clearly: "Politicians and government officials need to look into the future of the financial system. Only in this case will they acknowledge that in order to successfully confront crises, radical reforms are simply necessary. Any more cautious transformation is tantamount to rearranging the deck-chairs on the sinking Titanic[138]. J. Stiglitz, a recipient

---

[138] Roubini N., "Crisis Economics: A Crash Course in the Future of Finance", M., EKSMO, 2011 (in Russian language); p., 244.

of the Nobel Memorial Prize in Economic Sciences and head of the group of independent international experts at the UN, expressed his opinion no less clearly: "The goal of reforming the modern system of international relations should be the more perfect operation of the economic system in order to support the general welfare. This implies simultaneous fulfillment of long-term goals, such as sustainable and balanced growth, creation of new jobs in accordance with the principles of 'decent work', responsible use of national natural resources, reduction of greenhouse gas emissions, as well as solution of everyday problems caused by food and financial crises and global poverty... It is imperative to respond quickly and adequately to the current crisis, and at the same time to start the long-term reform that is necessary to create a more global, prosperous and balanced world economy. The goal should be to rule out the possibility of such global crises in the future".[139]

Another recipient of Nobel Memorial Prize in Economics, a Professor of Princeton University, P. Krugman evaluated the current situation in the world economy rather sharply and also proposed radical reforms based on successful historical experience. In his work "End this Depression Now!" he notes the following: "In my opinion, the most reasonable view of the ongoing economic crisis is to recognize the fact of depression ... in essence, we are dealing with the same type of situation, which was described by John Maynard Keynes in the 30's of the 20th century: The economy is in a state of chronically reduced activity for a long time without showing any noticeable trends to improvement nor to the final collapse. Of course, this situation is unacceptable... Hence, it is very important to take measures for a real, complete economic recovery. And something else: we know, or at least *must know* how to do it. Despite all the differences in details due to economic, technological and social changes that have occurred over 75 years, the troubles we are experiencing are very similar to those that occurred in the 30's of last century, and we know what high-ranking politicians did then - the analysis of Keynes and other economists shows how to respond to the difficulties today".[140]

---

[139] Stiglitz J., "On the Reform of the International Monetary and Financial System: Lessons from the Global Crisis". Report of the UN Financial Mechanism Commission, M., «MezhdunarodnyeOtnosheniya"», 2012 (in Russian language); pp., 48-50.

[140] Krugman P., "The Way Out of the Slump!",M., «Azbuka-Attykus», 2013 (in Russian language); pp., 8-9.

Politicians, statesmen and civil servants, unlike economists, are forced to take into account in their activities the influence of various factors, including those of various lobby groups, therefore, usually, modern leaders show great caution in approaches to economic and social reform. However, most political figures, both in power and in opposition, recognize the need for profound reforms, though they do not have unity as to the directions and timing of these reforms as well as the use of certain instruments of influence.

Now the idea of deep reforms is actively supported at the international level, in particular, it pervades virtually all documents adopted at meetings of ministers and leaders of G20 countries. It is supported by the IMF as well. Thus, according to IMF Managing Director K. Lagard, the situation with possible development of the global economy is as follows: "Five years ago, the world economy avoided the second Great Depression. Five years later the path has not yet been travelled to the end, but the fog of the crisis is rising, and we see that after the crisis we have to overcome several new transition processes. Two of them stand out: *the transition to new structures of economic growth* and *the transition to a different type of financial sector*"[141].

European policy makers also talk about the need for systemic reforms. German Federal Chancellor Angela Merkel intends to dedicate her third term as chancellor to eliminating 'structural flaws' in the mechanism for preventing crises. A. Merkel noted that "we need to eliminate the reasons that led to the current situation in the European Union and the Eurozone"[142].

M. Schultz, the Speaker of the European Parliament, also stated clearly enough that it was necessary to make changes to the economic policy when he addressed heads of states and governments at the EU summit in 2013: "since the last summit in the spring of last year, two million people have lost their jobs, youth unemployment continues to grow increasing to an alarming scale in some member states of the union, in many EU countries even more people are below the poverty line, while the real economy is still struggling to get funding for its expansion... Therefore, we adhere to our position: budget

[141]   Lagarde C. "Managing the New Transitions in the Global Economy", an Address at George Washington University, Washington DC, October 3, 2013., www.imf.org (in Russian language);

[142]   Angela Merkel as the main anti-crisis manager of the EU, DeutscheWelle, Topics of the Day: Politics and Society, www. dw.de

consolidation should go hand in hand with investments that foster growth...
without growth there is no strong economy, without a strong economy there
are no jobs and without new jobs there is no increase in state revenues"[143].

Thus, most economists and politicians agree that the goal of economic
development at the present stage is to build a stable, balanced, socially focused
economy capable of overcoming increasing disparities and negative external
influences. To achieve this goal, it is necessary to be guided by the following
fundamental principles, on which most scientists and experts agree:

First, actions to overcome the crisis and reform the economy should be
coordinated at the regional, national and international levels, because "in a
globally integrated world, the consequences of actions in one country affect
other countries. Too often, these external factors are not taken into account
when making decisions in domestic national policies."[144]

Second, it is necessary to achieve a balance between the market and
management, as the ideas of deregulation and market self-regulation have
largely dominated in the economic policy agenda in the last decades, while
such aspects as significant information asymmetry in markets and the
tendency of markets, especially financial ones, towards failure, have been
ignored.

The global crisis clearly showed the need for an effective and tailored to the
challenges of time management, which will constantly change and take into
account (preferably in advance) the development of the economy and financial
markets as well as innovations.

Third, the modern economy and the activities of monetary authorities are
in badly need of greater transparency and accountability, which will help
solve many problems, such as information asymmetry, the effectiveness of

---

[143] M. Schultz, the Speaker of the European Parliament, criticized governance
bodies of the European Union for technocratic approach to overcoming
economic and financial crises, "EkonomicheskyeIzvestiya", www.eizvestia.com

[144] Stiglitz J., "On the Reform of the International Monetary and Financial System:
Lessons from the Global Crisis". Report of the UN Financial Mechanism
Commission, M., «MezhdunarodnyeOtnosheniya"», 2012 (in Russian language);
p., 56.

anti-crisis measures, moral risks, the choice of development priorities, the balance of public finances etc.

Fourth, it is necessary to ensure a higher level of coordination between short, medium and long-term measures of economic and social policies of states, both developed and developing. At present, quite often a conflict of different purposes is observed. For example, the consolidation of budgets curbs investment, while the consolidation in the banking sector further aggravates the problem of 'too large' financial institutions.

Fifth, it is necessary to consider carefully the consequences of all measures taken, including the processes of redistribution of incomes and expenditures of budgets at all levels, changes in interest rates, mandatory reserves, taxes, quotas, tariffs, etc.

Sixth, in today's interconnected and interdependent economy, it is very important to reduce global imbalances, including in crisis response measures.

Seventh, the development of an effective economic model requires the stimulation of intellectual diversity, the struggle of ideas and theories because "modern economic theory has questioned many of the ideas underlying market-based fundamentalism, including those saying that unregulated markets yield efficient results, or that markets are self-regulating and stable. The current economic crisis raised a number of other issues related to these doctrines, and emphasized the need for alternative theories and ideas".[145]

Thus, it is impossible to move towards sustainable and balanced growth unless a number of conditions are present in the economic and social policies of the state and intensive and comprehensive discussions are held in the scientific and professional communities. With regard to the economic policy, it is necessary to implement a set of structural measures, including those relating to industry, technology and innovation. It is also very important to reform monetary and financial policies, also make sure that all sectors and markets are regulated and supervised, in the first place the financial market.

---

[145] Stiglitz J., "On the Reform of the International Monetary and Financial System: Lessons from the Global Crisis". Report of the UN Financial Mechanism Commission, M., «MezhdunarodnyeOtnosheniya"», 2012 (in Russian language); p., 63.

5.2. Structural Transformations in the Economy

To a large extent, the global crisis was caused by deep structural imbalances in the economy of both developed and developing countries.

Developed countries should eliminate the developmental gap observed for the past decade in the real sector of the economy, in particularly, in the industrial sector. The most striking examples in this area are the decline of a number of centers in the automobile industry in the United States, the closure or transfer to developing countries of manufacturing enterprises in Europe. Thus, from 2000 to 2010, the United Kingdom moved from the 5th to 9th place in terms of the share of net material products in the global manufacturing industry, Germany - from 3 to 4, while Spain - from 11 to 14. At the same time, China rose from 4th to 2nd place, Brazil from 12 to 6, India - from 14 to 10. As a result, the share of manufacturing enterprises in GDP in the UK and France accounted for only 10%, Canada - 11%, the United States and Spain - 12%, while in China - 33%, South Korea - 28% and Indonesia – 25%.[146]

To overcome this situation, developed countries obviously need to elaborate long-term development programs for the national economy, in particular, the industrial sector. There must be an industrial policy in place at the level of countries and regions. Recent historical experience has demonstrated that such measures were successfully applied by developed countries for the development of the economy in the past, for example, in the post-war period. In a limited form the elements of fostering the industry development have been preserved to date.

In this regard, the experience of Germany, which in recent decades has pursued a quite effective industrial policy, is interesting and worth using. In Germany, on the eve of the merger, subsidies to support industry, primarily rail and water transport, the coal industry and shipbuilding, accounted for 5% of GDP. In 1969, the Federal Government adopted a document "Principles of Sectoral (Industry-Specific) Structural Policy", which is still effective.

---

[146]   McKinseyGlobalInstitute.

Germany's experience shows that it is advisable for a state to stimulate the rapid sectoral reform (which is particularly important in the context of increasing globalization).

In this direction, the following measures may be applied: targeted retraining and resettlement of the able-bodied population that lost their jobs; price control; assistance to firms engaged in the development and production of new advanced technical products, which are important for the national economy. Moreover, in order to keep a balance between economic reforms and social stability, if necessary, Germany slows down the processes of sectoral transformation. The state acts on the assumption that in a number of cases the market speeds up the structural reorganization in certain sectors too much, which can cause undesirable, negative and painful processes in them, for example, in the sphere of employment. In these cases, the state allows limited intervention in these processes. Corresponding measures are applied only until alternative employment opportunities occur in related industries.

Germany has actively pursued the state sectoral structural policy. For the past several decades the policy has focused on such areas as the implementation of large-scale scientific and technical projects of a fundamental nature (nuclear power, civil aviation, modern rail transport, etc.); adoption of an active policy in the field of environmental protection, which, among other things, is related to the selective impact of the activities on various spheres of the economy; support of small and medium-sized enterprises, including in the field of competition promotion policy.

If we look at the instruments of structural policy, in a broad sense, actually all measures applied by the state as part of the economic policy have a certain structural impact. At the same time, special tools can be used, for example, allocation of funds from the state budget to retrain private sector employees; subventions and lending for the modernization of productive capacity; tax cuts or full exemption; reduction of excess capacity through the payment of compensations.

In recent years, particularly in 2008, Germany made certain changes to the industrial policy. The Federal Ministry of Economics and Technology defined the industrial policy "as a standard policy[147]pursued in the interests of industry." Its main goal is to create favorable conditions for industrial innovation, investment and production. Part of this policy is to support specific projects in industry, including in high-tech and innovative areas. The standard policy, which is carried out at the federal, land and municipal levels, combines all types of structural policy. The most successful examples of the standard policy at the regional level are the western federal states - Bavaria, Baden-Württemberg, Bremen, Hamburg and the eastern - Saxony, Thuringia, Brandenburg as well as Berlin. Over the past decades, they have turned into regions of high-tech production. Moreover, often the local authorities play the key role in the implementation of this policy.

Among the innovations in the field of industrial policy, the process of clustering of German standards can be noted. The regional cluster is territorially grouped companies, connected with each other by cooperation and division of labor, which gives them the opportunity to strengthen their own and obtain additional competitive advantages. On the basis of such clusters, so-called competence networks and centers started developing in the regions of Germany, which represent attempts by business communities to gain additional advantages from the clustering of specific standards.

First of all, this refers to the sphere of innovation and production of high-tech products.

Their most important difference is the interregional nature of several key partners formed on the basis of regional clusters of cooperation associations. They pay special attention to the effective management of the technological chain for the development of the end product and, correspondingly, to the increased competitiveness of their participants. Such networks promote the transformation of regional clusters into innovative centers of national, European and even global importance and, correspondingly, to the growth of competitiveness of the regions in which they are located.

---

[147] Shtandort Policy – the policy of the state to create favorable framework conditions for the development of a specific economic and political territorial formation with the aim of attracting and retaining capital, goods, services and labor.

The innovation and technology policy is an important component of a successful industrial policy. Germany offers a number of positive examples in this area as well.

The innovative policy should be aimed at identifying key technologies, conducting R&D in these areas and putting the results into practice. In particular, Karlsruhe Institute of Technology (KIT), the major research institution in Germany and Europe, focused its activities on the following areas: energy (including renewable energy sources and nuclear energy safety), Nano technologies, elementary particles and the environment (including climate change). The foundation of large scientific centers and support for innovative SME are parallel strategies for the technological policies of Germany and the European Union. As these structures often complement each other and the state seeks to organize effective cooperation between them. In particular, the Federal Ministry for Research and Technology of Germany has been carrying out a program of cooperation between SME and scientific centers since 1999. It was called "Support for Innovative Networks" (InnoNet). To receive state support under this program, small and medium-sized enterprises must prove the introduction of products and participate in projects with their own capital.

It seems that Germany's experience of implementation of quite successful industrial policy, which is modernized in line with the development trends of the global economy, could be successfully applied by both developed and developing countries.

Investment is a rather important element of structural reforms in the economy. Its level should be sufficient for expanded reproduction on a new qualitative level. In recent years, the level of investment in developed countries has generally declined, so the government should make some efforts to change this trend. In addition to stimulating private investments, especially direct investments, the state should play a more active role in the investment process, in particular, through development banks and investment agencies. It seems that, despite serious problems in public finance, developed countries should find opportunities for investment, especially in infrastructure, high-tech and environmentally significant production.

Developing countries and countries with economies in transition also need structural reforms, although the situation in this area varies greatly across countries. Thus, there is a group of dynamically developing Asian countries, in particular, China, India, Indonesia, which have a fairly high level of investment, both foreign and national. They have radically upgraded the economy in recent years and are constantly increasing their exports. However, the high dependence of the economic growth of these countries on exports has become a very serious problem, since adverse external influences, for example, a decrease in the demand for their products in foreign markets for one reason or another (crisis impact, protectionist measures, currency wars) can negatively affect the macroeconomic environment in these countries. Therefore, for this group of countries it is very important to develop domestic demand to further diversify and upgrade the economy.

The countries in transition also face a serious task of diversifying and modernizing their economy. They need to consistently improve the investment climate, carry out comprehensive structural reforms, in particular, increase direct investment in industry and agriculture through public-private partnerships and development institutions and foster domestic demand. An important element in the formation of a stable economic system in these countries is institutional reforms aimed at the formation of a modern and international legal framework, increasing the effectiveness and transparency of all public and state institutions, including judicial and law enforcement agencies.

Overall, both developed and developing countries need to significantly change the structure of production and consumption, increase aggregate demand, including through the optimization of government spending, increase the volume and quality of investments, primarily directing them to the development of infrastructure, new technologies, ecology, quality of manpower, including education and health.

5.3 Monetary and Financial Policy in the New Economic Conditions

The success of economic reforms, including removal of structural imbalances, will largely depend on improvement of the monetary and financial policies and their adequacy to the challenges of the time. During the Great Depression, the situation was significantly exacerbated by the lack of an effective monetary policy that would be adequate to existing threats and aimed at overcoming the crisis. In particular, this caused a near collapse of the banking system. Taking into account the historical experience acquired during the recent crisis, monetary authorities actively used various monetary policy instruments to support the financial sector and the economy as a whole, including unprecedentedly low refinancing rates, large asset repurchase programs, and various forms of centralized loans. As the researcher of crises Professor N. Roubini notes, "The scale of rescue operations knew neither precedents nor national borders, since the *International Monetary Fund* joined the fight, and the Federal Reserve System began to lend to foreign central banks, supplying them and corporations worldwide with much needed dollars. This was the largest financial rescue operation in the modern world, if not in history."[148]At the same time, this rescue operation has caused side effects in the form of moral abuse, automatism in saving large financial institutions, etc.

In future, the monetary authorities, obviously, should always have at hand all the anti-crisis tools that have been used so far. However, the monetary policy should first of all play a preventive role, that is, it should smooth accumulating imbalances. Interest rates, nature of the collateral and other conditions of loans granted to banks by monetary authorities should encourage credit institutions to perform, primarily, their traditional and very important functions for society, such as settlements, savings and lending. It is also necessary to channel more resources through national, regional and international development institutions. Increased resources, powers and instruments used by such institutions as the *European Stabilization Mechanism, International Monetary Fund, World Bank*, and regional development banks, certainly would promote sustainable and balanced growth.

Success in building a new type of economy will depend on the synchronism and harmony of changes in the monetary and financial policies of states. In financial policy, it is very important to continue the course of improving public finances pursued in recent years in most countries. Despite the measures taken, reduction of the budget deficit and public debt remains to be an extremely urgent task, especially given the magnitude of this phenomenon.

---

[148] Roubini N., "Crisis Economics: A Crash Course in the Future of Finance", M., EKSMO, 2011 (in Russian language); p.244.

Thus, according to the *Bank for International Settlements*, as of June 2013, the volume of government securities traded on the world's financial market amounted to 43 trillion dollars, having increased by 80% since 2007.

According to many experts, the chronic budget deficit problem cannot be solved by means of automatic cost reduction, but rather by optimization of budget incomes and expenditures. If we talk about the revenue side of the budget and tax policy, it is important to preserve, and in a number of ways, to strengthen the redistributive role of the budget, which will ensure availability of sufficient resources to address such socio-economic problems as declining incomes and real purchasing demand of the population, income inequality and differences in the development levels of regions and countries.

Reserves for increasing government revenues are certainly available, because, for example, in the United States in the 1950's and 1960's, taxes on high incomes reached 91%, while at present they do not exceed 35%.[149] In addition, a rather heated discussion is also going on about additional taxes for the financial sector, in particular financial transactions, introduction of which would allow, on the one hand, to increase financial resources available to the state, and, on the other hand, restrict speculative operations in the currency and financial markets.

For the first time the idea of taxing financial transactions was proposed by J.M. Keynes. In 1972 it was raised again by the Nobel Prize winner in economics J. Tobin, proposing to set this tax in the amount of 0.05 - 1% of the turnover of all cross-border transactions. During the global crisis, this idea was quite broadly supported by politicians. Since 2011, introduction of such a tax has been discussed in practical terms in the EU countries. This measure was supported by the President of France Nicolas Sarkozy and German Federal Chancellor A. Merkel. President of the European Parliament M. Schulz also made clear statements in support of this tax: "I am a strong supporter of the tax on financial transactions. Its introduction will allow the industry where profits can be quite high, make a more significant contribution to the development of our society, improve the financial situation in many countries, and also provide an opportunity for finding means to stimulate

---

[149]   Rajan R., "Rift lines. Hidden cracks, still threatening the global economy", M., Publishing House of the Gaydar Institute, 2011 (in Russian language);

economic growth. In addition, the *Tobin Tax* will help to prevent financial speculation, which is one of the causes of the current crisis ... Ideally, a tax on financial transactions should be introduced around the world. The EU should fight for it at the G20 meetings."[150]

According to the calculations of the *European Commission*, the rate of such a tax of 0.01% would provide the EU countries with 57 billion euros.

In 2012, the *European Commission* issued an official proposal for introduction of a tax on financial transactions. It was proposed to set the tax rate of 0.01% for derivatives transactions and 0.1% for deals with shares, bonds, units of investment funds, money market instruments, repurchase agreements, and securities loan agreements. At the same time, individual EU states could, if desired, establish higher tax rates for financial transactions. It was planned to introduce this tax in 2014, but then this measure was postponed to a later date.

Improvement of the public finances will be facilitated by further policies to combat tax evasion. Thus, according to experts of the *European Commission*, only in the EU, budget losses caused by tax evasion are estimated at 1 trillion euros. For this reason, the EU recently made decisions on automatic exchange of information on deposits and toughened the law on collection of the tax on interests from bank deposits. In addition, efforts are being made to prevent the widespread practice of large enterprises which use gaps in national legislations to hide profits from taxation. There should also be a system for automatic exchange of client data with funds and insurance companies from those countries that are still considered to be tax havens. According to the German Federal Chancellor A. Merkel, such measures will be "a clear signal against tax fraud and some tax evasion methods which are now still legal." In addition, as A. Merkel noted, "we must ensure that companies pay taxes where they work. This involves fighting against tax havens".[151]

In practice, Luxembourg announced its readiness to join the system of automatic exchange of banking information from 2015. Measures to combat

---

[150] Schultz M., "Tax on financial transactions should be introduced around the world, RBC daily interview22.03.2012". www.rbcdaily.ru (in Russian language);

[151] The European Union ends bank secrecy, RBCDaily, 23.05.2013, www. rbcdaily.ru

tax evasion were also supported by Austria. However, as many experts note, it is very important that such measures are supported by Switzerland, as well as countries with a special tax regime outside the EU.

Besides increasing tax collections, it is also very important to optimize public spending, reducing those expenses that do not have an impact on social and economic development while maintaining the necessary level of support for the economy and the social sphere. In addition, along with direct government spending, it is advisable to apply state guarantees and various instruments of financial incentives, such as tax incentives. At the same time, it should be understood that "unlike the monetary policy measures that can be immediately implemented by the central bank, without the need to overcome the pressure from voters, adoption of fiscal measures takes time and the ability to abandon costly projects that do not bring any results, except inefficient use of resources. A perfect package of incentives leads to effective investments in the modernization of dilapidated infrastructure and contributes to future economic growth".[152]

Thus, as shown by historical experience, including recent years, skillful application of monetary and financial policy instruments can have a powerful revitalizing effect on the economy. However, it is very important to learn how to use these tools in a preventive manner, precluding emergence of a destructive crises. The experience of preventing crisis is not very extensive, however, there is every reason for moderate optimism in this matter.

5.4. Solution of the Moral Abuse Problem in Business

In order to build a sustainable economy, it is very important to solve the problem of moral abuse in business, which is closely linked with the existing systems of paying dividends to owners and bonuses to managers as well as with the general system of wages and incentives used by enterprises, especially in the financial sector.

In recent decades, the problems that have accumulated in corporate governance and corporate ethics contributed to the formation of a system of payments to

---

[152] Roubini N., "Crisis Economics: A Crash Course in the Future of Finance", M., EKSMO, 2011 (in Russian language); p., 180.

shareholders, managers and employees, which was not focused on long-term development goals of the company, but on obtaining extra-high payments through ultra-short-term operations. Such a vicious practice, according to 80% of market participants, has become one of the significant factors in the development of the global crisis.[153]

In recent decades, in the field of corporate governance, owners have lost control over the actions of managers, especially in financial institutions, since "traders and bankers know much more about the financial position of their companies than the shareholders to whom they report ... this lead to a situation, when complete absence of direct or indirect control by shareholders stimulates the traders and bankers to do crazy things for the sake of short-term profit and bonuses."[154]

However, quite often shareholders are very pleased with the fact that management of financial institutions is taking increased risks for the sake of receiving super profits, because in the case of financial institutions, a risky game is mainly implemented using borrowed funds and in case of large losses, the main losses are borne by creditors, while in the case of Systemic Significant Organizations - by taxpayers.

Experts and regulators are actively discussing such a vicious practice and looking for an antidote. Thus, in particular, the Financial Stability Board developed the Principles for Sound Compensation Practices[155] and several measures were proposed for solving this problem.

It is advisable to increase the role of the Board of Directors of financial institutions in the elaboration, functioning and control of the wage system. Unfortunately, at present most of the Boards of Directors of financial institutions believe that a wage system is not a part of the risk management. Remuneration committees created within the Boards of Directors pay significant attention to the remuneration of the most "senior" managers of

---

[153] "Report of the Group of Thirty, Financial reforms. Approaches to ensuring financial stability", 2009, January.

[154] Roubini N., "Crisis Economics: A Crash Course in the Future of Finance", M., EKSMO, 2011 (in Russian language); p.212.

[155] Financial Stability Board, Principles for Sound Compensation Practices, 2009 April, www.financialstabilityboard.org

financial institutions. Issues related to the remuneration of other employees are delegated to the management of the financial institution. Often, the HR department, which may not have all necessary powers, is formally responsible for the development and operation of the payroll system.

It is important to ensure independence, sufficient powers and a special procedure for remuneration (regardless of the performance of business units) of employees of the bank's supervisory units. They should also be involved as much as possible in the functioning of the wage system, in particular, through substantiated judgments about risks in order to adjust the payment of business units taking into account the level of risks taken.

An important task is to establish a direct link between remunerations and the level of risks taken. At the same time, it is necessary to take into account a number of circumstances such as: simultaneous application of reasoned judgment and quantitative estimates in assessing the level of risks; difficulties in accounting for certain risks, e.g. liquidity; and the need to ensure maximum objectivity in calculating remuneration adjustments for risks. In addition, a separate problem is related to the risk adjustments applied to non-fixed remuneration (for example, bonuses) of most senior managers of financial institutions who are responsible for overall risks of the institution and general results of its activities. The most difficult task is to quantify the combined risk of a financial institution and distribute it among top managers. A solution to this problem could be to establish a remuneration committee within the Board of Directors which would use a reasoned judgment when adjusting non-fixed remuneration of members of senior management based on risks taken.

In case of payrolls, it is also important to observe the principle of linking the due dates of employees' wages / other remunerations with the time horizons for the risk realization. In order to increase the sensitivity of newly paid bonuses to the risk realization results, such remunerations, paid based on the results of a certain financial period, should usually be sensitive to probable risk realization in a longer time horizon. Otherwise, employees will be motivated to expose the financial institution to risks, the risk realization probability of which exists, but is extremely insignificant in the near future.

One way to take into account the risk realization time horizons is to place part or whole non-fixed remuneration (paid both in cash and in shares) on escrow accounts. At the same time, the deposited non-fixed remuneration will be reviewed if the financial institution as a whole demonstrates inefficient activity or excessively high risks. It is also advisable that, in the event of the dismissal of employees, early payments of deferred rewards are not made.

Obviously, in the matter of the risk realization horizons and the rates of non-fixed remuneration recovery, differentiation by units and individual employees is necessary.

It is also advisable to abandon the "golden parachute" agreements that are insensitive to the financial institution's performance risks and involve substantial payments to dismissed managers. Such agreements create incentives for an irresponsible approach to accepting risks to which the received remuneration is not sensitive.

An important element of the system to combat moral abuse is control of remuneration systems by supervisory authorities. In case of revealing the shortcomings in the remuneration systems, the supervisory authorities should take all necessary measures, similar to those taken with respect to the identified shortcomings in the area of risk management and corporate governance. At the same time, the analysis of remuneration systems by supervisors should be strict and consistent. Supervisory authorities should include assessment of existing remuneration systems into the process of assessing the risks taken by financial institutions.

5.5. Reform of the Regulatory and Supervisory System

Sustainable economic development is inextricably linked with the effectiveness of regulation and supervision in all sectors of the economy, but especially in the financial sector, because due to the nature of the activity, all systemic risks, including credit, market, currency, operational, country and other risks, are accumulated there.

The reform of the regulatory and supervisory system must cover several important areas.

In order to ensure long-term and sustainable economic growth, it is very important to tackle the problem of countercyclical regulation designed to prevent a situation where regulatory norms negatively affect the economy by encouraging banks and other financial institutions to make excessive and risky investments during economic growth and to limit their activities (including credits) during the economic downturn.

There are various instruments that can be used in countercyclical regulation, such as mandatory standards of banks' activities, norms for creating mandatory reserves, and norms for capital accounts. At present the concept of countercyclical regulation is the central notion recognized by both international and national regulatory bodies. Now it is necessary to implement it in practice. This concept is supported by many experts. For example, Professor J. Stiglitz sees the situation as follows: "The changing standards of capital adequacy and provisioning, which raise and lower the bar depending on the business cycle, are the best mechanisms for countercyclical prudential regulation. Such countercyclical standards can be based on simple rules that, for example, provide for raising the level of capital as the asset growth rate increases. The norms set for provisioning automatically guarantee that the bank will retain more reserves as the lending increases".[156]

The principle which serves as a basis for the countercyclical application of the capital adequacy and mandatory reserves standard is as follows: the provisions cover the expected losses, while the capital secures unforeseen losses. Provisions for possible losses on loans can be formed for the entire period of the business cycle, based on historical experience. The magnitude of capital adequacy can be linked to a significant macroeconomic indicator, such as the annual growth rate of bank loans. In the event that the growth rates of bank loans exceed the ranges established by the regulatory authorities, the credit institution should increase the level of capital adequacy and/or provisions for possible losses. Conversely, the countercyclical requirements could be milder for a bank with low lending activity.

Many experts in the field of regulation, however, warn that the existing banking practice allows to hide loans on off-balance instruments, for example, through special investment vehicles (SIV). Therefore, it is very important

---

[156] Stiglitz J., "On the Reform of the International Monetary and Financial System: Lessons from the Global Crisis". Report of the UN Financial Mechanism Commission, M., «MezhdunarodnyeOtnosheniya"», 2012 (in Russian language); pp., 162-163.

to ensure that calculation of the capital adequacy ratio is done taking into account all financial instruments, on a consolidated basis.

The instruments that can also be used in counter-cyclical regulation include establishment of the ratio of the loan amount to collateral security, introduction of provision requirements for possible loan losses based on the macroeconomic and sectoral situation, and liquidity ratios. It is very important to establish a relatively low ratio of banks' own and borrowed funds (leverage), since, as practice shows, in case of a high level of leverage, even a small depreciation of assets results in virtual loss of capital by banks.

Another important area of regulatory reform is the focus on systemic risks, their distribution among financial sectors, and a lower level of systemic risks for financial institutions of greater public significance. Consistent and detailed implementation of the well-known thesis of *group 30*, led by the former Head of the Federal Reserve, P. Volcker, is required in order to establish new restrictions on the volume and types of risky activities of those institutions that bear the primary responsibility for maintaining proper functioning of financial infrastructure. Therefore, introduction of differentiated norms and standards for different types of financial institutions is advisable, although, at the same time, it is very important to control the systemic risks and risks associated with regulatory arbitrage.

In their practice, regulatory and supervisory authorities need to pay more attention to the control of such indicators of banking activity as the structure of income and expenses, profitability of certain operations and segments of banking activity, and profitability of assets and capital. These indicators can clearly show the nature and volume of risks accepted by banks, banking business' structure, management quality, and moral risks.

It is important to constantly improve regulatory norms for assessing the risks of banking activities, because until recently, obviously super-risky investments of banks in opaque structured products and speculative financial instruments were recognized as ultra-reliable in accordance with the methods applied by regulatory bodies. In this regard, it seems that improvement of the *Basel Accords* must also move in this direction.

The emergence of crises is often associated with excessive currency risks of individual enterprises and banks, and the entire economy as a whole. Therefore, it is very important to establish strict norms regarding unsecured currency risks.

The stability of the economy and the financial sector will be largely linked to the regulation of the derivatives market in the future. The colossal losses of banks and other financial institutions during the crisis in transactions with derivative financial instruments gave rise to the idea that "if banks have explicit or implicit state guarantees, it is necessary to prohibit all activities that could lead to significant risks - both individual and systemically significant."[157]

In spite of taken measures, in general, the market for derivative financial instruments still requires more serious regulation. In describing the situation in this area, IMF Managing Director Christine Lagarde described the continuing lack of transparency of this market as a colossal problem and noted that: "At the end of the last year, the total number of outstanding derivatives was $633 trillion, of which instruments circulated on organized exchanges equaled only 24 trillion US dollars. For proper oversight of the rest, it is imperative that countries and markets implement, without delay, concerted reform of derivatives."[158]

Thus, in the market for derivative financial instruments, the problem related to lack of information transparency needs to be solved as soon as possible, especially with regard to credit default swaps. Credit derivatives should firstly be placed at organized exchange sites, which will increase transparency of these transactions and ensure that the parties involved in the transactions have the means necessary to fulfill their obligations. It is also possible to transfer transactions with insufficiently standardized credit derivatives to clearing centers, but in this case, it is also necessary to strengthen supervision over the activities of such institutions in order to ensure that they have at

---

[157] Stiglitz J., "On the Reform of the International Monetary and Financial System: Lessons from the Global Crisis". Report of the UN Financial Mechanism Commission, M., «MezhdunarodnyeOtnosheniya"», 2012 (in Russian language); p., 170.

[158] Lagarde C. "Managing the New Transitions in the Global Economy", an Address at George Washington University, Washington DC, October 3, 2013., www.imf.org (in Russian language)

their disposal sufficient financial resources to guarantee the obligations of transaction participants.

It would also be advisable to register transactions with credit default swaps in a central database, and this information should be available to all interested parties.

As financial innovations develop rapidly, more systematic and tight control over new generations of these tools is needed, since "this is not the case when regulators should fear that punitive measures will to some extent harm economic growth. Not at all: by its very existence this segment of the financial market exposes the global economic stability to serious danger, and the sooner the legislators, politicians and regulators understand this, the better."[159]

For the stable functioning of the banking system, it is also necessary to significantly strengthen the protection of borrowers of consumer and mortgage loans, since the recent practice of providing insufficient information to borrowers, high interest rates on loans, and even a certain degree of automatism in lending, caused on the one hand, unreasonably high incomes of banks from issued loans, and on the other hand, excessive household debts, growth of their arrears, social tensions, and undermined trust to banking institutions. In addition, it is necessary to decisively get rid of the practice when the plight of poorly informed borrowers is further aggravated by the fact that lenders resort to the help of collector intermediaries who use unregulated and often illegal ways of repaying loans.

Another important systemic task for regulators is to ensure the level of competition necessary for sustainable development in the markets, including financial and banking services. In practice, "the inability to conduct anti-monopoly policies has led to an excessively high concentration in the financial sector."[160]

---

[159] Roubini N., "Crisis Economics: A Crash Course in the Future of Finance", M., EKSMO, 2011 (in Russian language); p.233.

[160] Stiglitz J., "On the Reform of the International Monetary and Financial System: Lessons from the Global Crisis". Report of the UN Financial Mechanism Commission, M., «MezhdunarodnyeOtnosheniya"», 2012 (in Russian language); p., 176.

Lack of competition in the banking and financial sector has led to the emergence of institutions, the amount and economic influence of which have become so large that they could carry out excessively risky policy without any fear of bankruptcy or financial restructuring at the expense of the owners. Such institutions were called "too large for restructuring." At the same time, in recent years, despite the fact that this situation played a role in the onset of the global crisis, large financial institutions have increased even more, primarily due to the consolidation process. So *JP Morgan Chase* absorbed *Bear Sterns* and *Washington Mutual, Bank of America* increased in size due to the *Countrywide* and *Merrill Lynch*, while *Wells Fargo* and *Citigroup* fought for the absorption of a huge bank *Wachovia*, because "both companies knew: whoever took over bank *Wachovia* (which finally went bankrupt) would strengthen its status as a backbone institution, significantly increasing the chances for receiving government assistance (eventually *Wells Fargo* won in this fight)."[161]

Experts and politicians offer various solutions to the problem of too large financial institutions. At the same time, most agree that the tools used during the crisis, such as saving all creditors and contractors of the company (for example, in the case of *AIG*) or the other extreme - full bankruptcy (*Lehman Brothers*) are too expensive and "we need a third method that would give the government the powers and opportunities for orderly and least painful liquidation of large companies in case of bankruptcy."[162]

Thus, according to a number of experts, it is necessary to have, outside the standard procedures, a special regime for the liquidation of large financial institutions. This could take place in the forms of "state custody" (for example, as it was done with *Fannie Mae* and *Freddie Mac*) or giving the government the authority to place such institutions in a competitive management regime that would minimize the negative impact of litigation in ordinary bankruptcy and more flexible liquidation of financial giants.

It is very important to develop and implement internationally coordinated oversight of large financial institutions. The first steps in this direction have

---

[161] Roubini N., "Crisis Economics: A Crash Course in the Future of Finance", M., EKSMO, 2011 (in Russian language); p.257.

[162] Roubini N., "Crisis Economics: A Crash Course in the Future of Finance", M., EKSMO, 2011 (in Russian language); p...,258.

already been made, in particular, there is a list of systemically important global financial institutions. In addition, at present regulators are trying to limit the growth and risks of large financial institutions, introducing for them increased capital adequacy standards. However, there is a lot to be done in this direction in a short time, and many experts doubt that a small group of regulators monitoring simultaneously the global financial market will be able to quickly and fully identify the problems that transnational financial conglomerates may have. So Professor N. Roubini believes that "an even more preferable option would be to pass a law authorizing regulators to split up those banks and other financial institutions that become so large, influential and systemic that their collapse would pose a serious threat to the entire financial system".[163]

In the global economy, the role of the largest international rating agencies is still very high, and their ratings during the crisis caused many questions and criticism. The reform of the regulation of rating agencies has to be resolutely continued. Along with the measures taken to reduce the monopolization of the rating services market, it is necessary to further increase the requirements of regulators to ensure greater transparency of the entire rating process, including the methods used by rating agencies, procedures for assigning and revising ratings, and financial relationships with customers. It may be advisable for the supervisory authorities to impose sanctions in case of obvious inconsistencies between the rating assessments and the real risk level of companies, regions or countries. In addition, the proposal of a number of experts, in particular Professor J. Stiglitz, that "regulators and other bodies responsible for risk management should less rely on external ratings" is worthy of attention, since "the contribution of rating agencies to cyclicity was no less than that of market prices, and their assessments used by the regulatory authorities, further exacerbated the cyclical nature of the bank lending process".[164]

Another important task of regulators is to reduce risks in the area of securitization. The solution of this problem lies in several areas. The principal

---

[163] Roubini N., "Crisis Economics: A Crash Course in the Future of Finance", M., EKSMO, 2011 (in Russian language); p. 264.

[164] Stiglitz J., "On the Reform of the International Monetary and Financial System: Lessons from the Global Crisis". Report of the UN Financial Mechanism Commission, M., «MezhdunarodnyeOtnosheniya"», 2012 (in Russian language); p., 184.

approach is to force all participants of the securitization process to take maximum account of risks and to assess the quality of the obligations underlying such schemes.

It may be advisable to establish at the legislative level that companies and banks that issue such securities and structure more complex financial products on their basis, should keep a part of such assets on their balance sheet. Steps in this direction have already been taken at the international level (in the decisions of the G20 summits), and at the level of a number of countries. So proposals are made that the participants of the securitization process keep on their balance sheets approximately 10% of the issued financial products. Although many researchers recognizing this measure as fair and limiting risks, they still note that on the eve of the crisis the institutions participating in the securitization process partly held on their balance sheet such assets and suffered losses together with all the players in this market. Therefore, the proposed approach is useful for limiting risks, but still cannot radically change the situation.

A significant step in improving the securitization process could be a significant increase of its transparency and standardization. Information on such financial products should be standardized and accessible to users in one place, for example, on a website organized with the participation of regulatory authorities. Although in the conditions when super-complex financial products are created and a complex financial pyramid is built on the basis of a group of basic assets (CDO in a square, a cube, etc.), risk assessment is practically impossible, since it requires evaluation of a huge number of assets and liabilities. Since such products are too far from the basic assets, it is advisable to significantly tighten the rules for placing such products on the financial market, and some experts even suggest excluding them from the financial turnover.

In the field of regulation and supervision, time remains to be extremely important. According to IMF Managing Director Christine Lagarde, as before, "a shadow banking system that attracts a large volume of more risky operations is a dangerous zone. In the United States, the non-banking sector is now twice as large as the banking sector. In China, about half of the new loans have been provided through the shadow banking system this year."[165]

To correct the current situation, it is necessary to establish strict regulatory requirements not only for systemically important financial institutions, but for all participants of the financial market, which will help to avoid loopholes in the legislation. Otherwise small organizations will start to be built around large financial institutions, capable of conducting more risky operations, which can adversely affect systemic risks. The massive bankruptcy of savings-and-loan associations in the United States in the late 1980s convincingly shows that improper regulation of even small credit institutions can lead to a large-scale crisis in the economy and the financial sphere. As the researcher of crises Professor N. Roubini rightly points out, "financial supervision should be carried out totally, otherwise we will again face a large number of regulatory arbitrations that lead to new crises".[166]

The effectiveness of the regulatory and supervisory system depends not only on legal norms, their quality and adequacy of existing challenges in global markets, but also on the activities of regulatory institutions themselves, their independence, professionalism, authority and responsibility. The situation in this area is also far from ideal, which is noted by many eminent researchers of crises. So Professor J. Stiglitz gives the following assessment: "The mistakes that led to the present crisis are not only regulatory errors, but also regulatory structures that did not always perform their functions effectively or did not seek to enforce their norms and rules. In the current crisis, the regulatory functions of many central banks were not performed at the highest level. They did not properly monitor the implementation of the regulatory mechanisms at their disposal, and they did not fulfill them themselves - did not warn their

---

[165] Lagarde C. "Managing the New Transitions in the Global Economy", an Address at George Washington University, Washington DC, October 3, 2013., www.imf.org (in Russian language)

[166] Roubini N., "Crisis Economics: A Crash Course in the Future of Finance", M., EKSMO, 2011 (in Russian language); p.246.

governments about the need to create additional regulatory bodies or reform the existing ones, if they were not effective."[167]

The problem of the independence of regulators from the interests of supervised structures, various groups of lobbyists and other state bodies is more or less characteristic to all states, although the degree of its severity is certainly very different across countries. At various times, different proposals were offered on how to reduce this negative impact on regulators. It is obvious that the independent status of the regulators, enshrined at the legislative level, and their organizational and financial independence can significantly increase the regulators' resistance to the negative impact of external forces. Although, of course, the maturity of democratic institutions in society as a whole, transparency and public control over all state institutions are of great importance.

In addition, in regulatory practice, one should strive for simple and transparent regulatory norms, and involve independent experts in the assessment of regulatory rules.

The effectiveness of regulators depends to a large extent on the human resources of these structures - professionalism and moral qualities of employees. Therefore, along with taking measures to ensure responsibility of employees, it is very important to provide the necessary level of remuneration, comparable with the incomes in the financial sector.

In addition, "a very important task aimed at limiting systemic risks is creation of mega regulators capable of controlling risks in various financial markets. This institutional transformation is especially important in the context of a significant erasure of the boundaries between banking and non-banking financial institutions."[168]

---

[167] Stiglitz J., "On the Reform of the International Monetary and Financial System: Lessons from the Global Crisis". Report of the UN Financial Mechanism Commission, M., «MezhdunarodnyeOtnosheniya"», 2012 (in Russian language); p., 192.

[168] Kovzanadze I., "Systemic risks in the world economy: institutional solutions are needed", «Finansy», M., 2012, № 3 (in Russian language); 2012, № 3.

5.6. Coordination of Efforts at the International Level

In the global economy, the role of coordinating the efforts of all countries in the field of economic policy, including regulation and supervision, is growing. It is important to understand that regulatory deficiencies in individual countries, regulatory arbitrage at the international level, inadequate or inefficient delineation of the functions of national, regional and international institutions can adversely affect both the economies of individual countries and global economic processes.

According to many experts, one of the key issues in the field of global regulation is the regulation of capital flows, especially speculative ones. As Professor J. Stiglitz points out, "more and more specialists agree that liberalization of capital markets can contribute to economic instability, especially in developing countries. More generally, a fully integrated global financial system may be more prone to instability than a system with "fuses"".[169]

The problem of regulating capital flows is especially acute for developing countries, since uncontrolled flows of "hot" money can negatively affect the financial and economic stability of these countries. Tools that can be used to achieve this goal include: prudential management of foreign borrowings, low-yield reserve ratios, limiting short-term capital flows, long-term taxation on capital outflows and control over the mismatch between amounts and terms of assets and liabilities of financial institutions.

The trade and payments imbalances remain a serious problem of the global economy. So a number of developing Asian countries have very high export growth rates and a significant trade surplus, while most developed countries have chronic deficits in foreign trade. This disproportion is particularly evident in the US-China trade relations, where the situation looks like this: "While the US domestic consumption is too high, in China it remains at a very low level. Further survival and growth of this economy depends to a great extent on cheap exports to the United States, which in turn is financed by sales of

---

[169] Stiglitz J., "On the Reform of the International Monetary and Financial System: Lessons from the Global Crisis". Report of the UN Financial Mechanism Commission, M., «MezhdunarodnyeOtnosheniya"», 2012 (in Russian language); p., 200.

debt obligations to China".[170]Overcoming this macroeconomic imbalance depends on the growth of private investments and reduction of the state budget deficit in the United States, strengthening of the Yuan exchange rate, and structural reforms aimed at reducing the saving rate and the growth of domestic consumption in China.

In general, to address global trade imbalances in developed countries, it is necessary to concentrate on structural reforms aimed at increasing investment, productivity, and economic growth, which will also help to improve the state of the trade and payment balance. If countries that have significant trade and payment imbalances do not pay proper attention to this problem, then it can become more acute and lead to a crisis that, according to many experts, could threaten global economic and political stability. A prominent specialist of crisis situations Professor N. Roubini gives a rather impressive picture of this crisis: "This crisis would be a consequence not so much of the instability of the capitalist system but of profound changes in the distribution of geopolitical power. If the usual financial crises can be compared to minor earthquakes, then the crisis caused by the need to equalize global imbalances - not to mention the accompanying defaults on sovereign debt and currency crashes - is an earthquake of unprecedented strength."[171]

The stability of the global economy is affected by the existence of "tax havens". Therefore, it is important to continue the consistent work on deoffshorization and to establish multilateral exchange of information on bank deposits and taxes between all countries. A number of experts are invited to develop an International Tax Treaty designed to strengthen the coordination of tax policies of developed and developing countries.

Changes in the global economic system in recent decades have significantly outpaced institutional development at the international level, which makes it very important and urgent to further develop international institutions and coordinate their activities.

---

[170] Roubini N., "Crisis Economics: A Crash Course in the Future of Finance", M., EKSMO, 2011 (in Russian language); p., 290.

[171] Roubini N., "Crisis Economics: A Crash Course in the Future of Finance", M., EKSMO, 2011 (in Russian language); p., 292.

A number of experts, for example, suggest a significant improvement in the mechanisms for providing financial assistance in accordance with the Monterrey Consensus of 2002 and the Paris Declaration of 2005. It is advisable that aid recipients actively participate in the development of the 'Action Plan' and the work of international institutions that provide financial assistance.

In order to increase the effectiveness of regulation at the international level, many experts propose to significantly expand the powers of the *Financial Stability Board* and the *Bank for International Settlements*. At the same time, these institutions need to ensure closer coordination of not only the central banks, but also the structures responsible for regulating corporations and securities markets.

It is necessary to provide the *World Bank* and regional development banks with sufficient financial resources, including for the implementation of countercyclical regulation. It is also very important to expand their powers and reform their policies and tools, based on the goals of a quick and adequate response to possible future crises.

Given the marked slowdown in world trade growth during the crisis, it is advisable to avoid trade protectionism in every possible way, including in such forms as defensive and anti-dumping duties, as well as the measures to regulate state purchases at the national level. In this respect, the WTO could play a significant positive role.

In the expert community, the possibility of creating new international institutions is actively discussed.

Thus, an expert group headed by Professor J. Stiglitz initiated creation of an International Commission of Experts, which could be entrusted with the task of assessing and monitoring systemic risks in the global economy. The commission could also engage in such a significant task as "early warning" about the problems in the world economy. In the future, it is proposed to establish a *Council for Global Economic Coordination* at the level corresponding to the *General Assembly* and the *UN Security Council*. It is proposed to give to this council the authority to assess development and guide the process of solving economic problems. The authors of the project believe that such an institution "should contribute to development, seek harmonization of the political tasks facing the major international organizations, and help to achieve consensus among states on solutions to global economic, social and environmental problems."[172]

In order to ensure sustainable development of the world economy, including developing countries, it is important to ensure procedures for the restructuring of public debts with an appropriate institutional framework. Such procedures should be effective, fair, transparent and limited in time. They should protect creditors and take into account the socio-economic situation of debtor countries. In addition, it is proposed to establish a permanent institutional structure in this field, for example, the *International Court for Restructuring the Public Debt*, which would ensure compliance with agreed international principles relating to the priority of claims, need for debt cancellation and distribution of the risks of assessing the cost of collateral.

Thus, close coordination of efforts at the national, regional and international levels is necessary to eliminate the dangerous disparities in the world economy, build an effective regulatory and supervisory system at the global level and ensure sustainable and long-term growth.

---

[172] Stiglitz J., "On the Reform of the International Monetary and Financial System: Lessons from the Global Crisis". Report of the UN Financial Mechanism Commission, M., «MezhdunarodnyeOtnosheniya"», 2012 (in Russian language); p., 224.

Conclusion

Possible Options for Development of Socio-economic Processes at the Global Level

The post-crisis development of the global economy is characterized by weak and unstable growth and persistent macroeconomic imbalances that, if confronted with certain circumstances, provoke emergence of a new crisis.

The global crisis has caused heated debate among economists, business people, state bodies and politicians about its causes, coping methods, and directions for further development of the economy and social sphere. In general, the criticism of the current economic model, oriented to a short-term speculative effect, was quite acute during the crisis. However, even now, when the macroeconomic situation has improved and the intensity of the discussion has decreased somewhat, most experts still agree with J.M. Keynes' assessment of the crisis economy: "The decadent international but individualistic capitalism ... is not a success. It is not intelligent. It is not beautiful. It is not just. It is not virtuous. And it doesn't deliver the goods. In short we dislike it, and we are beginning to despise it." [173]

At the same time, it should be noted that to a certain extent, scientists and politicians still share the views formed by the neoclassical and monetary economic schools and supported by the neoconservative politicians. In

---

[173] JohnMaynardKeynes. «National Self-Sufficiency». – Yale Review, 22 (1933). – P.760-761.

general, the essence of these views is that the economic system is capable of self-regulation and the state intervention in socio-economic processes should be minimal, since economic activity of state institutions is a priori ineffective. Proponents of the neo-conservative trend strongly oppose significant reforms in economic policy, regulation and supervision, believing that the crisis has been overcome and it is possible to continue to maintain an efficient and self-adjusting economic model.

Nevertheless, for most experts it is clear that changes in the current socio-economic model are necessary, but their views often differ regarding the prescriptions for reforms. Discussions in general are about the scope and timing of reforms. At the same time, it should be noted that in recent years quite radical views on the future of the world economic system have also become more popular.

Most authoritative experts in the field of macroeconomics, including such as J. Stiglitz, N. Roubini, P. Krugman, R. Rajan, offer long-term reforms in structural, financial and monetary policy, regulation and supervision, at all levels: national, regional and international. They are in favor of closer coordination of the activities of governments and central banks of developed and developing countries and overcoming the dangerous disparities in the global economy. This group of experts also advocates the establishment of serious mechanisms to prevent crises, including countercyclical regulation, strengthening forecasting and planning elements in economic policy, elimination of moral abuses in business and public administration, and significant institutional changes, including at the international level.

The views of reformer economists are to some extent supported by many politicians at all levels. Ideas about the need for significant reforms and more active international cooperation are constantly heard in the speeches of the heads of international financial institutions. Thus, according to IMF Managing Director Christine Lagarde, "transitional processes ... will likely play out over the rest of the decade, if not longer. They ... will require not only active national policy management, but also active international cooperation in the field of economic policy. So my main message today is: these new global transitions need a new global agenda."[174]

Program documents on reforming the global economy were adopted at G20 summits. To a large extent, the decisions taken are already being implemented at the country level, as well as by the *Financial Stability Board* and the *Basel Committee on Banking Supervision*.

Thus, the *Financial Stability Board* is consistently implementing measures in different areas which are important for global stability, such as development of a set of standards, improved regulation of systemically important financial institutions, identification of shadow banking institutions and creation of effective supervision over their activities, reform of the OTC directives market, reduction of financial institutions' dependence on external credit ratings and regulatory reform of insurance companies.

Within the *Basel Committee's* framework, a comprehensive reform of the regulation of financial institutions is carried out. Basel-III Accord provides for introduction of a number of new coefficients, e.g.: leverage, counter-cyclical capital buffers, and liquidity coverage, designed to limit the level of accepted risks.

In the past few years, significant reforms in the field of economic policy, regulation and supervision have begun in the United States, Britain and the European Union.

It is necessary to note the active institutional reforms carried out at the national and regional levels. The success was particularly notable in the institutional structure of the EU: recently the *European Stability Mechanism*, *European Banking Union*, and *European Fund for Strategic Investments* have been created and are actively developing.

At the same time, it is very important that all the goals set for reforming the global economy are implemented consistently, despite the improvement of the macroeconomic situation. Only in this case it will be possible to transform

---

[174] Lagarde C. "Managing the New Transitions in the Global Economy", an Address at George Washington University, Washington DC, October 3, 2013., www.imf.org (in Russian language)

the current global economy, burdened by disparities and contradictions, into a more harmonious, steadily developing and socially-oriented economy of the future.

Consistent implementation of such reforms is very important, taking into account that the crisis of 2007-2009, like the crisis of 1929-1933, caused a sharp deterioration of the social and economic situation in many countries and helped to strengthen extreme political ideas and trends (including in a number of developed countries), which creates certain political risks.

Long-term stable development cannot be ensured either by yesterday's conservative approach to complex contemporary problems, or by the simplified radical proposals of extreme political trends. Only successive reforms can lead to the formation of a new economic model built on the basis of accumulated scientific knowledge and practical experience.

References

1. Abalkin L., "From economic theory to the concept of a long-term strategy", «VoprosyEkonomiki», 2010, № 6 (in Russian language);

2. Acharya V., Richardson M., Restoring Financial Stability: How to Repair a Failed System, New York University Stern School of Business, 2009;

3. Albright M.; "Religion and world politics", Publishing House., «Alpina Publisher», M., 2007 (in Russian language);

4. Ananiashvili Y., "Econometrics", Tbilisi, 2014 (in Georgian language);

5. Aneiro M., Egan-Jones Welcomes QE3 By Cutting U.S. Credit Rating, Barron`s, September 14, 2012;

6. ArchvadzeI., "The Economy of Modern Georgia: Some Aspects of Development and Vulnerability, Economic and Statistical Analysis", Tbilisi, 2012 (in Georgian language);

7. Asatiani R., "Globalization, Economic Theory and Georgia", Tbilisi, 2010 (in Georgian language);

8. Aslanishvili D., "The causes of the economic crisis in Europe", TSU, Collection of research papers of P. Gugushvili Institute of Economy, Tbilisi, 2012 (in Georgian language);

9. Ayres R.U., Did the Fifth K-Wave Begin in 1990-1992? Has it been Aborted by Globalization? Kondratieff Waves, Warfare and World Security» /Ed. By T. C. Devezas/ - Amsterdam, 2006, IOS Press;

10. Bagehot W., Lombard Street: a description of the money market, www. book-lib.com;

11. Balcerowicz L., Socialism, Capitalism, Transformation, Budapest, CEU, 1995;

12. Bank for International Settlements. Statistics. www.bis.org/statistics;

13. Bank of England, Statistical Release. Money and Credit: December 2013, www.bankofengland.co.uk;

14. BarbakadzeKh., Kakashvili N., About effective company budgeting, Moldova State University, 2015;

15. Barth J. R., Caprio G., Jr., Levine R., Rethinking Bank Regulation: Till Angels Govern, Cambridge University Press, New York, 2006;

16. Basel Committee on Banking Supervision. Basel III phase – in arrangements, www.bis.org;

17. Bass K., Testimony before Subcommittee on Capital Markets, Insurance, and Government Sponsored Enterprises, 2007;

18. Beridze T., Employment and Unemployment during the Transition Period in Georgia. In: VI World Congress for Central and East European Studies, Helsinki, 2000;

19. Bernanke B., "Communication and Monetary Policy", Speech of the Chairman of the Board of Governors of the Federal Reserve System at the National Economists Club Annual Dinner, Washington, November 19, 2013., www.fedspeak.ru (in Russian language);

20. Bernanke B., "Lessons of the Financial Crisis for Banking Supervision", Speech of the Chairman of the Board of Governors of the Federal Reserve Systemat the Federal Reserve Bank of Chicago Conference on Bank Structure and Competition, Chicago,May 7, 2009., www.fedspeak.ru (in Russian language);

21. Board of Governors of the Federal Reserve System. Economic Re- search and Data. Money Stock Measures, www.federalreserve.gov;

22. Board of Governors of the Federal Reserve System. Economic Re- search & Data. Industrial Production and Capacity Utilization, G17, Release date: January 17, 2014, www.federalreserve.gov;

23. Brzezinski Z., "StrategicVision: Americaand theCrisisofGlobalPower", Translation from English, M., 2014 (in Russian language);

24. Caprio G, Jr., Vittas D., Reforming financial systems Historical implications for policy, Cambridge University Press, New York, 2006;

25. Caprio G., Hanson J. A., Litan R. E., Financial Crises: Lessons from the Past, Preparation for the Future, The World Bank, Washington, D. C. 2005;

26. Caprio G., Honohan P., Stiglitz J. E., Financial Liberalization: How Far, How Fast? Cambridge University Press, New York, 2001;

27. Chikava L., "Employment and unemployment in Georgia", Tbilisi, 2012 (in Georgian language);

28. Chikviladze M., Tendencies of economic development of Georgia, international scientific conference "modern information technologies in the conditions of economic globalization", collection of research papers№1, Tbilisi, November 20152012 (in Georgian language);

29. Chitanava N., "Metamorphoses and prospects of the Georgian economy", Tbilisi, 2012 (in Georgian language) 20152012 (in Georgian language);

30. Chutlashvili A., Main trends in the development of the financial sector and stimulation of economic growth, the international scientific conference "Innovation, Performance and Competitiveness in the Financial Sector", collection of research papers, State University of Moldova, Chisinau, October 2015 (in Georgian language);

31. Dzhgerenaya E., "New paradigm of world economy", «EkonomikaGruzyi», 2009, № 2 (in Russian language);

32. Eliava L., "Banking crises forecasting", Tbilisi, 2013 (in Georgian language);

33. European Central Bank. Monthly Bulletin, 2014, January, www.ecb.europa.eu;

34. Federal Deposit Insurance Corporation, Regulation & Examination. Temporary Liquidity Guarantee Program, www.fdic.gov;

35. Federal Deposit Insurance Corporation. Bank Data and Statistics. Loans and Leases FDIC-insured Commercial Banks US and Other Ar- eas, www.fdic.gov;

36. Financial Stability Board, Principles for Sound Compensation Practices, 2009 April, www.financialstabilityboard.org;

37. Friedman J., Kraus V., "Man-made financial crisis. Systemic risks and failure ofregulation" (translated from English), M., Publishing House., «YRISEN» и «Mysl», 2012 (in Russian language);

38. Gaganidze G., "Determination of the goods' export potential", «Economy and Business», 2014, №1 (in Georgian language);

39. Gamsakhurdia G., "The national concept of anti-crisis measures in Georgia", «Economy and Business», 2009, № 2 (in Georgian language);

40. GelashviliS., "Статистическое прогнозирование в современном бизнесе", Tbilisi, 2012 (in Georgian language);

41. Geostat, GDP and Other Indicators of National Accounts, www.geo-stat.ge;

42. Gotsiridze R., "Currency crisis: the causes of the devaluation of the lari and the expected consequences", Tbilisi, 1999 (in Georgian language);

43. Greenspan A, The Crisis, 2nd draft, Manuscript, 2010;

44. Greenspan A., "The Age of Turbulence: Adventures in a New World", M., 2009, Publishing House., «Alpina Business Books» (in Russian language);

45. Gvelesiani R., "Economic Policy", Tbilisi, 2012 (in Georgian language);

46. Hayek F., Denationalization of Money, L., 1976;

47. Iakobidze D., "Georgian and global financial crisis", Tbilisi, 2009 (in Georgian language);

48. IMF, Global Financial Stability Report: Containing Systemic Risks and Restoring Financial Soundness, April 2008;

49. IMF, World Economic Outlook databases, October 2013, www.imf. org;

50. JibutiM., "The impact of the 2008 Russian-Georgian war and the global financial crisis on business in Georgia", Tbilisi, 2009 (in Georgian language);

51. Jim'enez G., Saurina J., Credit cycles, Credit risk and Prudential regulation, Banco de Espana, 2006;

52. Jones S., How Moody's Faltered, Financial Times, October 17, 2008;

53. Jonson S., Kwak J., 13 Bankers: The Wall Street Takeovers and the Next Financial Meltdown, N Y., Pantheon, 2010;

54. Jorda O., When credit bites back, Federal Reserve Bank of San Francisko Working Paper, Nov. 2011;

55. Jourdon Ph., La monnaie unique europeenne et son lien au development economique et social coordonne: uneanalysecliometrique», These, Montpellier, 2008, Universite Montpellier; Papenhausen Ch., Causal Mechanisms of Long Waves, Futures 40;

56. Juglar C., Des Crises Commerciales et de leur retour periodique en France, en Angleterre et aux Etats-Unis, Paris, 1862, Guillaumin;

57. Kaas L., Azariadis K., Self-folfilling credit cycles, www.bis.org., Central Bank Research Hab. 24/10/2012;

58. Kakulia M., "The problems of the development of the monetary system in Georgia", Tbilisi, 2001 (in Georgian language);

59. Keynes J. M., National Self-Sufficiency, Yale Review, 22 (1933);

60. Keynes J.M., "The General Theory of Employment, Interest and Money" (anthology of classic economy), M., Publishing House., «Ekonov», 1993 (in Russian language);

61. Khaduri N., "Economic threats of post-war Georgia", «Economist», 2009, № 4 (in Georgian language);

62. Kharabadze E., Financial accounting, Tbilisi, 2013 (in Georgian language);

63. Kharaishvili E., "Problems of competition and competitiveness in the agri-food sector of Georgia", Tbilisi, 2011 (in Georgian language);

64. Khelaya G, "International monetary, credit and settlement relations", Tbilisi, 1996 (in Georgian language);

65. Kistauri L., Tsutskiridze G., "Risk management in commercial banks", Tbilisi, 2015 (in Georgian language);

66. Kling A., The Unintended Consequences of International Bank Capital Standards, Mercatus on Policy 44, 2009, April;

67. Kokiauri L., "Ten axioms for saving Georgian lari", Tbilisi, 2015 (in Georgian language);

68. Kondratyev N., "Big cycles of conjuncture and foresight theory.", M., 2002, Publishing House., «Ekonomika» (in Russian language);

69. Kovzanadze I., "Finance: ways out of the crisis", «Economist», M., 2003, №6 (in Russian language);

70. Kovzanadze I., "Lessons of the world crisis: need for a new model of economic regulation", «VoprosyEkonomiki», M., 2010, № 4 (in Russian language);

71. Kovzanadze I., "Methods for managing problem banks", «Finansy y credit», M., 2001, №16 (88) (in Russian language);"

72. Kovzanadze I., "Peculiarities of banking system development in the former socialist countries", «VoprosyEkonomiki», M., 2004, №5 (in Russian language);

73. Kovzanadze I., "Post-crisis development of the global banking sector: trends and prospects", «Dengy y credit», M., 2013, № 3 (in Russian language);

74. Kovzanadze I., "Restructuring of banking systems: strategy and tactics to overcome systemic crises", «Finansy», M., 2003, №3 (in Russian language);

75. Kovzanadze I., "Systemic banking crises in the context of financial globalization", Publishing House., TSU, Tbilisi, 2003 (in Russian language);

76. Kovzanadze I., "Systemic banking crises in the context of financial globalization", «VoprosyEkonomiki», M., 2002, № 8 (in Russian language);

77. Kovzanadze I., "Systemic risks in the world economy: institutional solutions are needed", «Finansy», M., 2012, № 3 (in Russian language);

78. Kovzanadze I., "The Monetary and Financial Mechanism of Emerging Market Economies in the Context of Globalization", «Finansy y credit», M., 2004, №23 (in Russian language);

79. Kovzanadze I., "The Monetary and Financial Mechanism of Emerging Market Economies in the Context of Globalization", «Dengy y credit», M., 2003, №2 (in Russian language);

80. Kovzanadze I., "Trends and prospects for the development of the economy and banking sector in the transformation countries", Publishing House., «FinansyyStatistika», M., 2005 (in Russian language);

81. Kovzanadze I., Economic and Banking System Development Trends and Prospects for Countries in Transition, iUniverse. Inc., New York, Bloomington, 2008;

82. Kovzanadze I., Kontridze G., "Modern banking, theory and practice", Tbilisi, 2014 (in Georgian language.,);

83. Kovzanadze I., Kontridze G., "Some problems of the Georgian banking system before the August events of 2008", «EkonomikaGruzyi», 2009, № 1 (in Georgian language);

84. Kovzanadze I., Systemic and Borderline Banking Crises: Lessons Learned for Future Prevention, iUniverrse Inc. New York, Bloomington, 2010;

85. Krugman P., "We need to talk about the determining role of the state in overcoming the crisis, the need for intervention in market mechanisms and manual operation", ZN.UA, 18.09.2017 https://zn.ua/macrolevel/nobelevskiy-laureat-pol-krugman-nuzhno-govorit-ob-opredelyayuschey-roli-gosudarstva-v-preodolenii-krizisa-o-neobhodimosti-vmeshatelstva-v-rynochnye-mehanizmy-i-ruchnogo-upravleniya-260407_.html (in Russian language);

86. Krugman P., "The Way Out of the Slump!", M., «Azbuka-Attykus», 2013 (in Russian language);

87. Krugman P., The Return of Depression Economics and the Crisis of 2008, New York, 2009;

88. Lagarde C. "Managing the New Transitions in the Global Economy", an Address at George Washington University, Washington DC, October 3, 2013., www.imf.org (in Russian language);

89. Lee Kuan; "From Third World to First: The Singapore Story" (1965–2000), Publishing House., «Mann, Ivanov y Ferber», 2013 (in Russian language);

90. Lewis M., "The Big game for short. Secret springs of financial disaster", Publishing House., «Alpina Publisher», M., 2011 (in Russian language);

91. Marshava K., "Modern problems of statistics", Tbilisi, 2012 (in Georgian language);

92. Martin H..Schumann X.., "Trap of globalization: an attack on prosperity and democracy"., M., Publishing House., «Alpina», 2001 (in Russian language);

93. Maslov O, "World Crisis 2007-2009: Who is to blame? Weekly Independent Analytical Review", www. polit.nnov.ru (in Russian language);

94. Mauldin J, TepperJ."Endgame: the end of the debt super-cycle and how it changes everything", Publishing House., «Mann, Ivanov y Ferber», 2013 (in Russian language);

95. MekvabishviliE., "Political-Economic Anatomy of the Global Financial Crisis", «Economy and Business», т., 8, №2, 2015 (in Georgian language);

96. MekvabishviliE., "World experience and prospects of crisis management (on the example of the global crisis of 2008-2009)", «Economy and Business», 2014, №2 (in Georgian language);

97. MekvabishviliI., "The basic principles of effective banking supervision", «Ekonomika », 2005, №11 (in Georgian language);

98. MeskhiyaY., Global economic crisis and macroeconomic stability problems in Georgia, «Economist», 2009, № 2 (in Georgian language);

99. Narmania D., "Peculiarities of banking risk management in the post-crisis period", «Economy and Business», 2011, № 3 (in Georgian language);

100. Papava V., "Georgian Economy - reforms and pseudo-reforms, Tbilisi, 2015 (in Georgian language);

101. Papava V., "Non-traditional economics", Tbilisi, 2011 (in Georgian language);

102. Patterson S., "Quanta. As wizards from mathematics earned billions and almost did not bring down the stock market"., Publishing House., «Mann, Ivanov y Ferber», 2013 (in Russian language);

103. Poszar Z., at al. Shadow Banking, Federal Reserve Bank of New York Staff Report 458, July 2010;

104. Rajan R., "Rift lines. Hidden cracks, still threatening the global economy", M., Publishing House of the Gaydar Institute, 2011 (in Russian language);

105. Regling K., "The eurozone crisis: Half or even two-third of the case is done", Interview to the news channel Euronews 01.08.2013 г, www.euronews.com (in Russian language);

106. Roubini N., "Crisis Economics: A Crash Course in the Future of Finance", M., EKSMO, 2011 (in Russian language);

107. Schultz M., "Tax on financial transactions should be introduced around the world, RBC daily interview22.03.2012". www.rbcdaily.ru (in Russian language);

108. Semilyutina N., "The US law on modernizing financial services" 1999., «Depositarium», 1999, № 10 (in Russian language);

109. Seninsky S., Banking Union of Europe, Radio Liberty, 20.12.2013, www.svoboda.org (in Russian language);

110. Shabanel P., "Implementation of Basel III standards: complexity, options and opportunities", Analytical Banking Journal, 2011, № 10 (in Russian language);

111. Shengelia T., Investment Environment in Georgia and the Prospects of its Development, In book: Focus on Science and Technology from a Georgian Perspective, New York, 2014;

112. SilagadzeA., Priorities for the Economy of Post-communist Georgia in the Context of the World Financial Crisis. Problems of Economic Transition, 2013, Vol., 56, № 8;

113. Snyder M., 10 Shocking Quotes About What QE3 Is Going To Do To America, Activist Post, September 15, 2012;

114. Soros G., "On Globalization", M., «Eksmo», 2004 (in Russian language);

115. Soto de U., "Money, bank credit and economic cycles", Chelyabinsk, 2008, Publishing House., «Socium» (in Russian language);

116. Stiglitz J., "On the Reform of the International Monetary and Financial System: Lessons from the Global Crisis". Report of the UN Financial Mechanism Commission, M., «MezhdunarodnyeOtnosheniya"», 2012 (in Russian language);

117. Stiglitz J., "Steep peak. America and the new economic order after the global crisis", M., «Eksmo», 2011 (in Russian language);

118. Taylor J., Monetary Policy, Economic Policy, and the Financial Crisis: An Empirical Analysis of What Went Wrong, In Friedman, 2011;

119. Todua N., "Marketing research of customer behavior in the Georgian market", Tbilisi, 2012 (in Georgian language);

120. Tugan-Baranovsky M., Periodic Industrial Crises, M., 2008, Directimedia Publishing (in Russian language);

121. Tukhasvili M., "The end of migration expansion and the "new migration policy" of Russia", Tbilisi, 2009 (in Georgian language);

122. US Department of Commerce. Bureau of Economic Analysis. National Economic Accounts. Gross Domestic Product. News Release, January 30, 2014, www.bea.gov;

123. Vee V., "History of world economy" 1945-1990, M., 1994, Publishing House., «Nauka» (in Russian language);

124. Wallison P., Cause and Effect: Government Policies and the Financial Crisis, Critical Review 21 (2-3);

125. Wallison P., Housing Initiatives and Other Policy Factors, In Friedman, 2011;

126. Wayne S., "Global Financial Crisis", Publishing House., «Alpina Publisher», M., 2009 (in Russian language);

127. Wesbury B., It is Not as Bad as You Think, N Y., Hoboken, John Wiley, 2010;

128. Yavlinsky A., "The recession of capitalism - hidden causes", Publishing House., "ID VSE", 2014 (in Russian language);

129. Zandi M., Financial Shock: A 360-Degree Look at the Subprime Mortgage Implosion, And Now to Avoid the Next Financial Crisis, N.J., FT Press, 2008;

130. www.bankofengland.co.uk;

131. www.bea.gov;

132. www.bis.org;

133. www.ebrd.com;

134. www.ecb.europa.eu;

135. www.fdic.gov;

136. www.federalreserve.gov;

137. www.fedspeak.ru;

138. www.financialstabilityboard.org;

139. www.ifc.org;

140. www.imf.org;

141. www.nbg.gov.ge;

142. www.oecd.org;
143. www.rbcdaily.ru;
144. www.statistics.ge;
145. www.worldbank.org.

www.ingramcontent.com/pod-product-compliance
Lightning Source LLC
Chambersburg PA
CBHW020738180526
45163CB00001B/277